Joe Cahill

A Life in the IRA

Brendan Anderson

PB

THE O'BRIEN PRESS

DUBLIN

First published 2002 by The O'Brien Press Ltd,
20 Victoria Road, Dublin 6, Ireland.
Tel: +353 1 4923333; Fax: +353 1 4922777
E-mail: books@obrien.ie
Website: www.obrien.ie
Reprinted 2002 (twice).
First published in paperback in 2003.
Reprinted 2004, 2005.

ISBN: 0-86278-836-6

British Library Cataloguing-in-Publication Data
Anderson, Brendan
Joe Cahill : a life in the IRA. - 2nd ed.
1.Cahill, Joe 2.Irish Republican Army 3.Nationalists - Northern
Ireland - Biography
4.Northern Ireland - History - 20th century
5.Northern Ireland - Politics and government - 20th century
I.Title
941.6'082'092

6 7 8 9 10 11 12
05 06 07 08

Editing, typesetting, layout and design: The O'Brien Press Ltd
Printing: Nørhaven Paperback A/S

DEDICATION

To Annie and Vi

ACKNOWLEDGEMENTS

This has been a difficult book to research and write and could not have been completed without the help and encouragement of many friends.

A very special thanks to David McKittrick and Richard McAuley; to David for reading the copy, for his sensible advice and invaluable suggestions; to Richard for all his help, for answering so many questions and for responding to so many demands on his time, invariably made during a crisis in the peace process. Thanks to Brendan Murphy for his encouragement, his not so gentle prodding and not least his wonderful photographs; to the learned and courteous staff of the Belfast Central Library's Irish Section who took so much trouble; to Yvonne Murphy and the staff of the Linenhall Library for their kindness and help; to *Irish News* librarian Kathleen Bell, to Chris Thornton, Fionnuala O'Connor, Dr Eamon Phoenix and Martina Purdy, all of whose kindness and advice was deeply appreciated. Thanks to Annie Cahill for her unfailing thoughtfulness and generosity, to my wife Vi for putting up with so much, to my family and all those relatives and friends who by their 'positive nagging' gave much-needed encouragement to an old hack during the difficult times. Thanks to the staff of O'Brien Press, in particular Damian Keenan for whom nothing was too much trouble. Thanks most of all to Elisha Anderson, the man who planted the seed of an idea all those years ago.

Cover photograph: Colman Doyle.
Back cover photograph: Joe Cahill in front of the Bobby Sands mural in Twinbrook, Belfast, on Easter Sunday morning, 23 April 2000. Photograph: An Phoblacht.

CONTENTS

FOREWORD

It would be difficult to find a book dealing with Irish history in the twentieth century which does not contain at least one, and usually several, references to Joe Cahill. He is invariably referred as one of the veteran republicans who re-established the IRA in the North after the trauma of events of 1969. Equally invariable will be a reference to his gun-smuggling exploits and to the fact that he was sentenced to death in 1942 for his part in an abortive IRA operation in which a policeman was killed.

But there has been so much more to Cahill's life, and this work attempts to recount some of those other, so far unpublished experiences. The book has taken almost three years to write and research and has involved an endless stream of interviews with Joe Cahill, his family, friends and associates. For an 'ordinary' octogenarian, this would have represented quite an ordeal, but Cahill cooperated fully and for the most part demonstrated an extraordinary degree of enthusiasm and patience – not to mention a wicked sense of humour.

It has not been possible to record every event in the life of an extremely active eighty-two-year-old, who, at time of writing, was still carrying on a punishing schedule of engagements and meetings. Joe Cahill has seen a lot in those eighty-two years – he was, for instance, born before the partition of Ireland and was three years old when the Irish civil war ended. Much has, of necessity, had to be left out.

This work does not pretend to be a complete account of Cahill's life. Legal and other constraints on him and his associates preclude the revelation of much information of great interest. It is, however, probably as complete an authorised biography as is likely to be published. The whole story cannot at present be told and, indeed, it is doubtful if it will ever be told. Cahill, however, has spoken frankly about those things that he is free to speak about. His is a fascinating story, of a man who put principles and ideals before self, before family and home life. It is probably true to say that if Joe Cahill had put as much time, energy and devotion into a business as he did into the republican movement, he would be a very rich man today.

Brendan Anderson, August 2002

PROLOGUE

The cold metal of a gun muzzle pressed against his temple and the words, 'Don't move,' were the first indications that Joe Cahill, chief of staff of the Irish Republican Army, had of the presence of intruders in the ship's galley.

These two words, spoken by a young Irish navy officer armed with a Browning automatic pistol, spelled the end of one of the IRA's most audacious gun-smuggling operations. Below their feet in the hold of the *Claudia*, five tons of weapons – a gift from Libya's Colonel Gaddafi – lay waiting to be unloaded at a tiny harbour a few hundred yards away on southern Ireland's Waterford coast.

Then a fit fifty-two-year-old, the Belfast republican and two colleagues had travelled back to Ireland on the 289-ton Cypriot-registered coaster after it had been loaded by Libyan security forces at Tripoli. A carefully laid plan involving the local IRA unit was set to move into gear as soon as the *Claudia*'s cargo of assault rifles, explosives, automatic pistols and ammunition was taken ashore at Helvick Head. The drivers of a small fleet of vehicles, including four or five lorries, had been tasked with whisking the weapons away from the coast to specially prepared dumps across the country.

It was March 1973, and the republican movement was in the process of bouncing back from a series of setbacks, including the arrests of several members of the leadership, north and south of the border. The *Claudia*'s cargo – with the promise of more to come from Libya – was eagerly awaited in the North.

A man who had fought against the British presence in Ireland since he was a teenager, Cahill had been arrested many times and was philosophical about the prospect of spending another term in prison. After his reprieve from the gallows at the age of twenty-two, he was, after all, living on borrowed time.

CHAPTER ONE
Birth of a Rebel

In March 1920, the notorious Black and Tans arrived from England to begin their campaign of destruction and violence in Ireland. Towards the end of the year the young republican Kevin Barry was hanged, and Royal Irish Constabulary (RIC) Auxiliaries put Cork city to the torch.

A flying column attached to the Volunteers' West Cork Brigade ambushed a convoy of Auxiliaries travelling in two lorries towards Kilmichael in late November. The Auxiliaries, all experienced ex-British Army officers with wartime service, lost eighteen men in the carefully planned attack.

That same year saw the appearance of the first of eleven children born to Joseph and Josephine Cahill, a young couple from west Belfast.

Their oldest son, Joe, was born on 19 May 1920, before the drawing of the border which partitioned Ireland's six northeastern counties from the rest of the country. Shortly after his eightieth birthday, Joe Cahill summed up his lifelong battle against British rule in his country in a simple sentence: 'I was born in a united Ireland and I want to die in a united Ireland.'

James Connolly, the Citizen Army leader executed by the British for his part in the 1916 Easter Rising, lived next door to Cahill's grandparents on the Falls Road. Joe Cahill's parents became good friends of the Connolly family. In later years, the younger Cahill came to know Connolly's daughters well and formed friendships, particularly with Nora Connolly, which lasted for more than half a century.

The Belfast which Cahill was born into looked, on the surface, like many Victorian cities across England. The cramped rows of houses in the mean little gas-lit, cobblestoned streets were hastily built in the late nineteenth century to accommodate the influx of country people arriving in the city to work in the linen, shipbuilding and rope-making industries.

Belfast, however, differed from Manchester or Birmingham in one vital respect – its savage sectarianism. Four years after Irish republicans catapulted their cause onto the pages of the world's press with the 1916 Easter Rising in Dublin, Belfast's Protestant community regarded the Catholic minority with deep suspicion, and often with loathing. The city's Catholics, long cast in the role of second-class citizens, waited in trepidation as plans emerged from the English parliament at Westminster concerning the partition of the island.

Their fears of being isolated and cut off from co-religionists in the southern counties proved to be well founded. The British government offered all nine Ulster counties to unionists, who rejected the plan on the grounds that the province would be ungovernable – meaning, of course, that it would contain too many Catholics for comfort.

Unionists demanded, and were granted, the present six counties of Northern Ireland. These included two – Tyrone and Fermanagh – with nationalist majorities, as well as Derry city and Newry town, both also with nationalist majorities. The Government of Ireland Act – better known as the 'partition act' – thus divided the country in two in December 1920. The new state was to be called Northern Ireland. The other Ulster counties of Cavan, Monaghan and Donegal, each overwhelmingly Catholic, were to be severed from the province and included with the twenty-three counties of Munster, Leinster and Connaught on the southern side of the new border.

The twenty-six counties south of the border were known as the Irish Free State after the signing of the Anglo-Irish Treaty, which ended the war of independence. Free State status was conferred through British legislation in 1922, and recognised the authority of

Dáil Éireann (the Irish parliament), while locking the South into the British Empire. The Treaty resulted in the Irish Civil War, with the IRA split along pro- and anti-Treaty lines. The pro-Treaty forces supported the Free State and were ultimately victorious. The term Free State was used until the late 1940s, when an Irish coalition government unilaterally declared the Irish Republic.

Although the revamped northern area had a large unionist majority, with 820,000 Protestants and 430,000 Catholics, it still posed problems for unionists. While Catholics accounted for just over one-third of the population, they had managed to do surprisingly well in the local government elections held throughout Ireland in January 1920. Under the proportional representation (PR) electoral system – ironically introduced by the British to counter the increasing Sinn Féin vote in the southern counties – northern nationalists gained control of several councils.

Derry city, under Protestant control since the siege of 1688, was now, to the consternation of the new unionist government, in the hands of a nationalist administration.

Unionists were eventually able to drastically reduce the influence of the nationalist vote, by abolishing PR and adopting a policy of flagrant gerrymandering (creating artificial electoral majorities by manipulating constituency boundaries) of local government boundaries to give them false majorities in many councils. In the meantime, however, they were in no mood to tolerate nationalist council successes. Sectarian violence, long a way of life – and death – for the minority community, was about to reach unprecedented levels.

The War of Independence, initially being prosecuted by what was to become the Irish Republican Army against the British Army in the south and west of Ireland, had spread to Ulster. The IRA comprised, in the main, Irish Volunteer veterans of the 1916 Rising. Its republican socialist counterpart, James Connolly's Irish Citizen Army, had largely disintegrated with the execution of its founder after the Rising. The role of southern republicans was clearly defined – they were simply to engage the occupying forces. In the new Northern Ireland, where Catholics were in a minority, the IRA's units were pressed into assuming the additional role of defending the nationalist population in a hostile state.

Tensions had been running high in Derry for months after the January elections and unionist resentment was spilling over into violence. A concerted attack was made on a Catholic area by the Ulster Volunteer Force (UVF), a Protestant paramilitary organisation. Armed RIC men and British soldiers with fixed bayonets charged and fired into the Catholic crowds which had formed. IRA volunteers returned fire, fatally wounding a Special Branch officer, the first RIC man to be killed in the new state of Northern Ireland.

As the violence spread to Belfast, the overwhelmingly Protestant Harland and Wolff shipyard workforce laid down their tools and held a meeting. The workers cheered as speakers urged loyalist hero Edward Carson MP to call out the UVF in the city. Carson, a Dublin-born lawyer and politician, was a fiery orator who had helped establish the UVF in 1913 to resist the Liberal government's plans to grant Home Rule, a limited form of self-government, to Ireland. When the First World War broke out, many UVF men responded to Carson's plea to enlist in the Army. The UVF men, now formed into the Thirty-sixth (Ulster) Division, died in their thousands in the trenches of France and Belgium.

A highly inflammatory speech by Carson at the traditional 12 July Orange rally at Finaghy, on the outskirts of Belfast, not only roused Protestant wrath against Catholics, but against any trade unionist, labour supporter or socialist who posed a challenge to the master–worker relationship.

On the eve of yet another anti-Catholic pogrom, Carson declared to the crowd at Finaghy that unionists would 'tolerate no Sinn Féin in Ulster'. This was followed by a concerted letter-writing campaign in the unionist press, alleging 'republican infiltration' of unionist firms and neighbourhoods.

Carson's words were taken at face value and, once more, murder stalked the streets of Belfast. Catholic workers were expelled from the shipyard – often at gunpoint, always violently. Some unfortunate nationalists were thrown into the tide, forced to swim for safety while being pelted with iron nuts and bolts. In all, some 10,000 Catholics and a small number of 'rotten Prods' (for example, Protestant trade unionists and socialists) were expelled from Belfast shipyard, and from the mills and engineering firms in Belfast, Lisburn and surrounding towns. Rioting and looting became commonplace and there were frequent attacks on Catholic ghettos, churches and businesses. Retaliation was met with reprisal, murder met with murder. To visit a neighbour or walk to a back-street grocery shop was to gamble with death.

In the first thirteen months of Joe Cahill's life, 455 people were killed in Belfast – 267 Catholics, 185 Protestants and three of unknown religion. More than 2,000 others were wounded. The new Cahill baby came into the world to the sound of gunfire and explosions, sounds which would echo in his ears for most of his life.

Joe Cahill was born in the family's rooms above a tiny printing house at 60 Divis Street, in the part of nationalist west Belfast closest to the city centre. Joseph senior, a jobbing compositor and printer, struggled to support his large family by setting and printing dance tickets, bookmakers' dockets, letterheads and advertising posters. That both parents were republican-minded is reflected in the fact that several of their children rose to prominence in the republican movement. Josephine Cahill, in particular, was always anxious to instil in her family a sense of Irishness and a love of all things Irish.

As the new century unfolded, Joseph became more involved with republicanism and joined the Irish National Volunteers, the group which joined the socialist Irish Citizen Army in the Easter

Rising in 1916. Increasingly, he found his time being taken up with printing republican material. In the years following the Rising, he applied for membership of the IRA, hoping to see active service, but was requested to stay on at the printing house because of the value of his work to the republican cause.

As a boy, Cahill junior, by now attending St Mary's Christian Brothers' primary school in nearby Barrack Street, was well used to strangers visiting his father's little business premises. He never tired of hearing the story about Eamon de Valera, the most senior surviving commandant of the Easter Rising, coming to the shop on behalf of the republican movement to congratulate Joseph senior on his work. The future taoiseach (prime minister) and president had come to Belfast to oppose local Irish Parliamentary Party MP Joe Devlin in the 1918 Westminster elections. Devlin, standing in the west Belfast Hibernian bastion of Falls, defeated de Valera by almost two to one.

In 1932 Joseph senior was arrested and charged with printing illegal literature – posters advertising a protest meeting. He was later acquitted. During the war years, he printed forged ration coupons, which were sold to help finance the republican movement.

Joe Cahill recalls that although his father could have been classed as a 'self-employed small businessman', the family nonetheless had their share of tough times.

'Our mother and father had eleven children, but two died. The printing gear took up all the ground floor. We lived in two rooms and a small return room on the first storey, and two other rooms on the second storey. The outside toilet was at the bottom of the backyard. Like most working-class people then, bath-time meant filling the tin bath in front of the fire on Saturday night.

'We got it tough at times. My father was a good worker but not a good businessman, and I remember when there would not have been a loaf of bread in the house. Mother, however, was a good manager and she would have made the shilling stretch. I remember, too, that the pawn shop was used quite often.

'My mother's father had a fairly good job. He was head water commissioner – whatever the hell that job entailed – down at the docks, and my mother would regularly bring us down to his office. He would always give me five shillings, a hell of a lot of money in those days. He knew damn well what I would do with the money. Probably that's why he gave it to me. As soon as we were outside, I handed it over to Mother.

'I would be sent to the Ormo Bakery shop on the Ormeau Road twice a week, at eight o'clock in the morning before school. It was around two miles to the bakery. I brought a pillowcase to fill with yesterday's bread, which could be bought cheaply. The women waiting to be served got to know me and, I suppose because I was so small and young, they would push me further up the queue to be served more quickly. They thought I was a great lad, and said things like, "You're not like them bastards of mine – I can't get them out of bed at this time of day."

'Mother could always have sent me to one of the bakeries in west Belfast, which were closer. There were a number in the area at that time, but I would have been recognised and there was a bit of family pride to be lost in being seen standing in a queue for cheap bread.'

Despite the hardship, Joe Cahill senior always managed to put aside a small sum of money to rent a seaside cottage every year, either just over the border in County Louth or on the beautiful Antrim coast to the north of Belfast. While their father worked in the printing house, joining them on occasional weekends, the Cahill children spent the summer frolicking on the beach or exploring the unspoiled countryside. It was during one of these rough-and-ready but idyllic summers that Joe Cahill almost drowned and developed a life-long aversion to the sea.

'My father had a theory that if we got a good holiday in the summer time, it saved doctors' bills in the winter and the rest of the year. We would have had a cottage either in Omeath, near

Dundalk, or in Glenarm, in the Glens of Antrim. We generally went away for the duration of the school holiday and sometimes we were even granted an extension from the school, which meant our break could last up to ten or twelve weeks.'

Cahill was around the little printing house from the age of eight, and acquired a good working knowledge of the trade over the next six years, occasionally helping his father to set up and print jobs. Once, when Joe senior was ill, he asked his oldest child to stay off school for the day to complete an urgent job.

'It was the chance I had been waiting for. I told my father that it was 19 May, I was fourteen and I wanted to leave school for good. My mother and father had a discussion about it. Mother wanted me to stay on, but Father left it up to me. So I went to the school and proudly presented myself to the headmaster, a Christian Brother. I told him I wanted to leave and start work in the printing trade. He looked at me for a moment and said, "Well, you never were the brightest anyway, Cahill." But he wished me well and told me I was very lucky to have a trade to go to. Before I could leave, however, he made me promise to continue studying at home and to return at the end of June to sit the final exam. At that stage, I would have promised him the sun, the moon and the stars, just to get out of school.

'I thought no more about the exam until a friend reminded me that we were to turn up at the school and bring a pencil. I had always been very nervous during examinations and had not performed very well. I supposed I was just not academically-minded. On that day, however, I did not give a damn how I did. It did not worry me at all. There were two boys who achieved ninety-seven percent that day – I was one of them. The headmaster, Brother "Fish" Aherne, told me he knew I always had it in me, and the examination result had proved that.'

From around the age of twelve, Cahill says, he became aware of the cancer of sectarianism that was part of the way of life in the northern counties in the 'hungry thirties'. Looking back, he now laments a lost opportunity to build on working-class solidarity, when Catholics and Protestants united briefly against the government, during what became known as the Outdoor Relief riots.

The ODR scheme, as it became known, tapped the vast reservoir of the unemployed, using them to carry out heavy labouring work, such as repairing roads and laying pavements. The pay was poor, barely enough to alleviate the appalling hardship. When authorities announced plans to cut the wages as an austerity measure, poverty, hunger and resentment boiled over. The ODR workers, Catholic and Protestant, united to embark on a strike which was to deteriorate into serious rioting.

The unionist government, acknowledged since its inception by unionists and nationalists alike as 'a Protestant parliament for a Protestant people', became worried at the possibility of united working-class support for the Labour movement. Provocative anti-Catholic speeches soon became the order of the day.

Working-class unity was short-lived; the North soon fell back into a familiar pattern of sectarian violence. Pilgrims on their way to Dublin for the 1932 Eucharistic Congress, an international Catholic religious event, were attacked. The sight of the little ghetto streets adorned with altars and bedecked with flags and bunting in the papal colours proved altogether too much for the bigots and ignited a spate of house burnings and evictions.

The recently formed and openly sectarian Ulster Protestant League was to fan the flames of discrimination for the next few years. Community violence reached a peak in 1935 when Cahill, who has always claimed to be staunchly opposed to any form of sectarianism, was fifteen years old. That summer of sectarian madness left eleven people dead.

'There was a great depth to the hatred of some loyalists,' says Cahill. 'One particular incident which sticks in my mind occurred in east Belfast, when St Anthony's Catholic church was being built, at Willowfield on the Cregagh Road. In May 1936, some guys climbed a tree on the site in the middle of the night and stuck a huge pig's head there. On the tree trunk they nailed a big sheet of cardboard painted with the words "Cured in Lourdes".

'Incidents like that notwithstanding, it had been great to see the unity between Catholic and Protestant in the early 1930s. Labour were playing a fairly big part at the time and it was a fine thing to see people uniting to better themselves. It was around this time that I began to think about the causes of division, why they existed. I had a lot of social ideas in my head at that time.

'The first organisation I joined was the Catholic Young Men's Society. They had a strong social conscience. One of their campaigns that I was involved in was against moneylenders, who leeched off the poor by charging extortionate interest rates. Most of the moneylenders and hire-purchase providers in Belfast were people with established businesses in other fields. The CYMS brought a case against one of these people, a test case to see if their high interest rates were legal. The case went on for months before the court finally ruled that moneylenders were not permitted to charge more than twelve-and-a-half percent interest, which was still very high but it was a start. That was my introduction to social campaigning.'

At the age of seventeen, Cahill – who had by then forsaken the printing trade to become an apprentice joiner – joined his local *slua*, or branch, of the republican scout movement, Na Fianna Éireann. The organisation was formed by Countess Constance Markievicz to offer nationalist youth an alternative to Lord Baden Powell's British Boy Scouts movement. While the Fianna was a genuine boy scout organisation, it made no secret of its republican orientation. Right up to the 1990s, Royal Ulster Constabulary (RUC) officers giving evidence in court cases often referred to the Fianna as 'the junior wing of the IRA'. It was not obligatory for Fianna boys to graduate to the IRA, but most regarded it as a natural step.

However, entry into the Fianna was no simple formality. Would-be Fianns (translated as soldiers or warriors) had to complete a rigorous education programme before being accepted.

'It was difficult enough to join the republican movement in those days. They put you through all sorts of tests to see if you were genuine. Even in the Fianna, you had to know and understand Irish history. The Fianna took part in scouting activities – not only normal scouting activities, but scouting for the IRA. If the IRA was holding a company parade, as they called it – which could be a gun lecture or whatever – it was our job to keep lookout.

'In our area, the IRA used a building at Springfield Avenue called the Green Hut. They often held gun lectures there – not that we would know lectures were going on there, of course. We were told there was a meeting being held, and our job was to watch in case the police came. We were posted at different street corners and would signal down the line if we saw police coming. I remember at least two occasions when the RUC were on their way to raid the Green Hut and we managed to get a warning to the parade. The cops would come marching down in military formation, and it was not a big job to deliver a message ahead of them. We had a system of signalling which consisted of whistling from one corner to another. When the raiding party arrived, they invariably found a couple of men innocently playing cards.'

Sometime between his eighteenth and nineteenth birthdays, Cahill transferred to the IRA, joining his local 'C' Company, a unit of around sixty volunteers based in the Clonard area of west Belfast. Once again he faced a lengthy entrance process, frequently being sent away to reflect on the possible consequences of life as an IRA volunteer:

'Again you had to go through classes in history, political awareness and security. It was a long process, because you had to do examinations. You were told what lay before you, what you could expect – membership of the IRA could mean being on the run, imprisonment or death. They asked you to think about all these things. They actually painted a very black picture of what could happen to you, then gave you time to think it over. That could happen perhaps two or three times, and when you came back and said "right," they gave you even more time to think about it.'

Cahill's first weapons lecture was not, however, to take place in the Green Hut. Even idealistic young IRA men had to eat and, with work scarce in Belfast, Cahill accepted an offer of a job in the border town of Newry, thirty-eight miles to the south. A cousin, one of his numerous relatives there, 'spoke for him' and he obtained employment as a door-to-door collector for Britannic Insurance.

The new job also meant a new IRA company. The officer commanding his Belfast unit arranged for his transfer to the south Down IRA.

'I went to my first weapons lecture in Newry. It was held in the Labour Hall in the town's Cornmarket. Each time the hall was booked, up to five or six units of the IRA would turn up for a night's training. We would split up into groups for instruction in various weapons, such as the rifle, Thompson sub-machine gun, revolver and grenade. Generally the first weapon that volunteers were trained in was the grenade, or Mills bomb.

'As this was my first lecture, I joined the squad which was to be trained in the use of the Mark 5 Mills bomb. The instructor was explaining that it had vertical and horizontal grooves cut in the metal to ensure greater fragmentation when it was detonated. He hadn't finished the sentence when there was an explosion. There was pandemonium. I was sitting on a chair beside the table. People were running everywhere – the shit was scared out of them. I didn't know a damn what had happened. I remember someone saying, "Is he dead?" I automatically started feeling my chest, arms and legs to see if he was referring to me.

'The explanation was not long in coming. In the middle of the crowd next to us was a guy lying out cold on the floor. They had been doing the rifle. Someone tossed the weapon to another man, who pressed the trigger as he caught it. There was a round in the breech and it was discharged. The bullet went through the soft hat of the man standing beside the culprit and lodged in the wall behind him. The man with the hat fainted. Everyone thought for a moment that he had been shot. When they discovered he wasn't shot, they brought him to. The OC gave off hell about the lack of discipline. He said the only one present who showed any sense of discipline was "that man over there", and he pointed at me. Then he said, "But that is only what you would expect from a Belfast man."

'I was walking home with him that night and he said, "Tell me the truth. Were you frightened?" I told him I was so shit-scared that I couldn't move off the chair, and he said, "Never you tell anyone that, after what I said about you in there." That was my first experience of weapons lectures.'

Cahill spent several months in Newry before returning home, but that period, although short, was to prove eventful. There was one particular plan the Belfast man played a role in, which, if it had succeeded, had the potential to change the whole nature of the Irish–British conflict.

On this occasion, Cahill and his comrades were mobilised and brought out of town to the countryside near the border. The IRA men were split into groups of four and five and placed at intervals along the border. They were told they would receive further instructions later.

However, the night passed without event and, as dawn was breaking, the men were stood down and told to go home. The main body of volunteers never did find out the reason for this mid-night escapade. However, Cahill, who had become friendly with the south Down leadership, was later told the little they knew of the operation:

'I learned afterwards what the purpose of the mission had been.

There had been some sort of agreement that units of the Free State army were going to invade the north. We were there to guide them in, to bring them across the border.'

According to Cahill's theory, which he admits is based only on anecdotal evidence, the man behind the border incursion plan was the then Free State minister for defence, Frank Aiken.

Born of south Armagh farming stock in 1898, Aiken enjoyed a long and chequered career and served as *tánaiste* (deputy prime minister) in the Republic from 1965 to 1969. He only retired from active politics ten years before his death in May 1983.

Educated at Newry's St Colman's College, he joined the Irish Volunteers and was appointed Sinn Féin organiser at the age of nineteen. Aiken was active in the War of Independence and was officer commanding the IRA's Fourth Northern Division, which operated in south Armagh and north Louth.

On the eve of the Civil War in May 1922, Aiken met pro- and anti-Treaty leaders Michael Collins and Eamon de Valera and told them the conflict would mean the total abandonment of nationalists on the northern side of the border. That meeting led to the Collins–de Valera pact, which almost averted the war by proposing a coalition government. When the pact collapsed, Aiken's Fourth Northern Division initially took a neutral stance before joining in the fight on behalf of the anti-Treaty forces. The young south Armagh man rose to become chief of staff of the IRA. He was to hold the position until 1925, a period which included some of the bloodiest episodes in Irish history. At the end of the Civil War in 1923, it was Aiken who gave the order to the IRA to cease fire and dump arms.

Although embracing constitutional politics – he joined Fianna Fáil when it was founded in 1926 and was elected TD for the border county of Louth the following year – Aiken always retained his basic republican principles. He often expressed concern for the beleaguered northern Catholic minority following partition.

A close friend and confidant of de Valera, Aiken held several ministerial posts and accepted the Defence portfolio when his party was elected to power in 1932.

In January 1938, de Valera travelled to London for negotiations with the British government on a wide ranges of issues. The Irish contingent was reported to be well pleased with the mainly successful outcome of the talks, which resulted in, among other things, the end of the economic war between the two countries. There was anger in some Irish government circles, however, that no progress had been made on the ending of partition. Aiken, who never lost his strong attachment for the people of his native south Armagh and the northern counties in general, was said to have been angered by British intransigence on the partition issue.

It was against this background, Cahill believes, that Aiken – acknowledged as being quite impulsive on occasions – decided to create an international incident. He would place the partition of his country back in the world spotlight by sending units of the Irish Army over the border.

Cahill, still in his teens and burning with the zeal of republican idealism, accepted Aiken's alleged role as being only what would be expected of any Irish person. In later years, however, he realised the significance of the abortive operation and made several attempts to uncover the whole story.

'I have tried since then,' he said, 'to find confirmation, but I can only get broad hints that the man responsible was minister of defence Frank Aiken. The men meant to come across the border were known as "Aiken's Volunteers", although I cannot get anyone to admit they were involved. People have said to me they have heard of the plan but were not part of it. I do know that, around that time, Aiken was sent to America. It was said that this was done either as part of his punishment or to get him out of the way for a while.'

It is true that Aiken had been instrumental, with the Free State government's consent and approval, in founding an armed group – the Volunteer Reserve – which became widely known as 'Aiken's Volunteers'. This organisation was proposed by Aiken in 1933 and inaugurated by taoiseach Eamon de Valera the following year. During the Dáil debate in February 1934, it was stated that the new volunteer force would be based on the Swiss army model of a small standing army supported by a larger group of mainly unpaid volunteers. In fact the new 11,500-strong force was aimed at drawing the teeth of the IRA and weakening the movement numerically, by recruiting young republican-minded people as a kind of army reserve or auxiliary force.

Aiken entertained the hope that the IRA would go over *en masse* to his new group, thus obviating the need for unpopular and draconian measures such as internment and the harsh military court system. Some IRA members did join Aiken's Volunteers, but not in the numbers he had hoped for. Unsurprisingly, the first forty-strong *slua*, or company, of the new volunteer force emerged from Dundalk in the north Louth–south Armagh area, where Aiken's record in the War of Independence and the Civil War had ensured him folk-hero status.

Whether the group that Cahill and his comrades had waited vainly for were indeed members of Aiken's Volunteers, or a separate group of selected members of the Free State army, is not known. Cahill, however, is adamant that, shortly after the incident, he was told privately of the incursion plans by his commanding officer and his adjutant.

Belfast historian Eamon Phoenix puts forward two possible dates for the incident described by Cahill:

'During the London talks of 1938, de Valera gained the return of Ireland's "Treaty ports", held by Britain since 1921, and ended economic hostilities between the two countries. He failed, however, to win concessions on partition. Strangely, Aiken, though minister of defence, was excluded from de Valera's delegation at the negotiations with British prime minister Neville Chamberlain. Some historians feel this was because Aiken was too republican or too strong on the northern question.

'Aiken's US visit was not until 1941 (during the Second World War when the south was neutral). In dating the proposed "invasion" which Joe Cahill recalls, there are two possibilities. In 1938, de Valera compared the nationalist areas along the border to the Sudetenland in Czechoslovakia which Hitler seized by force. Secondly, de Valera took a strong stand against the threat of conscription in the North in April 1939 and succeeded in preventing it. The plan could have been a contingency at that time.'

Cahill spent part of his time in Newry at a small hotel – 'it was as cheap as living in digs in those days' – and it was there he heard that two Irishmen, Peter Barnes and Jimmy McCormack, had been sentenced to death in England. The men had been found guilty of planting a bomb in Coventry, which had killed five people and seriously injured dozens more. An investigation by the IRA revealed that neither McCormack or Barnes was the man who had conveyed the bomb in a messenger's carrier bicycle to the busy street, before leaving it propped against the wall of a shop. It was common knowledge in republican circles at the time that Barnes and McCormack – Peter Barnes in particular – were on the periphery of the operation and that the real bomber later returned safely to Dublin.

'Feelings were running high in Ireland that Ash Wednesday in 1940 when they were to be hanged at Winston Green Prison in Birmingham. No one had gone to work that day. There were a few of us, including a couple of teachers from the Christian Brothers' school, sitting around the radio that morning, waiting to hear the BBC nine o'clock news. All of us were hoping for a last-minute reprieve. But when the news came on, we heard that Barnes and McCormack had been executed.

'I can still hear the bitter comments from the other people in the room. Several were muttering things like "British bastards". We talked of the terrible loneliness and sorrow of them walking to the scaffold and even the British news said they walked very bravely to their deaths. Little did I think that morning that just two years later I would be in a similar position and that the same hangman would be brought to Belfast to execute my best friend; the same hangman would also be brought to Ireland by the Free State government to hang another republican, Charlie Kerins.'

Six weeks later, Cahill was to take part in an another event which made a lasting impression on him – south Down IRA's Easter Rising commemoration parade. Republican parades were banned north of the border; those taking part risked imprisonment. The ban, however, appears to have made the IRA more determined to honour their dead; each year in the North dozens of parades would take place – some clandestinely, some quite openly.

At Easter 1940, however, the IRA was numerically strong in the Newry–south Down area and the local leadership did not anticipate any trouble.

'The south Down IRA was divided into several groups that Easter and we went to different parts of the area to hold our parades. The crowd I was attached to was ordered to mobilise late at night in the yard [quadrangle] of the Abbey Christian Brothers' school at Courtney Hill. We were to march from there to a house at Ballyholland where two IRA volunteers had been shot dead in the 1920s,' Cahill says.

There was a bit of excitement when the marchers came across two 'B Special' police constables. The Ulster Special Constabulary, long regarded by nationalists as a sectarian force, was formed in 1920 to pave the way for partition and to help seal off the new border. The force, 32,000-strong by 1922, was based on the Ulster Volunteer Force raised by loyalists to oppose Home Rule in the years before the Great War.

The Ulster Special Constabulary originally consisted of three sections: A, B and C Specials. Class A were full-time, B Specials were part-time and C Specials were to be mobilised in an emergency or doomsday situation. By 1926, the A and C Specials had been discarded and the B Specials came to be regarded by northern Protestants as their own force. They were disbanded in controversial circumstances by the British government in 1970 and their role taken over by the Ulster Defence Regiment.

When Cahill and the others came across the heavily outnumbered USC members, they 'took the men prisoner and relieved them of their weapons. They were held until dawn when the whole commemoration parade was over and then released,' he says.

'We continued marching to the house and the scene which followed made a deep and lasting impression on me. At the gable wall, by the light of a storm lantern, the 1916 Proclamation was read out. The Army [IRA] statement was also read, as was customary, and a few words were said to commemorate the republican dead. The whole episode was carried off well. There were upwards of one hundred of us and I can still hear the tramp of feet on the road that night.'

Cahill stayed in Newry until May of that year, when circumstances dictated a return to Belfast. His return was not in answer to a summons by republican superiors, but the result of a more mundane set of circumstances.

'I was not a good insurance collector and unfortunately I got the sack. I suppose it was because I had a social conscience. We had to go around the houses of ordinary working people who were paying for their own deaths. Sometimes, of course, they were unable to pay.

After a fixed number of weeks of non-payment, I was supposed to strike them off, which meant they were out of benefit. I found that a very hard thing to do, going to a house with a big family and the man not working and having to press them into paying a shilling a week, which was a considerable amount of money then.'

On occasion, Cahill would pay a defaulter's weekly premium from his own meagre wage, but eventually found himself subject to the law of diminishing returns.

'Often I would pay the shilling to keep them on the books in the hope of getting the money back later. Sometimes you did or sometimes you got sixpence. Eventually I was forced to take them off the books because the whole thing was eating into my own wages. I was not really pressing for new business and I eventually got the sack. I thanked my relative for getting me the job, asked my IRA company for a transfer and headed back to Belfast.'

CHAPTER TWO
The 'Prod Squad'

Back once more in Belfast, Cahill's C Company, and indeed the city's entire IRA membership, were shocked by news of a setback which was to throw the republican movement into turmoil. Then aged twenty-one, Cahill was among hundreds of volunteers ordered to attend a parade in an Irish dance hall at the bottom of the Falls Road, close to the city centre.

'The parade took place in the Tara Hall, above O'Kane's public house in King Street. The hall was packed. The parade was called to attention and stood at ease. We had no inkling of what was to happen next. The purpose of that parade was to read to volunteers a statement – the confession of Stephen Hayes, IRA chief of staff, that he had acted as an informer for the Irish government.'

Hayes had been seized in late June 1941 by northern IRA men who had been called in to investigate an alarming and ever-increasing number of arrests and failed operations.

If Stephen Hayes was not an informer, he was singularly unlucky. After he was appointed IRA chief of staff in April 1939, there followed a series of disastrous operations, which, coupled with the tough 'emergency' laws in the South, sent the IRA spiralling into serious decline. Arrests of volunteers were an almost everyday occurrence. Several important operations were foiled by Special Branch officers of the Garda Siochána (the Irish police force, literally Guardians of the Peace), resulting in the death or capture of many IRA volunteers. Republican personnel sent across the Irish Sea to take part in a bombing campaign found British police waiting for them at purportedly secret addresses. Such was the drain on manpower down south that a number of northerners found themselves rapidly promoted to high rank. Senior officers in the North refused to believe that so many failures were simply the result of coincidence, ill fortune or good police work. There had to be an informer, and a highly-placed informer at that, they reasoned.

Seán McCaughey, Liam Rice and Charlie McGlade were all members of the IRA's Belfast leadership. McCaughey was from Aughnacloy, County Tyrone, but spent much of his life in Belfast. A popular figure with the city's republican community, he was known as Father Seán because of his deceptively gentle demeanour. It was McCaughey who initially suspected the chief of staff of being an Irish government agent and he took Rice and McGlade into his confidence. There followed one of the most bizarre episodes in IRA history, an episode which is still the subject of debate among veteran republicans.

Convinced he was on the right track, McCaughey and his 'Belfast boys', as they came to be known, travelled to Dublin and gathered together a group of volunteers whose integrity they believed was beyond question. McCaughey then instigated an intelligence-gathering operation which he hoped would result in enough evidence to convict Hayes at an IRA court martial.

A typical ploy used by McCaughey was to feed addresses of republican safe houses to Hayes. Safe houses were the homes of sympathisers who permitted the IRA to hold meetings or conceal weapons and documents on their premises. McCaughey's team would then carry out around-the-clock surveillance on the houses, more often than not being able to report the time and date each building was raided by the Special Branch.

By the end of June 1941, the northerners were convinced they had a watertight case against Hayes. He was held by former comrades as he turned up for what he believed would be a routine meeting. The Wexford man was charged with treason and told that he would be court-martialled at a date to be decided.

Hayes's account of what followed next differs sharply from that of the IRA. What is agreed is that the captive was taken north, just short of the border, to the Cooley Mountains in County Louth.

From there he was taken south again, to a cottage in the Wicklow mountains. When it appeared their position there had been compromised, Hayes found himself on a night-time forced march over the mountains to the outskirts of Dublin city, and from there to Rathmines in the south of the city. Hayes and his captors were billeted in Castlewood Park, in a safe house used by IRA Headquarters staff. Throughout his ordeal, Hayes was lightly shackled with a chain around his ankles. This apparently hampered his movement but did not render him immobile.

The court martial of the hapless former chief of staff, with Seán McCaughey, the new IRA leader, prosecuting, began on the evening of 23 July and went on for around ten hours, ending at approximately seven the next morning. Hayes was found guilty of crimes for which the IRA had only one sentence – death. Stalling for time, he offered to write a full confession, but said he would need a considerable period to do so.

The IRA, in statements issued later, admitted to keeping Hayes on short rations for a while and subjecting him to continual interrogation after his abduction. Shortly afterwards, they insisted, he received the same food as his captors and, although still being questioned, was not harmed in any way. Hayes, however, would later claim that he was starved and beaten. His offer to write a statement of confession, he said, was made after he had been kept awake for twenty-four hours and threatened with being tortured to death.

The condemned man began to write what turned out to be a 150-page statement. Each time he was urged to finish, he managed to find another crime to confess to. Years later he was to insist that he was continually beaten and threatened as he wrote. On 8 September, a few days before he was due to be executed – he was to be shot on the third Sunday of the month, All-Ireland Final day – the former IRA leader took advantage of a serious lapse by his captors.

His guard, who had taken off his holstered gun for comfort and placed it on the mantelpiece, was called to the door. Hayes managed to grab the gun and holster. He shuffled as quickly as he could towards the bay window, then launched himself into the street. Passers-by watched in amazement as the dishevelled, hobbled figure, clutching a firearm tightly to his chest, shuffled, staggered and hopped his way into the nearby Rathmines Garda station.

Seán McCaughey had been picked up by Gardaí a few days before Hayes escaped. The northerner had just alighted from a tram at the corner of Castlewood Avenue, a few yards from the safe house, when he was arrested. When Hayes presented himself to Gardaí, the Special Branch could scarcely believe their luck. As the newly-reprieved man poured out his incredible story, detectives realised they now had more than enough evidence to convict the new chief of staff – and they did not even have to find him first.

The authorities wasted no time – before the month was out, McCaughey was charged, tried and sentenced to death. Evidence given by Hayes helped to convict the chief of staff. The death penalty, however, was shortly afterwards commuted to life imprisonment. From the day he entered Portlaoise Prison until his death on hunger and thirst strike almost five years later, the Tyrone man was held in solitary confinement, clad only in a blanket because he refused to be branded a common criminal by wearing prison clothing.

Stephen Hayes was sentenced to five years' imprisonment for his IRA activities – a strange reward, some republicans argue, if he had indeed been a government agent. In 1949 Hayes went to great pains to publicly deny each and every accusation made against him by McCaughey. He was to continue protesting his innocence of treachery against his colleagues right up to his death in 1974 at the age of seventy-eight.

As an idealistic twenty-one-year-old volunteer, Cahill accepted at face value the IRA statement that September evening in 1941. It was later, when he heard doubts being raised about Hayes's guilt, that he began to ask questions. But, apart from any other consideration, the fact that Hayes gave evidence in court against McCaughey was, for a republican, every bit as bad as informing.

As Cahill rose up through the ranks of the IRA and travelled extensively around the country, he took the opportunity to question everyone he met who had been involved in the Hayes affair. Although opinions differ sharply to this day, Cahill firmly believes that McCaughey and the Belfast Boys were correct:

'I have talked to people involved in the Hayes affair; I have been talking about it for the last thirty years and I have no doubt he was guilty. There was ample evidence against him. And even if there was a remote chance that he was not guilty, he gave evidence against Seán McCaughey. That in itself is unforgivable.

'Hayes was a very, very shrewd man. His written confession was, deliberately I believe, littered with wrong dates and meetings which never took place. For instance, he would write that he met a Special Branch man at a time and date when he knew he had been attending an Army Council meeting. This was a double bluff, intended to render his confession worthless.'

Graphic descriptions of McCaughey's painful and lingering death also did little to enhance Hayes's image in Cahill's mind:

'I talked to Seán's sisters, one in particular who had been with him right up to end. It was horrible listening to her. She said sometimes she felt like letting him die. His tongue was horribly swollen and she had to put a spoon on his tongue and press it down to let him breathe. She said she was tempted often to let him choke to death rather than go through that terrible agony. It was very, very sad to listen to.'

The IRA in the South took years to recover from the Hayes episode, but in the North the day-to-day reality of a British presence led to a greater determination to reorganise and carry on.

✠ ✠ ✠

When Cahill returned to Belfast, he was deemed experienced enough to take on a training and recruiting role, amongst other duties, with Northern Command's Belfast Battalion. Not long after his return from Newry, Cahill was bemused but delighted to be asked to work with one of the IRA's most unusual squads – the Special Unit, made up of Protestant republicans who wanted to play their part in the struggle.

For most of the IRA's history, its northern members tended to come mainly, but not exclusively, from the Catholic community. Apart from fighting for the reunification of Ireland, republicans in Belfast – and indeed in any part of the North where religious tensions existed – were also expected to defend their areas against sectarian attack, a role which would not immediately attract many members of the Protestant working class.

There were also the issues of gerrymandering and government-backed discrimination in employment and housing, issues which tended to affect the Catholic community more than their Protestant counterparts. So, while the IRA did not block membership of the organisation on religious grounds – indeed Protestant volunteers were warmly welcomed – it invariably drew most of its members from the Catholic side. Those non-Catholics who did join the republican movement in the late 1930s and early 1940s tended to be mainly middle-class intellectuals and socialists.

There had been one promising period when Protestants from Belfast's Shankill Road – an area which was and remains the heartland of northern loyalism – marched to the grave of Theobald Wolfe Tone, the 'father of Irish republicanism'. His grave, at Bodenstown in County Kildare, is a spot sacred to Irish republicans of every hue. Cahill was fourteen years old in June 1934, when he witnessed the breakdown of working-class Protestant and Catholic solidarity amid distasteful scenes at the annual republican march and commemoration.

Members of a newly-established James Connolly club, formed by unemployed Belfast Catholics and Protestants, carved their own little niche in history by taking part in the commemoration that year. Unfortunately, the group found themselves involved in a left-wing versus right-wing split in the IRA. The left-wingers, who were attempting to embrace republicans, communists and social-ists in the broad-based Republican Congress, welcomed the pres-ence of the Shankill Road men in the South. However, hidden tensions rose to the surface following the expulsion from the IRA of Republican Congress leaders Peadar O'Donnell and Michael Price. As the northern Connolly men waited at the assembly point at Sallins for the march to move off, attempts were made by Tip-perary IRA volunteers to seize the left-wing banners. Scuffles broke out and the pioneering socialists from Belfast were involved in a number of fist fights. Further violence occurred at the end of the march, although the only serious damage was to Protes-tant–Catholic solidarity.

Seven years later, the Special Unit was proving particularly valu-able to the IRA. Few of its members were, at least initially, known to the RUC Special Branch and so they could move around with a greater degree of freedom than the 'usual suspects'. The fact that most members of the unit lived in Protestant areas was also exploited to the full by the IRA. Republican quartermasters knew well that arms stored in a middle-class unionist neighbourhood would be a lot safer than in the home of a well-known republican who had perhaps been arrested several times.

Most of the Special Unit were, or had been, members of the Irish Union Movement founded by Denis Ireland, himself a Prot-estant and a republican in the old Ulster Presbyterian tradition. Ireland, a journalist, author and broadcaster, served with the

British Army in France and Greece during the First World War. He was well respected by the Irish government and he later accepted a nomination to the Senate, serving there from 1948 to 1951.

His Irish Union Movement brought together like-minded spirits, northern Protestants who sought the reunification of their country by peaceful means. Several members, however, who had studied Ireland's centuries-old relationship with England, came to believe that armed struggle was the only way to achieve their aim, and so joined the IRA.

Cahill's responsibilities around this time included providing weapons instruction for this group:

'After coming back from Newry, I was working actively with the Northern Command. I was involved greatly with the Special Unit in Belfast. Their membership was kept secret from almost everyone, although I had a fair amount of contact with them. They trained in a small hall in Waterford Street on the Falls Road, facing Dunville Park.

'Some were intellectuals, but others were not. Some were small businessmen – for example Billy Smith, who had a small printing house, a jobbing house, in McAuley Street in the Markets area. Another was Rex Thompson, from the Antrim Road in Belfast. His father was a commandant in the B Specials. Smith and Thompson were arrested at Thompson's house where, I regret to say, what had been regarded as a very safe IRA arms dump was captured.'

One of the most experienced and dedicated members of what became known unofficially as the 'prod squad' was John Graham. Graham, who was born in India where his father was a colonel in the British Army, had been studying to be a clergyman when he underwent a radical change of vocation and joined the IRA. In the mayhem which followed the rash of arrests of leading republicans in the early 1940s, his resourcefulness was recognised and he was promoted to officer commanding (OC) Belfast Battalion.

Along with his duties as OC, Graham had a hand in directing publicity for the republican movement, including sharing responsibility for producing the IRA newspaper, *Republican News*, with Kerry man Davy Fleming. Graham and Fleming were arrested in 1942 after a gun battle with the RUC at the Northern Command's publicity HQ, a house on Belfast's Crumlin Road, not far from Crumlin Road prison.

Graham was sentenced to twelve years for his part in the shootout. He and Cahill, who had been arrested earlier that year, had ample time to renew their friendship in Crumlin Road prison's A Wing.

'John Graham was a man I got to know extra well, because he came into jail while I was there. He was a member of the Church of Ireland. Most of the Special Unit were Church of Ireland. John always maintained that his church was the true Christian church in Ireland. Catholics, he said, were impostors and perverts. We had fierce arguments in jail, but he was very convincing in his claims that his was the true church. He said all the important religious relics were in the hands of the Church of Ireland and pointed to several examples, including the Book of Kells. And he was right – all the items he mentioned generally belonged to the Church of Ireland. It was the Catholic Church, John maintained, that had left the true church.

'When he was in Crumlin Road jail, the Church of Ireland chaplain, Pastor Buchanan, was appointed pastor of St Mary's on the Crumlin Road – the church John attended when he was free. During one visit, John's mother and sister told him of the new pastor – what a great man he was, and the changes he was making to the church. They told John about a beautiful picture which the new pastor had mounted in the porch of the church. John asked what the picture was and was told it was the Virgin Mary. John, a Church of Ireland elder, was furious and, from his prison cell, attempted to call a meeting of the elders to have Buchanan removed because he had erected symbols of "papish idolatry" in the church.

'I became very friendly with this man Buchanan. He would come into A Wing exercise yard and talk to as many people as possible. He had seen service in the Second World War and was taken prisoner by the Germans after the parachute drop at Arnhem. He told me he spent eleven months as a prisoner of war. Nine months out of that period, he said, was spent under medical care in what resembled a nuthouse. Despite his own unpleasant experiences, he once said to me, "How, in the name of God, can you face a life sentence in prison?"

'I met him several times after I came out of jail, and he always remained friendly with me. That included a few times after he was promoted – for the man John tried to have drummed out of his wee church on the Crumlin Road was to become Archbishop Alan Buchanan.'

CHAPTER THREE

In the Shadow of the Gallows

Early 1942 saw Joe Cahill serving as second-in-command, or adjutant, of C Company in the IRA's Second Belfast Battalion, based in the Clonard area in the west of the city.

His officer commanding was Tom Williams, a quiet, slightly built but totally committed eighteen-year-old volunteer and a close friend of Cahill. Williams's family had moved to the Falls Road area after being burned out of their north Belfast home during the pogroms of the 1920s. He was quite young to have been appointed to the position of OC, but his superiors on Second Battalion staff believed he had 'an old head on young shoulders' and was totally dependable.

Williams and Cahill's friendship stretched back to the days when they were in the Con Colbert *slua* of Na Fianna Éireann. When not attending IRA arms lectures or drilling at company parades, Cahill and Williams would often go to the cinema or to an Irish dancing session together, or take a walk along the Falls Road discussing republicanism and the reunification of their country. They had both been appointed to C Company staff after the arrest of several older volunteers, who were charged with taking part in a fund-raising robbery.

When the Second World War broke out and the Germans launched their bomb blitz, both young men, in response to an IRA order, joined the ARP (Air Raid Precautions), a government group organised on a neighbourhood basis. The ARP warden's job was to assist civilians during air raids and enforce the black-out measures aimed at making the German bombers' task more difficult.

'Placing volunteers in the ARP was an early attempt by the IRA to give leadership and aid to the nationalist population in a time of strife,' says Cahill. 'Tom and I, and dozens of others, had many a quiet chuckle at the idea of republicans walking around nationalist areas wearing official British uniform.'

As they talked and plotted and planned and trained in the winter and early spring of 1941–2, the young IRA men could not know that their friendship was to end in dramatic circumstances before many months had passed. Cahill says the events of Easter Sunday, 5 April 1942, have remained etched in his memory ever since.

'Every year the Stormont government invoked the Special Powers Act to impose a seven-day ban on all parades commemorating Easter Sunday,' he says.

The Special Powers Act, as the name suggests, gave Stormont authorities wide-ranging powers which they wielded without fear of legal redress. Under the act, the RUC could, for instance, have a person jailed for singing a rebel song, or declare a gathering of three people an illegal assembly.

'The IRA in each area devised a particular plan to enable them to defy the ban and hold a parade to honour the men and women who took part in the 1916 Rising. For example, the year before, a huge march was held at six o'clock in the morning to Cyprus Street, where a commemoration ceremony was held at the home of Joe McKelvey [a Belfast IRA man executed by pro-Treaty forces in 1922]. Thousands turned out for that.

'In 1942 it was decided, for the purposes of the Easter Sunday march, to divide Belfast into five areas. In three areas, diversions were to be created by firing shots over, but not at, an RUC patrol. The intention was to draw police into those three areas, to allow two commemoration parades to take place elsewhere. Our company area was one of those selected for a diversion,' Cahill says.

Williams elected to head the operation himself, and selected five men and two women as his team. A five-man squad – the eighteen-year-old Williams, Cahill, then aged twenty-one, Henry 'Dixie' Cordner (nineteen), Jimmy Perry (twenty-one) and John Oliver (twenty-one) – armed with four Webley revolvers and a Luger semi-automatic pistol, would go to a street corner that was passed regularly by an RUC mobile patrol. The five were to fire a volley of shots over the vehicle as it passed the corner of Kashmir Road and Clonard Gardens.

The assumption was that the RUC men would immediately speed off to the safety of their barracks, and then call in reinforcements to sweep the area. Meanwhile, Cahill and his colleagues were to rendezvous with C Company's quartermaster Pat Simpson (another eighteen-year-old), Madge Burns (nineteen) and sixteen-year-old Margaret Nolan, who were to dispose of the weapons. Williams's squad would then separate and go off in different directions. Simpson and the women would take the guns down a back alley and through the rear door of a safe house, the O'Brien family home at 53 Cawnpore Street. The bag containing the arms would be spirited away by the women, who would eventually return them to the dump.

Cahill says the plan began to unravel when the RUC patrol car did not race for the Springfield Road Barracks as anticipated, but instead drove around a corner. Three men – a sergeant and two constables – leaped from the vehicle, determined to pursue their attackers.

'We had taken up position at the corner of Cawnpore Street, behind an air-raid shelter. The patrol car came along and we fired shots over it. We learned later that one bullet penetrated the car, smashing a window, but no one inside was injured. It was proved afterwards that its trajectory was upwards and so could not have been a deliberate attempt to hit the occupants. After firing, we headed towards the spot where the guns were to be handed over to Pat Simpson and the girls.

'Tom and I were the last two to get to the mouth of the entry [a

Belfast term for a narrow alley], and we saw some commotion at the other end. Pat said the others had gone down the entry. We too went down, and entered the safe house by the back door, intending to get the others out. We should never have done that – it was never intended that anyone other than Pat and the girls should enter the house. But we decided to go in the back and leave by the front door. Inside, the woman of the house, Mrs O'Brien – she was a great woman – said, "Here, have some lemonade," and rather than offend her, we stopped to have a drink. As quickly as it takes to tell, the house was surrounded by RUC. Jimmy Perry said there were police coming down the back entry, someone else told us they were also at the front of the house.'

The first policeman to come into the back yard of the O'Briens' house was Constable Patrick Murphy, one of the four RUC men from the patrol car. Murphy, a Catholic who was based in Springfield Road RUC Barracks, lived in the nearby Beechmount area. He was known to the parishioners there, including some of the IRA men involved in the operation. They could not, however, have known that he was in the patrol car, and still less that he would follow them into the safe house.

Murphy had spotted someone entering one of the houses – from the bottom of the alley he could not be sure which house – and informed his sergeant, Archibald Lappin. Lappin then detailed Murphy to cover the entry, while he and another constable checked the dwellings in the area indicated by Murphy. Sergeant Lappin sounded his whistle and was quickly reinforced by two more constables.

It remains unclear why Constable Murphy did not wait for back-up before entering the backyard of number 53, but there is no doubting his bravery. Revolver in hand, he crossed the little yard and approached the scullery. Cahill says that Perry was the first to spot the RUC man. They rushed to retrieve and reload their weapons, which had been placed in a brown leather shopping bag, now lying on a cabinet top in the room adjoining the scullery.

'Jimmy Perry said, "Here they are, coming in the back," and he fired a warning shot through the window. A policeman came in shooting. Tom had taken up a position in the scullery and he was fired on and fell wounded. There was quite a fusillade of shots at that stage and the policeman fell to the floor, fatally wounded. I didn't know who he was – I didn't recognise the man. It was some time later when Tom said it was Paddy Murphy who had been shot.'

Cahill lived at the bottom of the Falls area, in Divis Street, which is close to the city centre and he would not, at that time, have been familiar with many police officers based in Clonard.

Murphy managed to fire three shots from his .45 Webley at close quarters before he was hit by five bullets, from the weapons of two of the republicans. Minutes later his colleagues found him laying face-down, with his revolver still grasped in his hand. All of Murphy's rounds had struck Tom Williams, who was wounded in the left thigh, hip and left arm. The constable was hit in the stomach and chest, with one round piercing his heart. A sixth bullet had hit his holster.

With their OC injured and unconscious and both lines of escape cut off, the remaining five IRA men and the two women had to decide whether to surrender or make a fight of it. Cahill, as company adjutant, immediately took over from the unconscious Williams.

'We decided to shoot it out. There was nothing to lose. We decided to take over the top of the house and defend it from there. This would enable the people of the house to get out the back. We advised Mr O'Brien to try to get his family out.'

Madge Burns and Margaret Nolan were left downstairs, in the somewhat forlorn hope that they could walk out with the O'Briens. Cahill and the others carried Williams to an upstairs room and laid the badly wounded teenager on a bed.

'Tom had come round and I asked him where he was shot. He said he didn't know, but his body felt as though it was burning all over. One of the lads came into the back room to us and said the cops were coming in the back door. I said, "Right, let's take up our positions," and went out onto the landing at the top of the stairs. I saw the police putting the man of the house and his six-year-old granddaughter up the stairs in front of them. They intended to use them as a shield.'

(The O'Briens' granddaughter, Marie Gilmore, grew up to be a committed republican and, under her married name of Marie Moore, made history in 1999 by becoming the first Sinn Féin deputy lord mayor of Belfast.)

Fearing that the non-combatants would be endangered by any further resistance, Cahill told the others they had no option but to give up.

'We shouted down that we were going to surrender and had put down our arms. They flew up the stairs and battered hell out of us. They gave us an awful lacing. A Special Branch man said, "Let's shoot that bastard on the bed. They [RUC superiors] will never know that Murphy didn't shoot him." I threw myself over Tom and said, "Over my dead body."'

All five, says Cahill, were systematically beaten. He himself sustained a fractured skull, several broken ribs and extensive bruising.

'The beating went on until a senior officer, a district inspector, came into the room and said, "Right, stop that. These men are now prisoners." One of the policemen wanted to take us to Springfield Road Barracks, where Constable Murphy had been based. Feelings would have been running high there and we would certainly have been beaten again. However, Tom was taken to the Royal Victoria hospital and we went to Townhall Street police barracks in the city centre, where arrested people are normally taken. We were taken out of our cells periodically for interrogation. There was no great degree of brutality in Townhall Street, but during questioning they stripped me to the waist and lit up cigarettes. They brought the burning tips as close to my body as possible without burning me. I couldn't turn away because they were all around me and I would have moved into a lit cigarette.'

Cahill's injuries made it impossible for him to walk for a time – he had to be carried to and from the interrogation room. An RUC sergeant came to his cell and attempted to draw out a statement of confession from him. When Cahill declined, the sergeant said he would persevere, promising to 'give him every opportunity' to confess.

'And so he did. Every hour, on the hour, he came to the cell to ask if I was ready to make a statement. When I refused, he simply said, "All right," closed the door and came back an hour later.'

The six men and two women were charged with the murder of Constable Murphy. Cahill and the other men were taken to Belfast prison on the Crumlin Road, while Margaret Nolan and Madge Burns were taken to the women's jail in Armagh city. (Madge Burns was to lose her brother, Jim 'Rocky' Burns, two years later, in a somewhat similar shoot-out with the RUC near St Mary's church in Belfast city centre.)

Belfast prison, or 'the Crum', as the now obsolete and disused jail is known to thousands of former inmates, was built in the Victorian period and consists of four wings, each containing three storeys or 'landings'. From the air, the main building of the old jail, which closed in 1995, resembles a huge rimless wheel. Its four wings radiate out like spokes from a central hub, the 'Circle', as it was known to staff and inmates. The Circle, which housed the prison chapel on its second landing, was not only the administrative centre but also the only way in and out of A, B, C, and D Wings. Republicans made up the bulk of the prison's occupants. Cahill and his friends were housed in C1, the ground floor section of C Wing. Convicted prisoners were kept in A Wing, and D Wing was reserved for internees – suspected republicans who could be detained indefinitely without trial.

Because of the seriousness of their charges, which carried the death penalty, and because warders required time to gauge the demeanour of the new prisoners, the men were first housed in what prison staff called 'strong cells'. Unlike normal cells, the doors on these rooms opened outwards, so as to make a surprise attack on warders more difficult. The furniture was fixed firmly to the wall or floor.

'You did not have a proper chair, nor a table,' says Cahill. 'The seat was a plank sticking out from the wall. The table was another plank, fixed to the wall. There was no proper bed, just a wooden board screwed to the floor. In most of the other cells, the windows opened in a little for ventilation, but in these strong cells the windows didn't move or open. There was a one-inch gap running along the top for ventilation.

'We were in there for maybe the first four or five days, and we could hear these people playing handball against the wall of the exercise yard. In fact, the windows were completely black on the outside with the ball striking so often. With no chair or stool to stand on to reach the window, I rolled up the mattress, rolled the blankets up tightly and piled them together in order to see out into the exercise yard. I managed to get up to the window and realised it was internees in the yard. One actually climbed up on the outside and cleaned the window in an attempt to see in. I couldn't stay up there long because the blankets would not support me; they kept sliding from under me.

'They shouted in to ask who I was. I wrote my name on a small piece of paper and held it through the slot. One guy jumped up and caught it. I was able to tell them which cells the other boys were in, and that Tom was in hospital. They slipped cigarettes in to me through the slot. It was a good line of communication with them.'

While on remand, the five were not permitted to mix with other prisoners. Cahill, as adjutant, had automatically assumed command of the unit in the OC's absence. Knowing they faced the hangman's noose, the thoughts of Cahill and the others unsurprisingly turned to plans of escape. There was little chance to confer together, because of strict rules governing association.

'Like most republicans, uppermost in our minds was the question: how do we get out of here? Even during exercise periods we could not converse. We had to walk in single file in a circle around the exercise yard. Talking was not allowed – they did not permit any communication at all.'

To have even a slim chance of escape, they at least needed to talk freely. They also realised that, apart from C Wing, they were not familiar with the layout of the extensive prison grounds. Sentenced prisoners often had the opportunity to converse while working, but republicans on remand were not forced to work – a concession won through vigorous protest over the years.

'We realised very quickly that if we were going to plan anything, we needed to talk. We decided to volunteer for work, hoping to explore the opportunities of escape. By pure accident, we were given the job of clearing the wood yard after the week's work. Every Saturday the yard was tidied up and the sawdust, chunks of trees and twigs were cleared away. We used a cart – a big, two-wheeled effort with a centre shaft. The prisoners were the horses; they pulled the cart along. We loaded the sawdust and other debris onto the wagon and set off to the back of the prison garden, where the rubbish was to be dumped against the wall.

'The warder who was accompanying us was a laid-back sort of a guy. I remember it was a really sunny day, around early June or late May, and he was walking with his hat in his hand and his hands behind his back. He was a south of Ireland man. He was one lazy man and kept telling us, "Take your time going up there, for I have plenty of time to pass."

'He had already told us where to dump the waste, so we sort of ran on in front with the cart and were soon well ahead of him. We were well out of his line of vision when we reached the wall and heeled the cart upright to empty it. I spotted immediately that the shaft near enough reached the top of the wall. The screw was still coming up around the outhouses and had not reached us yet.

'I speilied [an old Belfast term for climbing quickly] up the shaft and looked over the wall to freedom. Landscape Terrace, which runs at right angles to the Crumlin Road and bounds the west side of the jail, lay just a few yards away. I dropped back down and said, "Right, boys, we can get out here."

'Quick as lightning, we made our minds up and decided to go for it. One man grabbed a piece of scrap iron to knock out the screw when he came. Then the thought struck us that Tom would be coming out of hospital soon and there would be a good chance of the six of us escaping. We immediately postponed the idea.'

On their return to C Wing, they heard the warder praise the efforts of his new crew to the principal officer, and promise to have them back the following Saturday. But whether because of the praise or through instinct, the PO was suspicious. He soon became aware of the serious security lapse which had occurred, with important prisoners being allowed to reach the bottom of a perimeter wall without adequate supervision. For the rest of their remand period, they were not permitted to do the job in the wood yard again. Their movements were restricted to the wings and exercise yard.

Almost sixty years later, Cahill sighs as he recalls his dismal record at attempting to take unauthorised parole from jails in various parts of Ireland:

'He who hesitates is lost. It would have been some feat if the six of us had managed to get away, but I was never born to escape. I have been involved in several escapes – I have helped plan and prepare for them – but never, ever have I made a successful escape.

'At the time, it seemed very difficult to us to make an escape, but with hindsight I now realise that it should have been quite easy. At that time, it seemed that we were subject to massive security measures. But when I look at all the escapes which have taken place in recent years, in spite of really tough security, I believe we should have found it relatively easy. I often look back and wonder why in hell we ever stayed in there.'

Tom Williams's condition soon improved enough for him to be moved from the Royal Victoria hospital to the prison hospital. The men were delighted to be reunited with Williams, but found their young comrade somewhat distant and preoccupied.

'Tom joined us shortly after the failed escape attempt. He had been discharged from the hospital, but then had to spend a while in the prison hospital. I had been in charge since we were remanded; I immediately told Tom I was standing down and he was the OC once more. He seemed reluctant, and appeared to have something on his mind. He told us, and it pained him to do so, that he had made a statement to the RUC while he was in hospital,' says Cahill.

Williams knew he had broken one of the most basic rules for an IRA volunteer – never make a statement that might incriminate yourself or your colleagues. It is widely accepted in present-day republican circles, however, that he confessed from the most noble of motives. His statement, made after suffering a severe loss of blood and while believing himself to be dying, shows he heaped responsibility for Constable Murphy's death on himself, while minimising the role of the others. As OC of the abortive operation, Williams took full responsibility and claimed, falsely, that he had fired all of the shots in Murphy's direction. During the subsequent court case, it was proved that all the republican weapons had been fired except the Luger, which was found to be faulty. The shots which killed the policeman had come from two weapons.

'When Tom was in hospital,' says Cahill, 'he was under severe interrogation. They told him he was dying and asked him, why didn't he admit the shooting and have it over and done with? He resisted this. Tom told us when he came on to the wing that he had asked the doctor if he really was dying, and was told he was. We now believe there was no danger of him dying from the wounds.

'Tom said he told himself there were five others involved whose lives were at risk, and so he said to the cops that he accepted responsibility for the shooting. That was Tom Williams, that was the greatness of the man. His thoughts were always for others. It was against all the rules and regulations of the IRA for captured volunteers to make a statement. However, Tom believed he was doing no harm, but could do good for five others. He always said he regretted making the statement, right up until a few moments before he left us.'

The trial of the six men began at Belfast Crown Court on Crumlin Road, before Lord Justice Murphy, on 28 July 1942. It lasted just three days.

Williams, Cahill, Perry, Simpson, Oliver and Cordner were dressed in their Sunday best for the trial. The courthouse, also now defunct, stands directly opposite the old jail. Prisoners to be tried were taken along a tunnel under the Crumlin Road and held in a cell beneath the courtrooms. Strangers to the Number One Court were often startled to see the concealed panelled door opening in the back wall of the chamber, and the heads of the accused slowly appearing as they walked up the steps into the raised dock.

Murder charges against the two women had earlier been reduced. Madge Burns was released, but immediately rearrested. She was interned without trial in Armagh Jail where she was to endure a series of privations at the hands of prison authorities, including being hosed down in her cell with cold water. Margaret Nolan pleaded guilty to a lesser charge of being an accessory after the fact, and was released with a recorded sentence of one year and put under bail to be of good behaviour for three years.

There was no doubt that one of the IRA men had fired the shots which killed Patrick Murphy, and that another volunteer had also wounded him. The best that defence counsel Cecil Lavery could hope for was to convince the jury that the republicans had acted in self defence and without premeditation. However, the prosecution team, led by the Northern Ireland attorney general, were having none of it and pressed for six murder convictions, carrying mandatory death sentences.

The men in the dock knew that the chances of any of them being found not guilty of murder were exceedingly slim, not least because of the make-up and background of the legal forces ranged against them.

'The attorney general, John McDermott, had been a Unionist MP and had served as a cabinet minister in the Stormont government. He was in the B Specials a few years earlier. The judge, Lord Justice Murphy, had been a senior member of the Orange Order and had also been Unionist MP for Derry,' says Cahill.

Lavery, a distinguished senior counsel based in the Republic, did his best to prove that the accused men had been subjected to heavy beatings in the O'Brien house. Several police officers, however, said in evidence that they had been in the back bedroom with the republicans and had seen no violence inflicted on them.

Towards the end of the third day of the trial, the jury members were ready to consider their verdict. The accused, however, seemed to be largely unaffected by the gravity of their position. The *Belfast Telegraph* reported that, during lulls in the proceedings, 'the prisoners chatted among themselves in the dock and nodded smilingly to relatives in court.'

Lord Justice Murphy warned the jury before they retired that their deliberations could 'take a considerable time', and they had his permission to send messages to their families to inform them accordingly.

'All this,' says Cahill, 'gave us the impression that the jury would be out overnight and we would have to wait until the next day for the verdict. Obviously the prison authorities thought so too, because they provided bedding for us in the cell and sent over to the jail for a meal for us.

'The jury was out for less than three hours – two hours and five minutes was, I think, the official time. We had been entertaining ourselves in the cell by singing republican songs, and were settling down for the night when a senior cop came in and told us we were wanted up in the court. We were kind of surprised to be brought back so quickly, and were not sure whether someone wanted to make a legal point or something. We went up the steps into the dock and the judge came in. We were made to stand. The jury filed in and the clerk asked the jury foreman if they had reached a verdict. He said they had.'

The six IRA men were reported to have stood to attention while the verdict was read out. All were found guilty of the murder of Constable Patrick Murphy, but the jury made a recommendation of mercy in the case of eighteen-year-old Pat Simpson, because he apparently did not fire a weapon during the Cawnpore Street incident.

Asked by the judge if there was any reason why sentence of death should not be pronounced on them, Cahill, when his turn came, said: 'I am not guilty of murder. There was no premeditation or intention to take life. I wish to thank counsel for their splendid fight and I also wish, through the medium of the press, to thank everyone who made it possible to have such a splendid defence in this case.'

The others also denied premeditation or intention to murder, and thanked their counsel. Tom Williams, the last to speak, echoed the short statements of the others, but added the sombre line: 'I am not afraid to die.'

There was complete silence in the packed courtroom as Lord Justice Murphy sat back in his chair to allow his tipstaff, or attendant, to place the 'black cap' – in fact a small square of cloth – on the crown of his long wig. Cahill remembers that he and his comrades found it amusing that the judge should have 'a lady's wee black handkerchief on his head'.

Following the archaic formula used by the British judiciary to pass sentence of death, the judge said: 'The sentence and judgement of the court are, and it is hereby ordered, that you, and all of you, be taken from the bar of the court in which you now stand to the prison whence you came, and that on Tuesday, August 18, you be taken to the place of execution in the jail in which you are then confined and then and there hanged by the neck until you are dead and that your bodies be buried within the walls of the prison in which the aforesaid sentence of death should be executed upon you and may the Lord Almighty have mercy on your souls.'

A few seconds of silence followed the judge's speech, before the courtroom erupted into a cacophony of screams of disbelief from women and shouts of protest from men. Several women are reported to have fainted upon hearing the sentence. One prisoner – no one today remembers who – attempted to reassure relatives in the public gallery by shouting, 'There's nothing to worry about.'

After waving to families and friends, the six condemned men drew themselves up to their full height and stood to attention before executing a right turn. There was time for little else as they were grabbed by warders and unceremoniously bundled through the panelled door.

'We were literally pitched down the stairs from the dock and they hustled us away. I think the screws were afraid of trouble developing and they wanted to get us away as quickly as possible. I vaguely remember hearing the row in the court, with people screaming and shouting,' says Cahill.

Within hours of the verdict, the men's legal team had lodged an appeal and the August execution date was suspended. The multiple death sentence also signalled the beginning of a vigorous and widespread campaign to have the six men reprieved.

Taken back through the tunnel under the busy main road, the IRA men were admitted to the jail's reception area to be processed as convicted prisoners. Soon after arriving there, Cahill was told that one of the chaplains, Father Paddy McAllister, wanted to see him in a side room.

'I could see that Father McAllister was very upset. He told me he would have to make special arrangements for spiritual matters concerning us. He also said we would have to agree arrangements for daily Mass and matters of preparation, including a general confession. I told him the sooner all these things were done the better. He was, I realised, preparing us for death.'

Prisoners awaiting execution were normally housed in the death cell next to the gallows chamber, on the ground floor at the end of C Wing or, in prison parlance, C1. The six IRA volunteers represented the largest number of people sentenced to death together since the inception of the state of Northern Ireland. This presented accommodation problems for prison authorities, who were obliged to observe a strict set of regulations governing the treatment and execution of condemned prisoners.

Cahill and Williams were put in the death cell proper, the cell furthest from the entrance of the wing. Both men had named each other when asked separately by a principal officer (PO) if they wanted to share accommodation with any of the other men in particular. The others were located in double cells as close as possible to the death cell. Dixie Cordner was placed with John Oliver, and Jimmy Perry shared with Pat Simpson.

The death cells were larger than normal cells, as they also had to accommodate three warders. The prisoners' every move was watched, every minute, day and night – in case, as Cahill wryly observes, they attempted to kill themselves before the State did.

'The PO explained to us that first night that we would be living under strange circumstances,' Cahill said. 'We were not permitted to listen to the radio or receive newspapers. No matter where we went, we had to have warders with us – going to the toilet, going for a bath; they stood over you no matter what you were doing. They took away our belts, braces and shoelaces. A warder even shaved us. We were not allowed to have a necktie or be anywhere near sharp instruments – all of this in case we attempted suicide.'

The close attention of the warders notwithstanding, the condemned cell was bright and relatively comfortable and, uniquely for Belfast prison, had a built-in toilet. Furniture consisted of two hospital-style beds – larger than normal prison beds – five wooden chairs, two small tables and a large, unadorned wooden cabinet which covered most of the wall furthest from the door. The prisoners did not know at the time – and few occupants of the cell were ever in the position to reveal – that the cabinet was the prison authorities' attempt to show consideration for the feelings of the condemned men. Minutes before an execution, the cabinet would be pushed aside to reveal a door. A prisoner who took just six paces beyond that door would find himself standing in the middle of the trapdoor of Belfast prison's gallows.

As condemned men, the republicans were granted special privileges, including the right to wear their own clothes. They could also select from a wider range of specially prepared meals, and were offered two beers or whiskies each day. Although they were denied contact with IRA comrades, and indeed all other prisoners, and had to eat meals in their cells, they were able to use C Wing's exercise yard for two-hour periods after breakfast, dinner and tea.

'When we left our cells for any reason, the screw rang a hand bell. The other prisoners had been instructed to take cover or return to their cells when they heard the bell, and were not permitted to see us, let alone talk to us. We often kidded each other about this, and called ourselves "the lepers".'

The men formed even stronger bonds and their morale, considering the circumstances, was high. 'The priests came over every afternoon and we had some great sing-songs,' says Cahill.

To minimise chances of contact with others, they were not permitted to use the tiny prison chapel, but attended daily morning Mass and evening devotions in a cell in C Wing where the priests had set up a tiny altar. A Catholic warder was called in to act as altar server. The six were all practising Catholics, but Tom Williams was acknowledged by his comrades to be the most devout. Cahill says, however, that they all derived great solace from the Mass and the spiritual guidance of the prison chaplains.

'Without doubt, our religion was a big comfort to us. We drew strength and succour from that. Once we realised we were facing death, we settled down and accepted that we were going to die. We all had great peace of mind. I can only equate it with people who are facing their final serious illness and are resigned to death, are even happy that death is approaching.

'People often laugh when I tell them that one of the books we were permitted to read – and we did read it – was St Alphonsus's *Preparation for a Sanctimonious Death*. We read a bit of that every day and it was a great consolation.'

Cahill says he had reached the stage of being so well prepared for death that he had feelings of disappointment at the thought of a possible reprieve. 'I know it's hard to fathom but it's true. I don't think I have ever been so well prepared or ready to accept death since.'

With the appeal date fast approaching, their serene acceptance of fate was to be tested to the limit.

The prisoners were not required by law to attend their appeal on 21 August and, in fact, none were present to hear the six death sentences upheld. The new execution date was set for 2 September 1942, less than two weeks distant. Cahill says he remembers little about the appeal, because the condemned men knew there was little prospect of the verdicts being overturned or the sentences commuted. There was, however, an incident on that sunny

August day which he says he has never forgotten.

'The one thing I remember about the appeal is how we were notified of the result. The principal officer in charge of us during the day was PO Lancelot Thompson, a small guy, a callous and vicious wee bastard who was to reach high rank in the prison service. He came out to the exercise yard with a piece of paper in his hand. He held it up in front of us and said, "I have the result of your appeal here. It's all in legal jargon so it will mean nothing to you. But the outcome of it is that you will hang on the second of September." That man rose to relative prominence on the backs of republican prisoners, whom he treated very badly.'

The three appeal judges refused a defence request for leave to appeal to the British House of Lords. The prisoners had steeled themselves for this news and had, in fact, expected it. Outside the jail, however, the result added greater impetus to the reprieve campaign. With just a few days left before the executions, the enormity of six hangings was brought home to even the most disinterested and non-political.

Appeal committees were formed – not only in the North and South of Ireland, but also across the Irish Sea in every English, Scottish and Welsh city with a large Irish community. Petitions were organised in every parish in the North. Prominent politicians and churchmen in Ireland and England lent their support to appeals for clemency. The Vatican and the United States State Department added their support to the campaign.

A petition presented to the unionist government at Stormont contained 207,000 signatures. The president of the United States, Franklin D Roosevelt, was bombarded with telegrams – including one signed by the Irish jurist, politician and former IRA leader Seán McBride – appealing for his intervention.

Even those opposed to republicans and their cause knew that executing the young IRA men would provoke a violent reaction that could reach far beyond Belfast. The city was already a sectarian time bomb and the deaths of six volunteers would certainly have resulted in IRA retaliation. The Dublin government, meanwhile, was fighting its own battle with the IRA and could not have been pleased at the prospect of the upsurge of support for republicans which would surely follow hangings.

Backing for the reprieve campaign came from unexpected quarters. A series of letters appeared in the London *Times* from staunchly pro-establishment figures, such as retired Army generals and Ulster Unionists, appealing to the Westminster government to show leniency to the six.

American pressure was intense. The British ambassador to Dublin wrote to taoiseach Eamon de Valera, chiding him for his appeals to the US government to intervene and pointing out that a country at war, as Britain was, could ill afford to make gestures which could be interpreted as weakness. The ambassador conceded, however, that in this case it would be expedient to show some measure of clemency.

The Stormont and Westminster governments publicly presented a united front in the face of the international reprieve campaign. However, around the cabinet tables and in the committee rooms of the two parliaments, there is little doubt that the pressure was beginning to tell.

The Westminster government was said to have been firmly in favour of all six executions taking place, until Irish primate Cardinal MacRory intervened. The cardinal, who supported the reprieve campaign and had signed the petition, asked his English opposite number, Cardinal Hinsley, to use his influence with the British government to spare the men. Hinsley approached Brendan Bracken, an Irishman and a minister in Churchill's wartime coalition government who was extremely close to the British leader. The reason for Bracken's immense influence on Churchill – the subject of some resentment in the cabinet – has never been fully explained, but post-war media reports suggest that there was a sort of father–son relationship between the two.

Back in Belfast prison, Joe Cahill, Tom Williams and the four others were kept abreast of developments by their visitors. The IRA men appreciated the efforts made on their behalf, but entertained no great hope of a successful outcome to the reprieve campaign. On the Saturday before they were due to be executed – the hangings had been set for Wednesday – Cahill had what he describes as 'a serious conversation' with Williams:

'I said I believed that none of us were going to be reprieved and that Tom, as OC, should call a meeting and he should speak frankly with everybody about it. We arranged to hold the meeting on Sunday night, but it was never to take place.

'We were out in the exercise yard on Sunday afternoon when we were told we had a legal visit and were brought to what they called the solicitors' room. Talking to the others later, they told me they had felt, as I had, a sense that something big was about to happen, but we weren't sure what.

'Our solicitor, Desmond Marrinan, was waiting for us in the room. I remember Marrinan gazing at each of us in turn, then saying directly to Tom, "I have good news for everyone except you, Tom. You are going to die."

'There was an awful silence and it was Tom who broke that silence. He was the strong one amongst us. He said, "This is how I wanted it from the start." It was a dreadful shock for us all. In fact, I collapsed. I will never forget the atmosphere on that day. None of us at that stage ever expected to be reprieved.'

According to the reprieve papers signed by Stormont home affairs minister Sir Dawson Bates, Cahill, Oliver, Cordner and Perry were sentenced to penal servitude (imprisonment with compulsory labour) for the rest of their natural lives. Pat Simpson was sentenced to fifteen years' penal servitude.

The five were informed by a warder that relatives were waiting for them in the visiting area. Cahill said they were aware that they would soon be moved from C1 to A Wing, so they refused to go without an assurance that they would be permitted to see Williams before they left.

Almost sixty years later, Cahill still harbours bitter memories of what he perceives as an act of dishonour by the authorities:

'The governor would not agree at first and we made a bit of a protest. Eventually we were given a guarantee that we would each be allowed to visit Tom before Wednesday. We were choked up and we all hugged and embraced him before leaving to see our families. It was the last time I was to speak to him. They did not keep their promise. We were not permitted to visit him.'

Tom Williams returned to the death cell alone. Cahill came back from his visit to find that he had been moved across the corridor for the night to a single cell directly opposite. The five reprieved men felt little elation at having their lives spared. Their thoughts were with their doomed comrade. Pacing his new cell, Cahill's mind was in turmoil. A few feet away the man he loved as a brother had been left to face a lonely death at the hands of the British hangman.

Cahill was to catch just one more glimpse of his young comrade. Each cell was fitted with a spy-hole, used by warders to check on prisoners. The hole was covered on the outside by a piece of metal on a swivel, permitting the jail staff to lift the cover to observe the prisoner before letting it drop back into place. The spy-hole cover in Cahill's new cell had not been dropped – probably because the cell had been recently empty – and remained in the 'up' position, affording the prisoner a rare, albeit temporary and limited, view of the corridor.

'About six o'clock that Sunday night I heard footsteps and the door of the condemned cell being opened. I went over to the spy-hole and looked out. I saw Tom leaving his cell and walking to the entrance to the exercise yard, which was halfway up the wing. His head was held very high and he was whistling. He seemed very composed. I often thought about this, and I have formed the opinion that he was very happy in his mind at the way things turned out. That was the last time I saw him.'

The campaign to save the last condemned man intensified. Trojan efforts were made by solicitor Desmond Marrinan to secure a last-minute reprieve for the nineteen-year-old, who had celebrated his birthday on remand in prison.

The headline in the nationalist newspaper the *Irish News* on Tuesday, 1 September, read: 'Feverish last-minute efforts to save Williams. Country stirred, nation-wide campaign.' The lead story told of a dash to the North by Dublin mayor Alderman PS Doyle, at the request of his city's corporation. Doyle had a two-hour meeting with his Belfast counterpart, during which he pleaded for Williams to be spared. He left in despair after being told that the governor of Northern Ireland 'had already dealt with the matter' and further action by Belfast Council was not called for.

Also on the front page, the *Irish News* revealed that Dublin firemen had attempted to call in the markers by asking the Belfast Fire Brigade to press for clemency for Williams. Earlier in the war, Belfast fire crews had found themselves hopelessly undermanned when German bombers left large areas of the city blazing. Although citizens of a neutral country, Dublin firefighters made a high-speed dash to the stricken city and played a significant part in bringing the inferno under control.

In their telegrammed appeal, the Dublin firemen said: 'Comrades, we were privileged to associate ourselves with you when death fell upon you from the skies and we appeal to you to approach the Governor-General and your Government supporting our submission that while appreciating the clemency extended to five boys, that the gesture be completed by granting reprieve to Williams also.'

The campaign was brought to the attention of governments as far away as Australia and Russia, with the Armagh Labour Party sending an appeal to the Russian ambassador in London. Telegrams and letters were sent to the English king, George VI, and his prime minister, Winston Churchill. The appeals, however, fell on deaf ears. Tom Williams was doomed.

Desmond Marrinan visited Williams late on Monday night, telling him of the Dublin lord mayor's meeting in Belfast and generally trying to keep some spark of hope alive. Alderman Doyle, Marrinan said, was continuing his efforts and Tom should feel encouraged by this. Williams, in turn, told his solicitor that two priests, Father McEnaney and Father Alexis, had been with him most of the night. But, by all accounts, the teenager hardly needed the encouragement of the lawyer. He appeared to be in complete control of his emotions.

Williams spent part of Tuesday saying farewell to the relatives and friends who had been permitted to visit him. Much of the evening was taken up with praying in the company of the priests, and later with writing goodbye letters to his comrades and family. The *Irish News* reported that Father McAllister and Father Alexis left Tom Williams in good spirits late on Tuesday night. When they returned early the next morning, Williams smiled at them and said he had slept soundly.

The condemned man attended two Masses on the morning of his execution, one at 6.30 and another at 7.15. At the earlier Mass, celebrated by Father Alexis, he received Holy Viaticum, the Eucharist for those in danger of dying. At the second Mass he was given the Catholic Church's final blessing by Father McAllister. Afterwards he refused breakfast, saying that the body and blood of Christ were the final things he wanted to take before he died.

Williams then prayed with the two priests until shortly before eight o'clock when the executioner, Thomas Pierrepoint, and his assistant, his nephew Albert, entered the death cell. According to prison regulations, the cell was known at this stage of the proceedings as 'the pinioning room'. Williams was asked to stand and his arms were indeed pinioned with a long, buckled leather strap.

The wooden cabinet was pushed aside and Williams, accompanied by the priests, his guards and the executioners, unfalteringly walked the few steps from the cell to the trapdoor, praying calmly all the while. Contemporary newspaper accounts tell of Williams mounting the steps to the scaffold bravely to face his fate. While eyewitnesses confirm that the IRA volunteer did show extraordinary courage, there were, in fact, no steps to climb – Belfast prison's gallows was at ground level, with its trapdoor set into the floor.

Mercifully for the victim, the actual execution was over in a surprisingly short time. As the senior hangman placed a white hood over the young man's head, his assistant swiftly strapped his feet together. Pierrepoint senior tightened the noose around the teenager's neck and, seconds later, a lever was pushed forward. The two halves of the trapdoor jerked open and the victim fell through to the basement. Death, caused by a broken neck, was designed to be instantaneous.

In the dining area in D Wing, where the internees were attending a special Mass for Tom Williams, a poignant and touching farewell gesture was made. The celebrant was Father Oliver, one of the four priests who had administered to the six men. Official executions follow a strict timetable and, at the moment he deemed that Williams was standing on the gallows trapdoor, the priest raised the Host towards Heaven and scores of internees bowed their heads in silent prayer.

Father Malachy Murphy, parish priest of St Paul's church in west Belfast, remembers as a schoolboy being acutely aware of the execution. His Religious Education teacher at St Malachy's College was Father Paddy McAllister, the kindly and much-loved priest who had been the Catholic chaplain to Belfast prison at the time of the hanging.

One of the comforts the Catholic Church provides for a dying member is the last sacrament, or extreme unction, when the person close to death is anointed with holy oil. Father McAllister told his pupils, however, that a prisoner sentenced to hang, even as he stands on the trapdoor with a noose around his neck, is deemed to be healthy. It is only after the execution that the priest may administer the sacrament. It fell to Father McAllister to carry out the harrowing task of anointing Williams's body in the basement under the gallows.

Father Murphy, who was born and raised in west Belfast, said the death of the young IRA man had made an impact on young and old alike.

'I remember the execution of Tom Williams myself because my mother had us up at eight o'clock, kneeling before the Sacred Heart picture praying for him on the morning of his death. Four years later, in 1946, I was attending St Malachy's College where Father McAllister was our Religious Education teacher at one stage, and he told us the whole story. I remember it very vividly. We were sitting, mouths open, afraid to miss a single word, because the Tom Williams situation was very fresh in all our minds.

'Father McAllister requested that a hole be cut in the hood to allow Tom to be anointed on the forehead after he came through the trapdoor. But, in case Pierrepoint put the hood on the wrong way round, Father McAllister had two holes cut in it, one at the front and one at the back, so that no matter which way it was put on, he would still be able to anoint Tom.'

When Father McAllister had anointed Williams's body in the basement, a doctor examined the body and pronounced that death had taken place. Following regulations, the corpse was left alone for one hour, before being drawn up with the hangman's portable pulley and prepared for burial.

Cahill recalls that, on the morning of the execution, normal routine was suspended and all prisoners, political and criminal, were given the opportunity to attend special separate Masses:

'I had been moved to A Wing by this time and our special Mass was at half-past eight. The thing that struck me that morning was the terrible silence in the prison. I have a vague recollection of that awful eerie stillness being broken only when I heard snatches of Orange songs, party songs [sectarian songs, perceived to be insulting to Catholics], being sung outside the prison.

'At half-past eight the doors were opened and we headed up to the prison chapel, still in complete silence. The only sounds to be heard on the way to the chapel were footsteps and sobbing, hundreds of men sobbing over the loss of a comrade. Father McEnaney celebrated the Mass. Sitting in the front row along with us, the long-term prisoners, were Father McAllister and Father Alexis.

'Father McEnaney was in such a state that he was not able to complete the Mass. Towards the end he was emotionally overcome and Father Alexis said the final prayers from his position off-altar. When the Mass was over a warder told us that Father McAllister wanted to speak to us. There was a wee vestry at the side of the altar and the five of us went in. Father McAllister, Father Alexis and Father McEnaney were already there.

'Although we were told that Father McAllister wanted to see us, we found that he could not speak. It was father Alexis who addressed us. He said he had witnessed the greatest bravery in his life that morning. There was not a quiver in Tom's body. He said the only people trembling were the executioners and the priests. He said we should pray – not for Tom, but pray to him, for he was surely in Heaven.'

The republican prisoners did not go to work, but spent the rest of the day in their cells in prayer and fasting. Cahill's mourning was interrupted just once that Tuesday:

'I was in A1 and in the cell above me was a guy called Kevin McQuillan. Around twelve noon, he rapped the floor and shouted, "Joe, quick, get up to your window." From my cell window I could see a gap between A Wing exercise yard and B Wing. You could look straight across to the hospital. What he wanted me to see was

Tom's funeral heading towards the grave at the back of the hospital. Warders were carrying Tom's coffin and the three priests were with them. They were out of sight in a few seconds.'

Cahill and the others were somewhat consoled when they later heard that the warders, selected because they were Catholics, had acted with respect and had stood to attention at the graveside.

When a prisoner was condemned to death, part of his punishment included being buried in unconsecrated ground, in an unmarked grave within the prison walls. The exact position of Tom Williams's grave was to be a matter of some conjecture fifty years later, when Cahill headed a campaign to have his friend's remains exhumed and reinterred in the Republican Plot in Belfast's Milltown cemetery.

'Tom's death is something I have never got over,' he says. 'It has lived with me ever since. I still feel that Tom is very close to me, even though we were separated by his death. Probably the hardest thing in my life was parting from him.'

Meanwhile, Cahill's 'vague recollection' of hearing sectarian chanting had indeed been correct. Hundreds of Catholics had been gathering around the jail since dawn. Police kept them from the immediate vicinity of the prison, but the crowd came as close as they were permitted. As the execution time approached, they knelt to say the rosary. Their prayers were interrupted when a loyalist crowd began to sing insulting songs and chant sectarian slogans. In between songs, as the loyalists paused for breath, could be heard the soft intonation of Hail Marys and Our Fathers.

Elsewhere, the death of the IRA man led to a more violent reaction. The following day saw the resumption of an IRA campaign that had been put on hold during the reprieve campaign. In County Antrim a police barracks was bombed. RUC men were fired on in County Fermanagh. An RUC officer and a B Special constable were killed by the IRA in County Derry.

An era had ended, another was about to begin.

CHAPTER FOUR
The Prison Years

The morning after the execution of Tom Williams, the five reprieved men had their civilian clothes taken from them and were supplied with prison uniforms. They were then taken to A Wing to begin their sentences.

'The uniform,' says Cahill, 'consisted of a dreary grey-coloured suit, a grey shirt, a vest and long johns. The boots and suit were made by prisoners in the jail workshops.'

They were now convicts, a term applied by prison authorities to anyone sentenced to three years or over. Almost sixty years later, Cahill's convict number rolls easily off his tongue: 'I was number 356C.'

Republicans, however, as a point of principle, never accepted criminal status and always referred to themselves as political prisoners, or prisoners of war (POWs). In keeping with their demands for POW status, generations of IRA prisoners referred to their jail as a 'prisoner of war camp'. Thus they had a Camp staff and Camp council. Many protests, often involving suffering and hardship, were embarked upon to win concessions which were enjoyed by IRA members and criminals alike. Each tiny victory – an extra letter, a few more minutes of free association, the holding of a commemoration parade in the exercise yard – took the republicans, they believed, a step closer to achieving political status.

In the early months in A Wing, the five received much sympathy and support from other prisoners, who recognised that they had undergone a prolonged and traumatic ordeal and emerged from it only to face the prospect of spending many years in jail.

On the positive side, Cahill and his friends were eased into the harsh prison regime by older and more experienced republicans, who taught them how to survive – and sometimes even manipulate – the soul-destroying regime which they believed was deliberately designed to break the physical and mental health of inmates. The existence of an IRA command structure meant that when the new felons arrived on the wing they experienced an immediate feeling of belonging. They were able to draw strength and comfort from being among others of similar principles and political beliefs.

Solidarity was often tested to the limit. The IRA's insistence on its members being regarded as political prisoners, and their refusal to conform and behave as what would later be called 'ordinary decent criminals', led to regular confrontation with the jail authorities. Protests took many forms, including refusal to work, refusal to wear prison clothes, refusal to leave a cell and the ultimate weapon of republican prisoners, refusal to eat – the hunger strike.

Many warders had no particular axe to grind with republicans and, according to Cahill, carried out their jobs with a reasonable degree of fairness and compassion. Some even turned a blind eye to the occasional contraband cigarette or newspaper changing hands during Mass. In prison parlance these were known as 'half--decent screws'. Every republican prisoner, however, has at least one horror story of a warder who appeared to derive pleasure from harrying, harassing and bullying the most vulnerable inmates. In cases perceived as extreme by prisoners, a message would be sent to the IRA on the outside asking for 'action' to be taken against the offending warder. That action, inevitably, would be an attempt on the prison officer's life.

Several warders were targeted by the IRA over the years. On one occasion during the 1940s, the wrong officer was killed. The warder who had incurred the anger of prisoners was amongst a group of off-duty officers cycling along Albert Street in nationalist west Belfast. Most of the group stopped at a newspaper shop and one man – the wrong man as it transpired – rode on alone into an ambush. A few yards down the street the ambush party, believing the approaching cyclist to be their target, opened fire, killing the man instantly. Somewhat unusually, several internees complained afterwards that the victim had been one of the 'half-decent screws' and had not deserved his fate. The men's protests were noted and as a result the IRA held an inquiry into the killing.

Official prison punishments included withdrawal of privileges (mail, parcels, the daily cigarette, etc.) and being sentenced to a number of days 'on the boards' – solitary confinement, with all furniture and bedding removed from the cell during the day. At night the prisoner was provided with a mattress and blanket. His bed was the wooden board which gave that particular punishment its name. Solitary confinement was usually accompanied by a period on 'number one' diet – a few ounces of bread and a jug of water served three times a day.

Other weapons in the official arsenal included the 'birch' and the 'cat', both of which Cahill was to hear more of before he had served his first full year in jail.

The novice A Wing convicts, Cahill, Cordner, Perry, Simpson and Oliver, were soon to discover they had a lot to learn. Almost sixty years later, the finest details of prison life remain etched in Cahill's memory:

'The day began officially at 8am when the cells doors were opened and we slopped out, that is, emptied the chamber pots. We then washed in the cell, using a jug of cold water and a basin. Breakfast was also taken in the cell.'

A typical breakfast, says Cahill, would consist of porridge, eight ounces of bread, a little cube of margarine and a pint of tea or half a pint of milk.

'At nine o'clock we began work, and continued until eleven o'clock. This was followed by an hour in the exercise yard, then back to the cell for two hours. Dinner was taken in the cell during this period. This was the main meal of the day and was typically potatoes with cabbage or peas. Stew was served on Monday and Thursday. On Monday it was corned beef stew, which I didn't mind too much. On Friday you could either have fish or rice, and milk.'

The two-hour afternoon work period ended at 4pm, when the prisoners were taken back to their cells for tea. This was likely to be a boiled egg, bread, sometimes a small portion of jam and 'occasionally, a sausage'. This was followed by one hour of free association for certain inmates.

Prisoners were not permitted association with each other during their first six months of incarceration. For the second six months, they were granted one hour on two evenings each week. In the second year, this rose to four evenings. Those who had served three years or over were permitted two hours free association on six evenings. By 7pm everyone was back in their cell, where they remained locked up until the next morning. Lock-up was even earlier on Sunday when, after two two-hour exercise periods, the prisoners were back in their cells at 4pm.

Certain luxuries, such as cigarettes and pipe tobacco, were available, but had to be earned.

'We got either one cigarette or seven leaves of pipe tobacco a day. We earned that by working. A leaf was based on a slice of plug tobacco. The prison authorities deemed that an ounce plug of Warhorse could be sliced into forty-nine leaves. We were permitted an ounce per week, the equivalent of seven leaves each day.'

(Warhorse was arguably the strongest and most foul-smelling brand of pipe tobacco available in Belfast, where it was manufactured.)

'We were not permitted cigarette papers. Some men chewed the tobacco, others shredded it in the palm of their hand and rolled it in toilet paper to make a cigarette. Generally people took the seven leaves, because they could do more with it. Non-smokers would take the cigarette and give it to a smoker, who was able to mix the cigarette tobacco with the Warhorse.'

Cahill says the near-ideal situation arose if two smokers opted for the pipe tobacco, with a non-smoker contributing his cigarette. The cigarette was divided between the smokers, who mixed the lighter tobacco with the Warhorse.

'Out of the seven leaves and half a cigarette you could manage to make three cigarettes, and a fourth from the three butts; so, if you were careful, you could have four cigarettes a day.'

There were strict rules governing the numbers of letters and parcels which prisoners could receive. Long-term prisoners in A Wing were permitted one letter and one visit every three months during the first year of incarceration, and a letter and visit every month thereafter.

The intimacy and pleasure derived from a letter from a relative or friend, Cahill said, was invaded and spoiled by the prison censors, whose rules were regarded as so ridiculous that many prisoners refused to write and told their families to do likewise.

'It was not just a matter of a blue pencil being used to obliterate words or phrases. The censors cut whole sentences out with scissors. With the writing paper being used on both sides, passages on the reverse were also cut which had nothing to do with whatever was deemed to be forbidden. The whole letter was destroyed and made no sense. It became so ridiculous that I refused to write or accept letters.'

In the early years of his sentence, Cahill and his friends were only allowed to receive parcels from relatives every twelve months. These restrictions, however, eased in the late 1940s.

'Relatives were initially permitted to send in a special parcel at Christmas, Easter and Halloween. At Christmas you could get perhaps fifty cigarettes, forty at Easter and the same at Halloween. You stretched them out for as long as possible. That went on until the last few years of my sentence when we fought for, and won, the right to have parcels of fruit sent in weekly.

'I think the reason they decided to make the concession was because our health was deteriorating; the fruit was meant to compensate for the poor prison diet. The food was really bad. The whole system could be described as punishment more than correction. That, in my opinion, summed up their attitude.'

In prison, even the tiniest and normally inconsequential minutiae of life became battlegrounds between prisoners and the authorities.

Prisoners were not permitted matches or cigarette lighters, and had to ask warders to light their single legal cigarette at the permitted smoking time. That created a problem for those who managed to obtain extra tobacco.

Once again ingenuity was called for. For most smokers, the perennial problem of obtaining a light was solved by making a tinder box. Historically, the tinder box – in common usage before the advent of the match – contained a piece of metal, a flint and some tinder, an easily combustible material such as wood shavings or fine straw. The metal was struck against the flint to produce sparks, which eventually ignited the tinder.

Cahill says the prisoners improvised on this principle, using any material to hand.

'The tinder box was as small a metal box as you could get, usually a flat, round shoe-polish tin. It had to be something that could be easily hidden in the cell. The tinder was a piece of cloth which had been charred black. The cloth was brought to its burnt state by using a razor blade to chip at a tiny piece of flint, the type used in a cigarette lighter. This created sparks which landed on the dry cloth in the polish tin. When the sparks caught, you blew gently on the cloth until it glowed red. It was then extinguished by putting the lid on the tin.'

The cloth was easy to ignite after the initial stage. When a light was required, only a few sparks from the flint were required to bring the cloth to a satisfying glow. The cloth tinder generally lasted around a week, while the flint would have to be replaced after about a month.

Making tinder in the cell was a smoky and risky business and the republicans were glad to avail of an unofficial service provided by friends who worked in the tailors' shop. During his period in the shop, Cahill had access to both cloth and heat and was able to supply all the smokers on the wing. When a fresh batch of tinder was required, Cahill would volunteer to forego his morning period in the exercise yard and remain behind to 'cut cloth'. The warder in charge, with whom Cahill had established a rapport, remained in the shop but turned a blind eye to the young IRA man's nefarious activities.

This criminal misuse of the finest British government linen was severely restricted, however, when the disciplinary officer (a particularly nasty species of warder, according to Cahill) chose to work from his office between the tailors' shop and the boot shop.

'Once, during a security clampdown, we were having difficulty in getting tinder and no prisoners were permitted to stay in the shop during the exercise period. Before I left the shop, the screw asked me how we made tinder and offered to make some while we were at exercise. I explained the procedure and left. He was in the middle of burning the cloth when the door was rapped and the disciplinary officer shouted that he was wanted in the governor's office immediately. The screw wrapped the hot material in a piece of paper, stuffed it into his trousers pocket and rushed in to see the governor. He was standing in front of the governor when he felt his leg being burned. The governor kept sniffing and remarked that something seemed to be burning; the screw had to tell him that he must have put his pipe in his pocket while it was still lit.

'He still didn't mind us making a bit of tinder, but when I came back to the workshop, he said, "Joe Cahill, never, ever ask me to make that stuff for you again."'

Smuggling contraband into the jail was a risky and demanding business for visitors, who had to constantly invent methods of out-witting prison staff. Fortunately for the smokers, lighter flints are tiny. They would often be pushed deep into a tube of toothpaste which was sent in to internees, who then shared them with the sentenced men. Warders, too, were known to hand over a flint or two to prisoners.

Wooden matches were another luxury, but, with careful use of a razor blade, a single match could be quartered lengthwise to create four precious lights. Igniting the resulting extremely slen-der matches developed into something of an art form. When strik-ing on a wall, the little match was gripped between the thumb and second finger while the index finger had to be held to the head to support it until it flared into a tiny flame. The trick was to lift the index finger just before it was burned by the flare of the match.

The five new prisoners soon learned to use any and every resource to improve the quality of life in the austere Victorian jail. For example, Cahill says, the cast-iron pipes of the archaic heating system provided a ready-made telephone system.

'We each had a metal enamelled mug in our cell. Now, if you crouched on the floor and the bottom of this mug was placed against the heating pipes, you could speak into it and your voice would carry along the wing. When you wanted to receive a mes-sage, you put your ear to the mug. In that way you could have a conversation involving up to ten people. Unfortunately, it was not secure and the screws could hear. It was not unusual for the screw on night duty to come around, kicking the cell doors and shouting, "Get off those fucking pipes!"'

IRA staff members on the different wings needed to commu-nicate with each other, and Sunday Mass provided the main opportunity. As the prisoners settled into their seats, a note – written on toilet paper and folded into a tiny package – would be expertly and discreetly passed from one prisoner to another, even under the watchful eyes of prison officers.

Often the prisoners with the most up-to-date information about events on the outside were the detainees housed in C Wing. These were men who had been arrested but whose internment documents had not yet been signed by the Stormont minister of home affairs. They were normally detained for around twenty-one days before being moved to D Wing to join the internees.

Any news on the IRA campaign brought in by the detainees was eagerly pounced on by the sentenced men. Everyone wanted to know how things were going on the outside – who had been captured, who was on the run, how the situation was in Derry or Dublin and whether the British or Germans were winning the war.

Cahill says the internees in D Wing had more access to news from the outside world than sentenced prisoners. These men, who 'had not been charged, let alone found guilty of any offence,' were not forced to work, had a less rigorous regime and were treated more or less as prisoners of war. As such, Cahill says, they received newspapers more often than convicted IRA men and had the use of a radio in their mess hall.

'All republicans were, of course, anti-British, but sometimes we had a bit of a laugh at the expense of the internees. When things were going well for Germany in the war, the internees all became Germans. When they were doing badly, they all became Reds and switched their support to the Russians.'

Wartime partisanship occasionally caused fraught feelings between prisoners and staff, for example, when republicans learned of a British defeat. Internees often pinned up makeshift maps on their cell walls, marking the scenes and outcomes of the various land and sea battles. When they heard of the sinking of the battlecruiser HMS *Hood*, the pride of the Royal Navy, a huge cheer rang out around D wing and internees banged their metal cups on the heating pipes in celebration. For the warders, the majority of whom were of the unionist tradition, the sinking of the ship by the German pocket battleship *Bismarck*, with the loss of around 1,300 men, was a tragedy of enormous proportions. The incident, in May 1941, led to several days of bitterness and acrimony in the jail.

Men from the same wing were seated together in the chapel, making it difficult for prisoners from different wings to communicate. On occasion this led to a message being passed along the floor by foot from the back of the little chapel to the front. Many deeply religious prisoners felt bad about such activities taking place during the Mass, but in the main they were able to console themselves with the notion that under the circumstances, God would understand.

'There was always a way,' says Cahill, 'of getting a message or a bit of tobacco from one cell to another. At night, when we were locked up and not supposed to have contact with anyone, we very often used a line, a piece of strong string, to achieve this. Each cell window contained twenty-four small panes of glass. At least two of these panes were always kept broken, partly for ventilation and partly for communication. The gap was just large enough to put your arm through. Using a weighted string, it was possible to transfer messages, tobacco, cigarettes, books or newspapers – in fact, anything that could be passed through the gap. The cord, which was particularly strong, was taken from the workshop, where it was used in the stitching of mailbags.

'We would make a package for transfer and tie it to the end of the string, which was as long as possible. Once it was through the broken window, you could swing it to the cells on either side. The other person would be expecting it and put his arm out of his window to catch the line and pull it in to retrieve the item. If you were in a cell on the middle floor, you could receive stuff from above and swing it to cells on the left or right, or drop it down to the windows on the first landing.

'It was very useful, particularly on Sunday when we got the

newspapers in and we were able to pass them on after they were read. Nearly everybody had a line in their cell and it was something the screws would look for when they came raiding. They liked to deprive you of that little bit of pleasure.'

These anecdotes related by the ''forties men', as Cahill's generation came to be known, were handed down over the years and the ideas adapted and improved upon by republican prisoners in the 1970s and 1980s. In Long Kesh jail, twelve miles west of Belfast, republican inmates thirty years later used a refined version of the line system during the long-term prison protest there. These men refused to wear prison uniform and were confined to their cells, naked except for a blanket. Their 'line' was a thread, carefully unravelled from the blanket. A button, usually purloined, was fastened to the thread, and this was flicked under the cell door, across the corridor and under the door opposite. Once a line had been established, it could be lengthened and used to pass 'comms' (communications – messages written in tiny block capitals on cigarette paper and folded to the size of a pea), tobacco or even a precious ballpoint refill.

Long Kesh cell blocks were single-storey buildings, and a line could also be passed in the traditional arm-out-the-window method by swinging it to the prisoner next door. He would add a thread to it and pass it to the next man. Eventually a line was established along the full outside length of the block and used to pass contraband in either direction. The ubiquitous toothpaste tube made an excellent pencil, which was used by the men to record Irish lessons (shouted out by a fluent speaker from his cell) on the wall.

It was an attempt to establish another, more serious line of communication that almost landed Cahill in serious trouble. Regular and reliable contact with the IRA on the outside was vital and republican prisoners occasionally cultivated prison officers in a bid to enlist them as messengers.

Occasionally, says Cahill, a good-natured warder would deliver a message if he believed it to be a purely personal note to a prisoner's family. He adds, however, that prisoners also used a number of 'rogue officers', who undertook to deliver messages for payment.

After losing a long-term reliable messenger, a prison officer, Cahill was detailed by the wing OC to find a replacement.

'The screw who had been doing it had gone – retired or shifted to another prison. Communication with the outside at this particular time was very important, because we were not taking visits and it was imperative that we get news of what was happening out to the leadership.

'I was an altar server at this time, along with Dixie Cordner. The screw who looked after the chapel was a Catholic who lived in Ardoyne [a staunchly Catholic area of north Belfast]. I think he may have been Dublin-born. I was fairly friendly with him through serving Mass and I often had quite a bit of conversation with him.

'The OC asked me what I thought of this screw as a possible communication carrier and if I thought I could get him to take a letter out for me. I said yes, I believed so, and I would ask him to take a personal letter out to try him out. After confession on Thursday – in preparation for the next day's First Friday Mass – I was talking to him and asked if there was any chance of him taking a letter out for me. I did not say whether it was personal or otherwise and I said this was strictly just between him and me.

'He replied that things were so tight in A Wing that he would be afraid to attempt it. I told him that was fair enough and asked him to forget about it. I reported back to the OC, who advised waiting for a while as he felt there might just a chance that the screw would get back to me.'

Cahill did not have long to wait. That afternoon he heard a warder on the ground floor shout to a colleague outside the tailors' shop on the second landing that the PO 'wants to talk to Cahill, send him down'.

'I went down and was brought to the PO's office at the top of A Wing. The PO was George "Red" Morrison. I had a suspicion that the screw had told him what had happened earlier, that I asked him to take a letter out. Morrison told me to sit down. I said I would stand.

'He went straight to the point and inquired if I had asked an officer to take a letter out of the prison for delivery. I said that was correct, I had.'

The conversation, Cahill recalls, ended abruptly after a few questions from the PO.

'You are not denying it?' PO Morrison asked.

'Why would I deny it, when this boy has already told you?'

'Was it for the IRA?'

Cahill, indicating that he was not prepared to be questioned further, said: 'I asked him to take a letter out for me. That's it, end of story. Do what you like, that's it.'

The PO, says Cahill, could scarcely contain his delight.

'I remember he looked straight at me and said something like, "I have waited a long time to get you, Cahill, and I can hardly wait until tomorrow to personally put you on report and bring you before the governor – I will throw the fucking book at you."'

During association that night, Cahill gave his OC a report of the incident. The OC was of the opinion that Cahill would receive twenty-one days' bread and water. Therefore, in line with standard republican practice, a formal protest would have to be made and plans laid for an unofficial protest.

'Next morning,' says Cahill, 'we went to chapel for the First Friday Mass. Father McAllister was the chaplain and he came rushing in, late as usual and out of breath, and said, "Good morning, boys. That was a terrible thing that happened last night."'

Dixie Cordner, Cahill says, politely asked the priest to elaborate.

'George Morrison dropped dead as he walked out through the prison gate,' said Father McAllister.

Cahill says his immediate and automatic response was: 'Thank God.'

This elicited a strange and uncomprehending look from the gentle chaplain, who, by way of admonition, said: 'You are not being very charitable, Joe.'

Before Cahill could reply, Dixie Cordner told the chaplain: 'If you had been in Joe's position, Father, I don't think you would have been very charitable either.'

Cahill learned shortly afterwards that PO Morrison had gone off duty immediately after their conversation, without compiling his report.

✠ ✠ ✠

In the first few weeks of his sentence, Cahill had been taken under the wing of a senior republican who was to become a lifelong friend. Jimmy Steele, a leading member of the movement in Belfast, was an IRA staff member, a totally committed and dedicated republican who won widespread respect both inside and outside the organisation.

A natural writer, the north Belfast man was the author of several republican pamphlets and booklets and was the first editor of the *Republican News*. During his frequent periods in prison, using the illicit 'jail mail' system, he acted as literary critic and mentor to the aspiring authors, poets and dramatists of A and D Wings. Even in prison he managed to write articles which were smuggled out and printed in the IRA's *War News* and *An tÓglach* (The Soldier). A small man of slight build who had never really enjoyed good health, Steele was nonetheless a veteran of dozens of jail protests, and was described by comrades as 'Steele by name and steel by nature'.

Jimmy Steele was born in 1907 and had his first experience of prison when, as a sixteen-year-old Fianna boy, he was arrested with his brother and detained for a period. By the time of his death in

August 1970, he had spent almost twenty years in jail for his republican activities. He had held practically every senior position in the Northern Command, and was a former adjutant general of the IRA. Completely uncompromising in his republicanism, Steele immediately reported back to the IRA for active service each time he was released. When he first met Cahill, he was serving a ten-year sentence imposed in 1940.

'Jimmy and I became very close friends in jail,' says Cahill. 'When I was first arrested, he was on the IRA staff on A Wing and he used to write notes to me. They were passed to us at Mass, just letters of encouragement and asking if there was anything he could do to help. When I went to A Wing, I worked in the tailors' shop and Jimmy worked in the laundry. I was attending Irish classes in the jail and he was the teacher.

'If you did not know Jimmy Steele's occupation – he was a plasterer – you would think he was a teacher or an academic. He never used bad language and was a pioneer [a Catholic society whose members abstained from alcohol to atone for the excessive drinking of others]. He was very small, just 5ft 3in or 5ft 4in. In fact he used to tell a story about himself: He had been brought from the jail through the tunnel to the room under the court. There were several cops and warders there. Steele was sitting there unnoticed while a couple of cops were talking. One said, "Where's this Steele man?" The sergeant said, "Oh, I know all about him. He's a great big tough guy. They haven't brought him over yet."

'Jimmy was sitting listening to all this. Eventually one of the screws came down from the court and said, "Right, Jimmy, you come up now," and Jimmy stood up, all five-foot-four of him. The sergeant was left with a very red face.'

Along with all his other duties, Steele also found time to explore the nooks and crannies of the prison for possible escape routes. IRA escapes were not only intended to return essential personnel to the outside, but also as a blow to the establishment and a morale boost for supporters. The extensive publicity surrounding a successful escape, especially of high-profile prisoners, invariably led to an increased number of young men and women seeking membership of the IRA and Cumann na mBan, the women's wing of the republican movement.

Shortly before Christmas 1942, the IRA staff in A Wing became aware of a serious security lapse on the part of prison authorities. A prisoner had spotted an old trapdoor in the ceiling of the toilets on the top landing, the Threes. The only obstacle to the roof-space was a heavy padlock on the trapdoor cover.

It was decided that the wing OC, a County Armagh man named Pat Donnelly, together with Jimmy Steele, Derry man Hugh McAteer and Ned Maguire from Belfast would attempt to escape. The skills of Maguire, a roof slater by trade, would enhance their chances of breaking through onto the roof with a minimum of fuss and noise. McAteer, recently chief of staff of the IRA, had been handed down a fifteen-year sentence. Donnelly was serving twelve years and Maguire six.

The plan, the leadership believed, stood such a good chance of success that they arranged for a 'second wave' to use the same route, providing that the first four could make a clean getaway without causing the alarm to be raised. The date for the breakout was set as 15 January. Cahill says that while a number of accounts of the incident have been published, it is not widely known that two teams of republicans were meant to escape that day.

Those selected for the second team were Cahill, John Graham (former leader of the Prod Squad and OC Belfast Battalion until his capture three months previously) and Davy Fleming, who had travelled from his native County Kerry to fight in the North.

'Jimmy Steele and the others were to go at half-past eight in the morning, not long after the cells were opened. If all went well, John, Davy and myself were meant to make our attempt while going to the workshops at nine o'clock,' says Cahill.

Steele and his team worked surreptitiously for several weeks making equipment for the escape. Rope ladders were fashioned from strips of bed sheets, which had been torn lengthwise and stitched end-to-end with waxed string from the bag shop. A metal grappling iron was fashioned from the foot of a bed and tied to a sheet rope. The hook of this instrument was swathed in bandages, both to cut down on noise and to ensure that it snagged on the barbed wire on top of the perimeter wall. To place the hook at the chosen spot on the wall the men used broom handles to make an extending pole. Each section was fitted with a leather connecting joint or ferrule which had been made in the boot shop.

One side of A Wing faced the busy Crumlin Road, but in between lay a vegetable and flower garden, a twenty-foot perimeter wall and then a row of warders' cottages. If the prisoners made it to the main road, they intended to mingle with pedestrians and make their way towards the city centre.

Singly and at short intervals, Steele's team asked permission to visit the toilets. Once all four were together, they pushed a table to a spot under the trapdoor and stood on it to break the padlock. After all four had climbed into the roof-space, they replaced the trapdoor while other prisoners removed the table.

Maguire, the slater, then removed several tiles, enabling the men to climb out onto the roof, from where they used the sheet-rope to descend the three storeys to the exercise yard. Once on the ground, another prisoner, who had been hiding the pole in his cell, pushed the sections through the window where they were collected by the escapers. The four then ran to the perimeter wall and, using the assembled pole, attempted to place the hook on the barbed wire, only to discover that the instrument was several feet short. Maguire stood on McAteer's shoulders and, balancing precariously, had the pole handed up to him by one of the others. He carefully secured the hook on the wall top, ensuring that it was snagged on the wire.

Donnelly, Steele and Maguire managed to climb the wall, negotiate the barbed wire and drop down into the lane behind the warders' homes. Hugh McAteer, when almost at the top of the wall, lost his grip and fell back into the yard, badly injuring an ankle. Despite that injury and a hand ripped by the barbed wire, McAteer persisted until he too had topped the wall and dropped to the outside. Their main fear now was that they would be spotted by any off-duty warder who happened to glance through his rear window.

McAteer had become separated from the others and at one stage walked into a group of warders going on duty. He kept his head, however, and managed to avoid being recognised. The others, meanwhile, made their way to the North Queen Street district, about a mile from the jail. Steele was now on home ground. He had been born in the area, spent his boyhood and youth there and drilled with Na Fianna Éireann in the adjoining New Lodge district. It was Steele who now led his friends to an empty safe house, where he arranged for food to be delivered. McAteer, limping and in severe pain, was picked up by a sympathiser and guided to North Queen Street, where he too was taken to the safe house.

Back in the jail, the second team had waited anxiously for any sign that their colleagues' escape bid had been discovered. Despite the flowing adrenaline and suppressed excitement, Cahill, Graham and Fleming forced themselves to follow their normal routine, slopping out, washing and eating breakfast in their cells, as the seconds ticked towards nine o'clock when it would be their turn to go over the wall. Each man, just before heading off to his respective workshop, was to slip away to the toilets on the Threes landing. When they had assembled together, they would follow in the others' footsteps, using the materials that had been left behind.

Once again, Cahill's early release plans were thwarted. There were only minutes to go before prisoners headed to the workshops, and the cell doors had still not been opened. In fact, the doors were not to be opened until much later. Along the wing, Fleming and Graham shared Cahill's sinking feeling as they realised that a very real chance of gaining freedom was slipping away.

'In between the first four going and us attempting to go,' says Cahill, 'the escape was discovered. We had no chance at all. We were actually locked in our cells at the time we were supposed to be going over the wall. We found out shortly afterwards how the escape had been discovered – as the four men went over the wall at the back of the warders' cottages, they were spotted by a young lad, a warder's son, who was preparing to go to school. This boy's father was eventually to become governor of Crumlin Road jail. Unfortunately the boy just happened to look out the window at the wrong moment. He shouted to his father that men were coming over the prison wall. Jimmy and the others got clean away, but the alarm was raised and we were trapped inside.'

A massive manhunt was launched throughout the North, and a £3,000 reward offered for information leading to the capture of all or any of the escapers. It was not to be the last time that members of the escape team were to make headlines in following weeks.

Steele, Donnelly, McAteer and Maguire spent a few days in the safe house before Belfast Battalion staff arranged for them to be taken to separate billets. Donnelly and Maguire eventually made their way to Dublin, while McAteer and Steele remained in Belfast.

✠   ✠   ✠

The IRA in the South was in turmoil during this period, with the Free State government going to extreme lengths to prove that a neutral stance in the World War was not synonymous with taking a soft line on republican activists. The situation was not much better in the North.

Kerry man Charlie Kerins had succeeded Hugh McAteer as chief of staff. He was elated at the news of the escape, but waited until the fuss had died down before travelling to Belfast four weeks later with Archie Doyle, another member of IRA General Headquarters staff. A one-day Army Convention was held in Ballymacarrett in east Belfast, a loyalist area where police would not expect to come upon an IRA meeting. Kerins, described by Cahill as a born fighter and die-hard republican, recognised that McAteer's talents as an organiser and administrator were needed at that moment and he handed over the leadership to the Derry man. Other appointments were also made. Doyle and Kerins stayed in Belfast for two weeks before returning south. In December of the following year, 1944, Kerins was to share the fate of Tom Williams when, at the age of twenty-six, he was hanged after being sentenced to death by a military court in the South. The same hangman, Thomas Pierrepoint, carried out both executions.

The breakout from Belfast prison had provided a huge and much-needed boost to the morale of the republican movement, and McAteer and Steele were determined to build on that. They learned that an escape tunnel in Derry jail was at an advanced stage – IRA prisoners had been digging for five months – and a large-scale republican exodus was planned. The pair threw themselves into the logistics of the operation.

On 20 March 1943, the day before the escape, Jimmy Steele and Belfast republican Liam Burke travelled north to Derry in a hired furniture van, intended to be used to transport the escapers. The next morning, a Sunday, at a small house in Harding Street, an amazed family watched as a steady stream of IRA men, twenty-one in all, trooped in from their back yard, passed through the house and ran off down the street to the parked van.

Cahill later spoke to the first man out of the tunnel:

'Brendan O'Boyle told me the tunnel came up through the floor of the family's coal shed and he was covered in coal dust. He was the first into the family's home and his appearance scared the wits out of the woman of the house.'

(O'Boyle later broke away from the mainstream republican movement to head up a dissident group. He was killed in 1952 by his own bomb, which exploded as he tried to blow up the telephone exchange at Stormont, seat of the unionist government.)

Most of the escapers were subsequently picked up by the RUC or the Gardaí, but the prestige of the IRA in the North was significantly enhanced.

Some weeks later, with Easter just a few days away, McAteer and Steele searched for a way to beat the Stormont government's ban on republican ceremonies and marches commemorating the 1916 Rising. The RUC, knowing the IRA was committed to holding some form of ceremony in Belfast, saturated nationalist areas with mobile and foot patrols.

Cahill and the other republican prisoners in Crumlin Road jail heard with delight of the next propaganda coup. On Easter Saturday, as police patrolled the Falls Road and the maze of side streets, armed IRA volunteers slipped into Broadway cinema. During a break between films, a well-rehearsed drill was carried out. As the projectionist and other staff were held at gunpoint, a message was inserted into the projector and flashed onto the screen.

There were a few seconds of silence as startled patrons read: 'This cinema has been commandeered by the Irish Republican Army for the purpose of holding an Easter Commemoration in memory of those who died for Ireland. The Proclamation of the Republic will be read by Commandant General Steele and the statement from the Army Council will be read by Lieutenant General McAteer.'

The audience erupted into wild applause as McAteer and Steele mounted the steps to the stage and read from the documents. Simultaneously, an IRA statement on the cinema takeover was sent to local newspapers. Despite having patrols within yards of the republican leaders, the first that senior RUC officers heard of the operation was when journalists contacted them for more details.

With so many leaders in prison, North and South, those who remained free found the increased workload forcing them to take ever greater chances. Pat Donnelly was still free at the end of the war, but Ned Maguire, who had returned north to assist in the Derry escape, was arrested by Gardaí twelve weeks afterwards in Donegal. Jimmy Steele was recaptured in May and was back in A Wing by August, with a sentence of twelve years for possessing a gun and ammunition. Hugh McAteer lasted until November, when he was caught leaving St Paul's church on the Falls Road. The arrest of the chief of staff effectively signalled the end of the IRA's 1940s campaign in Belfast.

✠ ✠ ✠

Back in Belfast jail, republican prisoners were paying a price for the success of the January escape. Cahill says that the Stormont government, angered and embarrassed by the breakout, ordered an investigation. Some weeks later the regime was tightened considerably, and what republicans describe as a 'reign of terror' began, which was to last for almost three years.

'Following the escape, an inquiry was instigated,' says Cahill. 'The result was that the PO in charge of the wing and six warders were removed. Previously, prisoners held their own commemoration parade at Easter or when they received news of the death of a volunteer on active service. In general, outside of what we called Thompson's "reign of terror" period, the screws ignored our parades, which could take the form of a silent march around the yard for twenty minutes or perhaps the OC would call for a minute's silence in the mess hall.

'Following the removal of the screws, a new squad of warders was put in under a gentleman by the name of Lancelot Thompson, who rose from being a B Special based in Derry jail to become governor of Crumlin Road jail. He was one bad boy. He was known for his vindictiveness against republicans – very mean, very petty in his outlook. He liked to deprive you of anything that he could. And the type of warder he had under him was always very anti-republican. None of them, of course, was pro-republican, but some were fair and were just doing a job. These boys were in it to try to break republican prisoners.

'There were few commemorations held during that period. If a parade was held, everyone connected with it was automatically sentenced to one day's confinement. If someone made a speech, and the speaker could be identified, he would get three days' bread and water. Usually we stood around the speaker in an attempt to shield him.'

In mid-June, the Camp staff decided on yet another push for political status and sanctioned a 'strip strike', during which IRA inmates would demand the right to wear their own clothes and refuse to dress in prison uniform. Cahill, John Graham, Jimmy Steele, Davy Fleming and Gerry Adams, father of the present Sinn Féin president, were among twenty-two men who volunteered to take part.

The heating system in the old jail had been turned off for the summer and, even though the strike began in June, the republicans knew the thick black stone walls never really lost their winter chill. At 7.30am each morning, warders removed the strikers' clothes, beds and bedding, chair and table. Bedding was returned at night, leaving the prisoners to either stand all day or sit on the cold stone floor. It was the cold which was to be Cahill's undoing.

'On the first day of the strip strike, after the screws had removed everything from my cell, I was left with a towel about two foot square to cover myself. The prison never really warmed up and, without clothes, the freezing cold penetrated to the bone. I only lasted one day and collapsed. That was the last thing I remembered until I came to and found I was lying on a bed in the cell, all my clothes on and a medical orderly, a screw, was spooning whiskey into me. As far as I was concerned, that was the finish of the strike for me.'

Despite the hardship, the strip strike lasted until September. It was called off because censorship and news of the war had kept the protest out of the newspapers. With the republicans receiving little or no publicity, no pressure was being exerted on the unionist government and the exercise proved futile.

The 'reign of terror' continued. Cahill, incurring the displeasure of prison authorities, received his first experience of solitary confinement and the number one diet. After so many years, he says, it is difficult to remember details of his offence, but he believes it was 'fairly trivial'.

'You didn't have to do much to be punished in those days. I remember being taken to the punishment cells – small, bare cells without a bed, table or chair. At night the mattress was thrown in and you lay on the floor. Food and drink consisted of a mug of water and four ounces of dry bread three times a day – number one diet. During those three days, the prisoner was not allowed out of the cell and had no contact with other prisoners. If you were lucky, maybe once or twice during that punishment the orderly, when he was bringing your water, would attempt to slip in an extra bit of bread.'

Although punishments such as solitary confinement and number one diet became commonplace after the escape, they did not engender the same degree of bitterness and resentment which surrounded the use of the birch and the cat. Judges often sentenced young men to a prison term plus several strokes of the birch or cat. Both forms of punishment were severe and designed to humiliate, but the cat was reputed to be the more painful of the two.

The birch, as the name suggests, was a collection of rough twigs fashioned into a fearsome instrument capable of cutting, tearing and bruising the bared buttocks of the victim.

The cat (cat-o'-nine-tails as it is historically known) was a type of whip, originally used to punish offenders in the Royal Navy in the days of sail. The cat was fashioned from nine cord lashes, which were knotted for maximum effect. The victim was stripped to the waist and tied, spreadeagled, to a specially constructed triangular frame. The stipulated number of lashes were then administered, in the presence of a doctor.

Students of the conflict between republicans and the British, Cahill says, are often surprised to learn that medieval punishments like the birch and cat were still being used on prisoners as late as the mid-1940s. An added refinement to these punishments was the psychological pressure of not knowing when the sentence was to be carried out.

Cahill and his friends had been in A Wing for eleven months when three members of Na Fianna Éireann were brought into the jail to begin their sentences. The teenagers had been arrested at a Fianna training camp, where the RUC had discovered a gun. Two had been sentenced to twelve years penal servitude and twelve strokes of the birch, while the third received ten years and twelve lashes of the cat. (The three Fianns, and the newly recaptured Jimmy Steele, were sentenced at the same court session by Lord Justice Murphy, the judge who had passed the death sentence on Williams, Cahill and the others.)

'I did not experience the cat or the birch myself,' says Cahill, 'but we talked to those lads later. They knew they were going to be whipped or birched but they were not told the date. That appeared to be part of the punishment, an attempt to keep them in a state of anxiety. The screws took so long that we began to think they were going to let the matter drop. But in December, not long before Christmas, they were brought out of their cells and taken to C Wing, where they were ordered to strip to the waist and left in a cell for a while.

'They were eventually taken separately to a basement. The lad who was to receive the cat was tied to a triangular frame. The flogging then took place, with the governor counting the strokes aloud and a doctor checking the prisoner's heartbeat after every lash.'

Veteran Belfast republican Liam Burke, a contemporary of Cahill's, was OC of A Wing when the Fianns were sentenced. Burke interviewed the teenagers shortly after they were beaten, and lodged complaints with the prison authorities and a prisons watchdog body. His account of the incident is related in Uinseann MacEoin's *The IRA in the Twilight Years 1923–1948*.

After being held half-naked in the unheated cell in C Wing, Burke said, the teenagers were removed one at a time and escorted through rows of off-duty warders – possibly there as voyeurs, Burke claims – to an underground boiler house.

'There, they [the men who were to be birched] were suspended by rings, hands and feet, inches over the ground,' Burke continues. 'A man with a hood over his head then administered the whipping. Each stroke was counted by the prison governor ... The boiler house was filled with warders: it was not clear if their attendance was on the governor's orders or if they had volunteered. After each flogging, each victim was taken down and escorted back to his cell. The only medical treatment received was a thin gauze bandage over the bleeding parts.

'The following morning I examined the men and found each bleeding. James Mooney, who had received the cat, was quite badly cut upon the chest, while Joe Doyle and Arthur Steele were lacerated on the buttocks. I complained to the governor on the next day about the barbarity of this punishment, about the unnecessary attendance of so many warders, the lack of proper medical attention, but his answer was that he *acted in accordance with Home Office instructions and the sentence of the court* [MacEoin's italics]. My

Above: Cahill in British ARP (Air Raid Precautions) uniform following the outbreak of World War II. Joining the ARP, republicans believed, gave them the opportunity to openly give leadership and assistance to their community.

Above right: Lieutenant General Jimmy Steele, IRA, at Mullingar Cathedral in 1969, for the reinterment of the two republican soldiers, Barnes and McCormick, who were hanged in England in February 1939. Steele was dismissed from the IRA for a speech in which he was heavily critical of the direction being taken by the republican movement. He joined Cahill in re-establishing the IRA in Belfast later that year. Photograph: An Phoblacht.

Right: Joe and Annie Cahill on their honeymoon in Dublin, April 1956. This picture was taken by a street photographer.

FORM 14.

IN THE COURT OF CRIMINAL APPEAL IN NORTHERN IRELAND.

REX. *v.*   **JOSEPH CAHILL,**

(Appellant).

UPON CONSIDERATION being this day had by the Court of

Criminal Appeal, as duly constituted for the hearing of Appeals under

the Criminal Appeal (Northern Ireland) Act, 1930, of the Appeal of the

above-named Appellant against   **conviction.**

The Court doth determine the same and d dismiss the said

Appeal.   AND THE COURT DOTH APPOINT Wednesday,
the   2nd   day of September , 1   for the
execution of the sentence of Death upon the said JOSEPH
CAHILL instead of the date appointed by the Judge at the
trial.

Dated this   **21st**   day of   **August,**   19 **42,**

registrar.

The official document, dated 21 August 1942, informing Cahill that his appeal
against the death sentence had failed.

Good. Bye Joe, but do not fret. It is the way that I wished for. & prayed for. Do not forget me in your prayers. And if. Please God I reach heaven I will look after you always. + your parents & relatives Sept 1942 Till we meet again my brave comrade, Good Bye & may God look after you always. Tom.

Above: The last few lines of Tom Williams's final note to Joe Cahill, written on the day before Williams was executed.
Right: A final letter from Tom Williams to Joseph and Josephine Cahill, parents of Joe, before his execution.

H.M. PRISON BELFAST

Dear Mrs Cahill,

Just a very short note to let you know that I am keeping well & hope that you, your husband & family are same. I wish to thank you for your kindness you & your family have shown to me & my friends during these last trying months. Your son Joe could be nothing else but brave having such a fine & grand mother & father as he has. And hell is also very thankfull for the kindness given unselfishly to her by you & your family.

So I'll close here, sincerely hoping you will understand this note as it is my heart speaking to you. God bless your Irish heart. Yours Truly

Give my love to all your family.

Your Son's comrade
Tom.

Above left and right: Joe Cahill in 1968/69, when he was site foreman during the construction of Corpus Christi church in Ballymurphy, west Belfast.
Below left: Joe Cahill with his mother and father, Josephine and Joseph, at a cottage in the Wicklow mountains. Cahill was often on the run and met his family in secret in the cottage, which was loaned by a supporter. The premises were also used for meetings of the IRA Army Council.
Below right: Cahill performing the unveiling ceremony at the new County Antrim Memorial Plot in Milltown cemetery in 1966. A grave in the plot was reserved for Cahill's executed comrade Tom Williams, pending his exhumation from the grounds of Belfast's Crumlin Road prison. Williams's family objected, however, and the teenager was buried in his mother Mary's grave a short distance away.

Above: CS gas is fired over the barricades, Bogside, Derry, 12 August 1969. Photograph: Colman Doyle. **Below:** Members of the B Specials (more properly the Ulster Special Constabulary) in Derry city as the Battle of the Bogside drew to a close. The handkerchiefs are to protect against CS gas used by security forces against Bogside residents. Pick-axe handles were issued to the B Specials, who found their police issue batons no match for the hurls used by nationalists. Photograph: Colman Doyle.

Above: Four IRA volunteers pause for a photograph. They are armed with M1 carbines, a Thompson sub-machine gun and a Stirling sub-machine gun.
Photograph: Colman Doyle.
Below: Daithí Ó Conaill (left) and Jimmy Drumm at the historic 1986 *Ard Fheis*, when delegates voted to remove the abstentionist rule for
Dáil elections. Photograph: An Phoblacht.

Scenes such as this, with RUC and British soldiers mingling with masked members of the Ulster Defence Association in Portadown, caused unease amongst nationalists and led to accusations that security forces showed an undue tolerance of loyalist paramilitaries. Photograph: Colman Doyle.

Above left: Cathal Goulding, whose perceived abandonment of armed struggle led traditional republicans to break away and re-establish the movement in the North. Photograph: An Phoblacht. **Above right**: Seán MacStiofáin, first chief of staff of the Provisional IRA. Photograph: Colman Doyle. **Below:** The presence of children on the streets usually meant a quiet spell on sentry duty for British troops. Officers often warned their men to be extra vigilant when the streets suddenly became deserted. In the background is an army sangar (an observation post) and a corrugated timber fence. These 'temporary' structures were later raised and strengthened, to become part of Belfast's notorious peace-line. Photograph: Colman Doyle.

complaint to the Board of Visiting Justices received the same answer.'

Once again, the older republicans talked the youngsters through the after-effects of their ordeal. Burke was able to record that there was no evidence, during their sentence or in later years, that the young men had suffered long-term physical or mental damage. But little is sacrosanct in jail – not for long at any rate – and even this unsavoury episode provided a laugh for their comrades.

Cahill remembers being seated close to one of the birching victims in the visiting room in the following weeks. 'The lad's mother tried to spare his feelings, but at the same time wanted to know if his injuries had healed. She was obviously concerned about him, but always asked, "How is your back now, son?" He tolerated this as long as he could, until she asked about his back once too often and he exploded, yelling at her, "I told you dozens of times, Mother, it was not my back, it was my arse."'

In March the following year, 1944, amid worsening conditions, the IRA staff decided to launch a hunger strike. Prisoners were invited to volunteer and the usual tactics would be followed. Rather than have dozens of prisoners fasting at once, the republicans would build up the pressure by having small teams refuse food in a phased operation. Hugh McAteer, Pat McCotter (another victim of the cat) and Liam Burke made up the first team. The three men were, or had been, members of the Camp staff and were regarded as high-profile. They were all dedicated republicans; there was no doubting their commitment to fast to death if necessary.

They were followed onto the strike a few days later by a team led by Jimmy Steele. This process continued until eighteen men were refusing food. Cahill's team began fasting on day sixteen. By the time the leaders had been without food for more than forty days, it had become painfully obvious that the hunger strike was going to suffer the same fate as the strip strike the previous year. Little or no news of the fasting men was reaching the newspapers, and a decision was taken to bring them off hunger strike on day forty-four.

'Normally when someone came off hunger strike, he was fed only milk until he was examined by the doctor, who had to confirm the prisoner was able to take solids. When our hunger strike ended, the man in the cell above me, Joe Doyle, rapped the floor and said, "Get up to your window." A line was lowered and four ounces of bread came down. The line went up again and Joe shouted down to ask if I would like some cornflakes and dropped down a half-box, just small enough to retrieve through the window. I ate the bread right away and munched away all night at the cornflakes, with the occasional sip of water. Damn the bit of harm it did me,' Cahill says.

The IRA prisoners eventually did win some concessions, but not the right to wear their own clothes. As the situation gradually began to improve, the prisoners in A Wing were provided with a dining room. Also, restrictions were eased on the number and type of books permitted into the jail. And with more association came a raft of classes in a wide range of subjects. The craft culture so beloved by republican prisoners also blossomed.

Republican handicraft sessions produced attractive items which were eagerly sought on the outside. Prisoners' relatives treasured the objects, which were often the result of weeks or even months of painstaking work. One item which many prisoners made for wives and girlfriends was a finger ring crafted from a florin (a two-shilling coin with a high silver content). This was gently but incessantly tapped and worked into a smaller and thicker shape. The centre of the coin was then pared out with a penknife until it was roughly ring-shaped. At this stage it was again tapped, until it reached its final shape. It was then engraved – usually with an intricate Celtic design – using a sewing needle as a chisel.

'Leatherwork, too, was always a popular occupation and there was a great demand for those items as well. We became expert at making belts, purses, wallets and handbags. Several men took up embroidery,' says Cahill.

Many handicraft items were balloted in bars and republican clubs to raise money for the Green Cross, or the Prisoners' Dependants Fund as it became known in later years.

✠ ✠ ✠

Being imprisoned during the German bombing of Belfast, Cahill says, was a nerve-racking experience, although it did have its moments of humour. The city was severely damaged in April 1941, the year before Cahill's arrest. Almost 800 people died in two Luftwaffe raids that month and much of Belfast city centre was devastated. The carnage was never to reach such proportions again, although the city was bombed many times before the war ended. On these occasions, prisoners and warders were packed into a tunnel linking two parts of the prison, which provided a makeshift air-raid shelter. Here they awaited the all-clear siren.

'Once when the prisoners were down there, the bombs started dropping on and around the jail. There was one particular screw who was a real bigot, he hated Catholics. He used to watch the internees saying the rosary in their canteen in D Wing. However, when the bombing started getting a bit rough and he thought he was going to be killed, he yelled at the internees, "Quick, quick, fuck yez, say the rosary to save us."'

Although republicans, for reasons of discipline and identity, tended to keep a little distance between themselves and other prisoners, they shared some wings and there was a certain degree of intermingling. It was also not uncommon for the groups to help each other out. Non-republicans tended to respect IRA prisoners, who not only took a stand against the authorities but were also prepared to suffer hardships to win concessions which benefited the entire prison population. In return, orderlies – short-term prisoners, who performed cleaning and other duties – often used their slightly higher degree of freedom to smuggle messages and contraband from one republican wing to another.

In the years after the Second World War, Cahill came into contact with a significant number of young non-republican prisoners.

'There had been a raft of break-ins and robberies in Belfast after the war. Normally the youngsters, if they were caught and brought before the Magistrate's Court, would get perhaps six months in prison or a period in borstal – certainly no more than two years in jail, which was the upper limit that a magistrate could impose. But after the war, the Stormont government decided to teach these young people a lesson. This resulted in the offenders being brought before the City Commission, which was a higher court and could impose longer sentences. We had an influx of youngsters coming into the jail who were nothing like hardened criminals but had nonetheless been sentenced to three, four or five years.

'We felt it was a bit rough that these kids were thrown into jail and left to rot away for so many years. There was absolutely no attempt by the authorities to educate them or wean them away from their evil ways. A few of us – Dixie Cordner and myself and some others – got talking to them in an attempt to get them to see sense. Their first reaction, inevitably, was, "Who the eff are you to talk? Sure, you're doing life."

'But we persisted and pointed to some of the old lags as examples of how the kids could end up. We showed them one old boy who had spent forty years in jail. He had spent more of his life inside than out. And there were three or four cases almost as bad. There were around thirty of these youngsters, and we had a go at them all. We normally began by just chatting to them and then later offering them advice. At first they just sort of listened. Some had difficulty in listening, but they would go away and come back in a day or two, or a few days, maybe wanting to hear more.

'Of that thirty or so, twenty-seven did not come back in. It was very satisfying. As well as something worthwhile to do while we were in jail, we got a great kick out of seeing the majority of them make good.'

✠ ✠ ✠

In March 1945, four months after McAteer was arrested, the IRA formally declared a ceasefire. Shortly afterwards, campaigners began to press the Westminster and Stormont governments to begin releasing prisoners. Most of the internees were freed in the years immediately after the war, but the last of the long-term sentenced republicans were not released until 1950.

In October 1949, Cahill, Perry, Oliver, Cordner and Simpson, five of the six men who had entered C Wing under sentence of death, walked through the prison gates as free men. The last of the 'forties men were released the following year – Hugh McAteer and Liam Burke were freed in August 1950 and Jimmy Steele a few weeks later.

Cahill felt there was something strange about his and his four friends' release. The decision seemed to be made very quickly and without the usual formalities:

'We went off to the workshops as usual that morning around ten o'clock. There had been no mention of releases; they seemed to have stopped for a while. I heard a warder shout up the stairs that I was to be brought down to the head of the wing. The other four were already standing there. We were brought up to see the governor. I said to the others, in a half joke, that we must be getting out. Normally, when sentenced men were getting out, they were told by the governor they were to be released within seven days, so they could tell their people and have clothes sent in.

'But that morning, the governor said to us, "Good news, boys, you are being released." It was a big shock, but a bigger shock was to come. He said, "I have been instructed to release you as soon as possible – hopefully you will be out by lunchtime."

'Jimmy Perry pointed out that our release was being rushed, and wanted to know why. The governor replied that he had no idea, but he had some formalities to complete and we would be released then. He said, "In fact, you will not be going back to the wing." It's strange looking back now; we were definitely unhappy about the circumstances of our release. Jimmy told the governor to hold our release back until the next day, because we needed to talk to the boys on the wing and also sort out our belongings.

'However, the governor said we could send a message to our friends, and he would make sure they got it. Everything belonging to us in our cells would be brought down to reception. He said he was aware that we had not had time to have our civilian clothes sent in – we had sent them out when we first went to A Wing – but he had made arrangements for that. The warder in charge – Mr Piper, the master tailor – would look after us. We then went to the reception area and had a shower.

'Piper was in reception when we went down, and had a newly made sports jacket and a pair of flannel trousers for each of us. I had been close to Piper and worked with him in the cage in the tailors' shop. He said he had known for the last couple of days about our releases, but had been instructed not to say anything. He said he found it very hard to keep himself from telling us the news.'

The five were released shortly before noon. Their families, unaware of the sudden freedom thrust upon the men, were not there to meet them. After a brief look around, they walked across the Crumlin Road – this time over the tunnel – down Agnes Street, across the Shankill Road and along Northumberland Street to their own Falls Road.

'When we got to the Falls Road, I went left towards my home in Divis Street and the others turned right towards the Clonard area. We arranged to meet in my house later in the day.'

Cahill, acutely aware of his father's heart condition, had no wish to shock Joseph senior by walking boldly into the family home. He searched for a neighbour, to break the news of his release in a more gentle fashion, but could see no one that he knew. Eventually, he took the bull by the horns and pushed open the print-shop door. The doorbell tinkled out a warning to the family in the upstairs living quarters.

As Cahill walked gingerly upstairs to the living room, he met his father coming down. The older man took in the situation at once and, with typical understated Belfast humour, calmly asked his son: 'Shouldn't I know you, boy?'

'My mother heard this and came to see what was going on. She began making a fuss and threw her arms around my neck. My father told her, "The British hangman could not hang him, so don't you be trying to do it now."'

Shortly afterwards, the family had a laugh at the expense of another son, Frank, who had come home for lunch and was alarmed to find his older brother chatting with their parents. 'You bloody eejit,' Frank Cahill told Joe. 'Sure, this is the first place they will come to look for you.'

Following the end of the IRA's 1940s campaign, Cahill's parents had become involved in the campaign for the release of prisoners. By chance, on the morning of Cahill's release, Joseph and Josephine Cahill had been handed a letter by their local Labour MP Harry Diamond, who supported the campaign. The letter was a reply to Diamond from the Stormont minister of home affairs, outlining the unionist government's reaction to the Labour politician's appeal for the release of republican prisoners.

Considering the contents of the letter, Cahill's parents were doubly delighted and amazed at the suddenness of their son's release.

'I can't believe this,' Cahill senior told his son. 'This morning your mother and I were reading a letter from the minister of home affairs to Harry Diamond saying there are no political prisoners in the jail. The minister said the people Diamond mentioned were all criminal. He said some had a second chance in life to give up their activities. Burke, McAteer and Steele had escaped from prison and were caught again. Another, McCaffery, was caught with one of the biggest arms dumps ever found and he showed no remorse.'

Still quoting from the letter, Cahill's father continued: 'As for the last five names on your list [Cahill, Cordner, Oliver, Simpson and Perry], as far as I am concerned, they are convicted murderers and they will do every hour of their sentence, and, in Simpson's case, he will do fifteen years.'

✠ ✠ ✠

A few months later, Joe Cahill attended the 1916 Rising com-memoration, his first as a free man in eight years. It was with a heavy heart that he stood in Belfast's Milltown cemetery that Easter Sunday, listening to the reading of the Proclamation and a statement from the IRA Army Council. Deep in thought, his mind on another Easter Sunday back in 1942, he barely noticed the approach of a personable and well-dressed young man until he was tapped on the shoulder.

'He had a very nice young lady with him and a couple of kids. He introduced me to his wife as "the man who kept me out of jail". The lad was a Protestant from the Shankill Road, one of the youngsters we had tried to talk to in prison. He did not know where I lived, but he knew he would find me at the republican commemoration and he wanted to thank me.'

CHAPTER FIVE
Reporting Back

On the surface, post-war Belfast and its people had changed little since Cahill's arrest in 1942. Food was still rationed, decent jobs were still scarce and Britain still occupied the North.

In the days following his release, however, he began to detect a subtle change in the politics and attitudes of several old friends, including former prisoners.

'Many of the lads returned to the IRA within a few weeks of being released, but several others just seemed to drift away and find other interests.'

Cahill considered himself to be as committed to the republican cause as ever, but decided to permit himself an adjustment period while considering his future. He wanted, he says, to discover if seven-and-a-half years in jail had changed him in any significant way.

While the mainstream republican movement was dusting itself down and preparing to reorganise after the mauling of the 1940s, a number of tiny ultra-militant splinter groups sprang up.

'One of these groups, based in Belfast, carried out an attack in our area,' Cahill says. 'A grenade thrown at Springfield Road RUC barracks injured a policeman. Dixie Cordner and I were visiting an old friend, Tom Heenan, who was chairman of the Gaelic League [an organisation for the promotion of the Irish language] at the time. Tom lived in Violet Street, near the barracks, and we were sitting talking to him when we heard a bang. We hadn't a clue what it was, because there was no IRA activity at this time.

'We went to the door and met a policeman in the street. He told us he believed a gas main had exploded, and the three of us walked to the corner. There was a figure lying on the pavement close to the barracks. The policeman banged and banged on the barracks door, but the people inside would not open up. He kept shouting, "It's all right, it's Constable Walker."

'A few people had gathered by this time. The story was going around that an IRA man had been walking up the street with a grenade and it had exploded and the man lying on the street was the volunteer.'

Cahill and Cordner, fearing that the story was true, slipped away. They made several attempts to establish the injured man's identity, intending to inform his family and have his home cleared of any weapons or documents before the RUC raiding party arrived. The man's name, however, remained a mystery and they returned to the barracks area in the hope of gleaning more information.

'The injured man had been taken into the barracks. The story about the volunteer was persisting and we were anxious to know if it was true. At that moment the barrack door opened and a figure on a stretcher was carried out to the ambulance. An old woman with her head covered in a shawl pushed her way through the crowd, saying, "Let me through till I see if I know who the poor boy is, God bless him."

'The man's face was covered in blood and I could not see him properly, but the old woman recognised him as a policeman. She spat at the figure, saying, "It's oul' Smiling Peter himself, the oul' bastard." The cop was a Catholic who was anti-Catholic and anti-republican.

'There had been a case in the 1930s of a prison warder who had been shot at Divis Street. A man from Ardoyne was arrested and sentenced for the shooting. He successfully appealed the conviction on the grounds that he had been speaking to a policeman, a Constable Walker, some distance away at the time of the shooting. Now this Constable Walker was the same man who spoke to Dixie and me in Violet Street all those years later.

'I have often wondered what our chances would have been if we had been arrested at the scene of the grenade attack and we had offered the alibi that we were talking to Constable Walker – and both of us just out of jail after serving sentences for shooting a cop.'

After a few days out of prison, Cahill's thoughts turned to the question of earning a living. He had continued studying joinery in jail and had developed his skills to a respectable level by the time he was released. He admits, however, to being a little surprised and quite disappointed at having so much difficulty in finding employment in west Belfast.

'Perhaps a bit naively, I believed I would have no trouble walking into a job. After being handed down a life sentence, I half-expected employers to be a bit sympathetic. It was not so. No one wanted to employ me – Protestant employers because of my religion and background, and some Catholic employers who had contracts in loyalist areas and believed it would be too dangerous for me to work for them. There were also Catholic employers who exploited ex-prisoners by offering them poor wages, knowing they had to accept or starve.'

Following several unsuccessful applications, an offer of employment came from a most surprising source. The Belfast shipyard, with over ninety percent of its workforce Protestant, was long perceived by nationalists as a bastion of anti-Catholic sectarianism and a haven for hardline loyalists.

'The possibility of a job in the Harland and Wolff shipyards was raised by a friend after I told him I had trouble getting employment. He advised me to go down to the yard with him to a building called the Hut, which was the name for the office used by the department boss, invariably known as the Hat. All heads of departments were called Hats because they were required to wear a bowler hat, as a status symbol, I suppose.

'Inside the Hut, there was one man sitting at a table and another standing beside him. The standing man was advising the Hat by giving a slight nod or head-shake as each applicant came to the table. I was looking for a job as a joiner, which was what I had been doing before being arrested.

'After the seated man asked me a few questions, he expressed concern that my experience was in building and that I knew nothing about shipbuilding. I told him I realised the difference and that I knew about squares and set squares and all that sort of thing. Given a week, I said, I could work with anybody. I spotted the standing man nodding to him. I always remember the Hat saying that at least I was honest and not like those who came down to the yard attempting to bluff their way.

'I was told to return on Monday, prepared to start work and to bring my dole card [unemployment document], insurance card and a P45 [a tax statement from a previous employer]. I was met at the gates by the man who had nodded and he brought me into the office to hand in my cards. The only document I had was a dole card. I didn't even know what a P45 was – it sounded like some class of a revolver to me.'

Asked where he had worked recently, Cahill says he did not hesitate to tell the truth, that he had been in jail for almost eight years. During the first of two periods – eleven months and nine months – at Harland and Wolff, he worked on ships of the Castle Line, including the *Caernavon Castle* which was being refitted for her original role as a passenger liner after seeing war service as a troop carrier.

Although it must have been obvious to Cahill's Protestant and loyalist colleagues that he was a Catholic from the nationalist Falls Road area, he says he suffered little religious harassment and got on well with his fellow workers.

'They didn't really know me. Well, not until Easter 1962, when my photograph was taken at Milltown during the commemoration service and was published in the papers. I had made friends, great friends, in the yard and after the picture incident one man, a decent man from Bushmills who was then living on the Shankill

Road, told me, "Don't walk about the boat without your hammer and your hatchet in your belt."'

But there was little reaction to the newspaper picture, and Cahill was still able to associate with 'the black squad', an elite group composed entirely of staunchly loyalist workers who would have no love for an Irish republican.

'I still had the privilege, and it was a privilege, of boiling my tea can on the black squad's stove on the boat,' he says.

Cahill enjoyed working in the shipyard, and was even promoted – briefly, as it turned out. His new job as a marker-off entailed measuring and marking the positions for the ship's bulkheads. This was a step up from being a joiner, he says, and paid three pence an hour more.

'That lasted for four or five days, until the foreman came around and said he was sorry but I would have to go back on the tools. I asked if I had been inefficient, or had not been doing the job properly. He said I had been very efficient and he was glad to have me working for him, it was just that I kicked with the wrong foot. Apparently it was okay to have the odd Catholic around, as long as they didn't try to rise above their station.

'I more or less accepted it. I never knew any Catholic to get any further than a tradesman down there. Still, I had my first pay that Christmas of 1949.'

At around the time he started work in the shipyard, Cahill was approached by the OC of Belfast Battalion, and asked about his intentions regarding a return to active service. From being in the position of believing he was virtually unemployable, Cahill now found himself contemplating two job offers.

The failure of the 'forties wartime campaign had left the IRA on the rack. More than 1,500 republicans, or suspected republicans, had been incarcerated as internees or convicts in jails and prison camps in England and both parts of Ireland. The bombing campaign in England had fizzled out. Across the border, the southern government's tough measures – military courts, death sentences and internment – also took a heavy toll. With so many volunteers dead or imprisoned, the emasculation of the IRA's Southern Command was almost complete. Northern Command fared just as badly, and at one stage had just one volunteer available for active service in Belfast. The coalition government had taken the South out of the British Commonwealth and announced a republic in 1949. However, this was by no means the all-Ireland socialist republic envisaged by the signatories of the 1916 Proclamation, and was therefore not acceptable to Cahill and the vast majority of his contemporaries. In the North, Cahill found that the post-war position of nationalists had improved little.

'Republicans operated an abstentionist policy towards Westminster, Leinster House and Stormont. [Cahill, like most republicans of his generation, uses the term Leinster House when referring to the seat of government in the Republic, rather than the more correct Dáil Éireann or simply Dáil. For a republican of the old school, to refer to 'the Dáil' would suggest full recognition of what he regards as a partitionist regime.] The Stormont government was not only partitionist, but republicans also knew how futile it would be for nationalists to attempt to change it from within. Gerrymandering continued; sectarian speeches by unionist ministers continued to stir up hatred towards Catholics. From the end of the war until the early 1950s, there had been several attempts, mainly inspired by the various shades of Labour supporters, to have some form of representation other than right-wing conservative unionism in the Stormont and Westminster governments. All failed.'

In November 1945 the Anti-Partition League, a loose group of nationalist-minded politicians, labour supporters, business people and clergy, had been organised in an attempt to present a united front in the Westminster and Stormont elections of that year. The League's candidates for each set of elections had limited success.

Cahill says that during campaigning League members were often attacked by unionist mobs. When they held parades, he says, they were batoned by the RUC.

'When people took to the streets,' Cahill says, 'their protests were immediately, often brutally, suppressed by the RUC on the orders of the unionist government. Constitutional politics had been tried and had failed; peaceful protest had also failed.'

It was in this mood of growing frustration that the 'forties men began to talk of preparing for another campaign.

'When I came out of jail in 1949 there was no doubt the republican movement had been almost defeated during the war through imprisonment and internment. The IRA was at a low ebb, but almost immediately released prisoners decided to reorganise.

'The OC of Belfast was Frank McKearney, an ex-prisoner whom I knew very well. He asked me what I intended to do. I said I thought I should take a break from things, just to see what effect prison had on me, whether I still had the same commitment. He said that was the proper thing to do, but added, "If I know you, Joe, before a month is up you will be reporting back for active service."

'I did try to test myself on the whole thing. Before going into jail, I would not have thought about going to a modern dance. At that time we were into all things Irish – *céilí* dances and Irish language classes. Most of the guys I knocked about with before I went into jail were in the IRA. After they were released, some just drifted, but even so we always remained very friendly. Their way of life was entirely different to what it was before they went into jail. Some were now drinking and going to modern dances, or English dances as we called them. I told them I thought this was all very strange. They said I should try this broader outlook and that I would probably enjoy it.

'I did go to a few dances, but it was completely alien to me and I certainly could not take to English dances. McKearney was right –

before a month was up, I reported back to the IRA.'

Cahill also joined Sinn Féin around this time, and was very active in working towards the party's stated aim of establishing a branch in every parish in every town and village in Ireland. Sinn Féin was enjoying a new lease of life, after being resuscitated from its low point in the mid-1940s. This revival was largely due to the efforts of released prisoners in the South, who cast around for a political vehicle to lift republicanism from the doldrums. A commission had been set up to look at existing political organisations or, if necessary, to establish a new political party. The commission's report, to the surprise of many, revealed that Sinn Féin remained in existence. This was largely due to the efforts of the indomitable Dublin woman Margaret Buckley, who had remained as president throughout the war years and, with the help of a few dedicated colleagues, kept the party ticking over.

The report found that the party, although on the point of oblivion, was capable of being rebuilt. It recommended that volunteers be instructed to join Sinn Féin and work to put the party on the road to recovery.

In 1951 Mrs Buckley lost the presidency to Pádraig MacLógáin, OC of South Armagh during the War of Independence and one of the party's most formidable political intellects. Cahill, who was present at the *Ard Fheis* (annual conference) that year, says that Mrs Buckley bowed to the inevitable with considerable grace and thanked delegates for voting her into the position of vice-president. MacLógáin was then in a position to act as liaison officer between the IRA and Sinn Féin.

MacLógáin was one of the trio known as the 'Three Macs' – the others were Tomás McCurtáin and Tony Magan – who played an important part in giving the rejuvenated IRA direction and impetus in the late 1940s and the 1950s.

Tony Magan, a farmer from County Meath, was known as a tough militarist and disciplinarian, with a sharp tactical mind. He demanded the highest standards from volunteers, but was always concerned about their welfare.

Tomás McCurtáin, son of the lord mayor of Cork who was killed by the Black and Tans, was as uncompromising a republican as his father. The younger McCurtáin, like Cahill, had been sentenced to death, following an incident in which a policeman was killed in Cork city in 1940. The Garda detective, one of a group attempting to arrest McCurtáin, had been struck by a bullet fired during the scuffle and died the next day. McCurtáin was reprieved by the Fianna Fáil government and his sentence commuted to life imprisonment.

'There were those,' says Cahill, 'who claimed that the Three Macs were more interested in politics than fighting and were reluctant to commit the Army to a new campaign, but I am convinced that is not true. In fact, they believed in a joint policy of armed struggle along with a political strategy. MacLógáin was a great thinker and he always maintained that the only way to build up the support of the people was by carrying out spectacular operations and by contesting elections on an abstentionist basis. There was no talk of entering partitionist assemblies or Westminster. MacLógáin, McCurtáin and Magan were diehards as far as those things were concerned.'

The tactics of the Three Macs, as described by Cahill, were strikingly similar to the policies forged by the republican leadership of the 1980s and 1990s. A close parallel could be drawn between the attitude of the Three Macs and a speech by former Sinn Féin director of publicity Danny Morrison. Addressing the party's 1981 *Ard Fheis*, Morrison said: 'Who here really believes that we can win the war through the ballot box? But will anyone here object if, with a ballot paper in this hand and an Armalite in this hand, we take power in Ireland?'

The IRA Constitution is the code of practice and conduct by which every volunteer, from chief of staff to the rawest recruit, is expected to live. Updated in the 1980s and now known as the 'green book', it states that one of the IRA's objectives is 'to support the establishment of an Irish Socialist Republic based on the 1916 Proclamation'. One of the recommended means of achieving this is to 'wage revolutionary armed struggle'. Quite simply, every IRA activity, apart from its defence of northern nationalists during pogroms, was and is geared towards achieving a thirty-two-county republic and ending British involvement in Ireland's six north-eastern counties.

Each time a campaign was called off – whether through a lack of weapons or support, unsustainable casualties or large numbers imprisoned – the IRA would inevitably be ordered to cease hostilities and dump arms. Sooner or later, and just as inevitably, republicans representing IRA units from all over Ireland would be called to an Army Convention and a twelve-member Army Executive elected. This body is required, within forty-eight hours of the end of the Convention, to elect seven volunteers from the IRA's active list to an Army Council.

The Army Council is then deemed to be the IRA's supreme authority when the Convention is not sitting. Its members are responsible for appointing a chief of staff, who in turn selects a General Headquarters staff to oversee the day-to-day running of the organisation. Preparations will then begin for a new campaign.

This was the situation after the 1940s campaign. However, in the early 1950s, unlike the previous decade, leadership of the IRA was now firmly in the hands of the southerners who had breathed new life into the movement. Northern and Southern Commands had faded away, along with the dynamic of the previous campaign, and would not be resurrected for several years. The line of command now came directly from Dublin, with battalion areas in the North commanded by well-trained young southerners.

While some northerners, Cahill included, thought local volunteers may have had a better understanding of the situation, they accepted the new order without demur and set to work recruiting and training new members, gathering intelligence, planning arms raids and selecting military and police barracks for attacks.

Back at the Belfast shipyard, Cahill meanwhile toiled away at his 'weekday job', occasionally wondering what his employers would make of their new joiner's spare-time activities. In his spare time and at weekends – and quite often during Harland and Wolff's time as well – Cahill was recruiting, training and gathering intelligence for the IRA. The free-and-easy attitude to timekeeping and attendance at the shipyard was abused to an alarming extent by many workers. Harland and Wolff veterans have anecdotes by the dozen of absentee workers being checked in by friends, sometimes for days at a time, without being missed. There are also accounts of apprentices who were absent so often that they were unable to do their job properly at the end of a five-year training period.

'That was one of the advantages of working in the shipyard – you could slip off for a half-day fairly often and there was always someone to cover for you. People collected their boards [daily attendance records] from the office in the morning and threw it in at night; no one noticed where they were in between. Lots of men were at it.'

While other workers used their illicit free time for relatively innocuous visits to the cinema or the bookmakers, Cahill was engaged in more clandestine activities.

'I used to cycle around Belfast, particularly around the British military camps, observing and taking notes,' he says.

The IRA, constantly plagued by a shortage of weapons, was not averse to raiding British Army camps, and intelligence reports compiled by people like Cahill were often the basis for these arms raids.

'Intelligence gathering at that time was not a big deal and not particularly dangerous, because there was no great security on

Army camps. I carried out intelligence checks on Girdwood Barracks in Holywood and the British Army's headquarters at Thiepval Barracks in Lisburn. There were also several TA [Territorial Army Volunteer Reserve] camps in and around Belfast – for example, there was one attached to Queen's University. It was part of the normal work of a volunteer to gather intelligence.'

Later, after leaving the shipyard, he was to travel further afield, helping to organise and strengthen IRA companies across the North. Travelling by bus or train, Cahill visited Derry, Fermanagh, Tyrone, south Down and south Armagh. Often he found units which were extremely keen and well-intentioned, but in disarray and without a proper command structure. In such cases, he would stay in the home of a sympathiser, or book into a guest house or a cheap hotel, and spend a few days in the company area. To account for his arrival in a strange town or village, a public meeting would be arranged. Cahill would pose as a Sinn Féin spokesman who had travelled from Belfast to address the meeting. Inevitably, he and the local IRA leaders would be approached afterwards by young men and women who wanted to do more than listen to politicians.

Travelling IRA organisers such as Cahill were expected to handle practically any problem in each company area. It was not unusual for an organiser to help with recruiting and education in one area, instruct volunteers in the use of a variety of weapons while giving a crash course to a training officer in a second, and act as OC until a suitable candidate was trained up in a third.

During his latter years in jail and in the early 1950s, Cahill became increasingly convinced that the republican physical-force tradition would not, on its own, solve the problem of partition and the British presence in Ireland. His support for the IRA ceasefires and the Irish peace process of the 1990s was, he says, rooted in political discussions with a wide range of people, including non-republicans, trade unionists, socialists and Protestant clergymen. Sinn Féin's 1986 decision to contest Dáil elections, and take seats if victorious, was no great culture shock to Cahill, who spoke very strongly in favour of the move at the party's *Ard Fheis* that year. He had, after all, been discussing that very possibility since 1950.

Even at that early date, Cahill reasoned that while the people of the South might not support the armed struggle, there was every likelihood that they would support Sinn Féin members who took their seats and fought in the Dáil to improve the lot of their electorate. Many of his comrades agreed with fighting elections to gauge support, but drew the line at taking seats in the Dáil at Leinster House.

'I had realised for some time that there would have to be a rethink on policy. Along with the military side of things, there had to be a strong political side. I was always convinced that politically we would not make progress in the South unless we took seats in Leinster House. To me, it was not a principle, it was a tactic. I listened to many people, including Northern Ireland Labour party members, who said they could never understand abstentionism. I learned that they had no fear of a united Ireland. It encouraged me to know that, even in those days, some Protestants would think that way.'

The very thought of taking seats in Stormont or Westminster was anathema to republicans at the time, including Cahill. The Special Powers Act, which forbade republican assemblies, demonstrations or processions, made normal electioneering impossible.

Speaking at the age of eighty-one, Cahill still harbours bitter memories of the clever little machiavellian ploy of insisting that applicants for government jobs should take an oath of allegiance to the British Crown.

'There was no way you could work politically in the North then. There was an awful lot against us: laws were against us; the lack of opportunity to preach politics; Sinn Féin was banned, as were public meetings and processions. The laws were totally oppressive. I could see absolutely no advantage in trying for Stormont.

'Another major bugbear was the oath of allegiance to the British Crown. That applied to teachers, nurses and civil servants and even domestics. Any nationalist or Catholic wanting to work in what's now called the public sector had to take the oath of allegiance. Even the few Catholics who managed to go through university had great difficulty in finding employment, and no chance at all if they were not prepared to taken the oath to the Crown.'

The oath of allegiance Cahill refers to was introduced by the northern government in 1922 and was compulsory for all civil servants. The oath was imposed despite vigorous objections by senior members of the South's provisional government, most notably Michael Collins. While most Catholic teachers found the oath objectionable, they had little option but to subscribe to it. A small number refused and lost their jobs. Many others went south to work there. The oath remained in force until 1973, when it was removed by the Whitelaw administration.

Cahill cites the case of friend and fellow republican Joe McGurk, a trained teacher whose principles would not permit him to take the oath:

'By refusing to swear allegiance to the Crown, McGurk effectively ruled himself out of the running for a teaching job and was forced to take on work for which he was over-qualified – sometimes as a bookmaker's clerk, occasionally as an office clerk. He was a totally dedicated volunteer and one of the most interned men in Ireland.'

McGurk's account of a meeting with the great nationalist leader 'Wee Joe' Devlin made a deep impression on Cahill. Devlin, a constitutional politician, represented nationalists at Westminster and, after partition, at Stormont.

'I remember Joe Devlin sent for Joe McGurk. It was more or less a deathbed statement by Wee Joe. He told Joe McGurk he had wasted his life and achieved very little by attending Stormont, and would advise anyone thinking of going to Stormont not to do it.

McGurk was a very honest man, and I have no doubts at all about the authenticity of his story.'

Meanwhile Cahill, now aged thirty, was active enough to attract the interest of RUC Special Branch. In 1951, the Branch deemed it prudent to have him and several comrades taken off the streets for the duration – plus a few extra days – of a visit to Belfast by a member of the British royal family.

The law under which the republicans were jailed was the all-embracing Special Powers Act, a piece of legislation so powerful that police officers invoking it could even afford to ignore a writ of *habeas corpus*. It had been used in the 1940s to imprison two young Newry women – Lily Farrell and Rose O'Hanlon – for selling Easter lilies, the republican symbol of the 1916 Rising. Under the Special Powers Act, it was illegal to play a recording of a republican song or fly the Irish tricolour. Newspapers of the time are liberally sprinkled with court reports of people being fined or even jailed for shouting, 'Up the rebels.'

'The surprising thing,' says Cahill, 'was that many nationalists seemed to accept this sort of thing from the Stormont government. Thirteen of us were arrested that year and held for a week in Crumlin Road jail. That was a regular thing – every time there was a royal visit, they put you out of the way for a week.'

The anger and resentment caused by lifting men off the streets and jailing them for a week was lost on prison authorities, who insisted on punishing detainees further by imposing a remand prisoner regime, rather than permitting them to spend the seven days under relatively relaxed 'internee conditions'.

'They wanted us to take remand exercise – that is, walking around the exercise yard in single file with no talking. At this stage remand prisoners were limited to two cigarettes in the morning and another two in the evening. We were expected to eat nothing but jail food – no parcels. We told them we would not accept these conditions. They ignored us and simply left us locked up. There was no redress or appeal. I suppose we did not mind a big lot, because we knew it was only for a week.'

In May 1951, the IRA leadership appointed a military council to oversee the planning of a new campaign. One month later, republicans carried out an arms raid on Ebrington military barracks in Derry, netting six machine guns, two Bren guns, twenty Sten guns, twenty Lee Enfield rifles and a quantity of ammunition. This was to prove the first of several – successful and unsuccessful – such attacks by the IRA in Ireland and England between 1951 and 1955.

The IRA planned a series of protest operations to mark the coronation of Queen Elizabeth in June 1953. Cahill was employed in the construction industry at the time. As usual, he had been earmarked by Special Branch for arrest and detention during the period, but a building site accident foiled police plans.

'I was working for a building contractor in a County Antrim cement plant when I was hit on the head with a scaffolding bar. I was taken to Larne hospital to be treated for a fractured skull, and a while later was sent to recover in a convalescent home at Cairndhu on the Antrim coast. There had been a lot of raiding in Belfast at the time. The RUC searched my home in Divis Street and asked where I was. Of course no one would tell them.

'After leaving my house, they went around the corner to the home of Joe McGurk in Institution Place. On his mantelpiece was a "get well" postcard, which he was just about to mail. It was addressed to "Joe Cahill, Cairndhu Convalescent Home, Cairndhu, County Antrim". The Branch couldn't believe their luck and came down to Cairndhu to see if I really was there. They didn't bother me when they discovered I was still ill. However, they questioned the matron and it upset her very much. She told me the Special Branch had inquiring about me. I told her not to worry, because it was part and parcel of everyday life for republicans.'

Whatever the matron's politics, she certainly did not let it interfere with her duty to her patients. Spotting Cahill sitting in the lounge where the coronation was being shown on television, she called him to the corridor and discreetly asked if he was happy enough watching it.

'I told her I was, and that I actually wanted to see it. She then brought me an armchair and I had the best seat in the house. Later in the week my mother and father came down to visit me and told me the RUC had been at the house. That's when I found out about Joe McGurk's "get well" card.'

Once he was fit enough, he left the convalescent home and travelled to Leixlip, just outside Dublin, where he spent a few days resting at an aunt's residence. Cahill didn't know it then, but a chance meeting with an attractive Belfast girl during this brief sojourn in the South was to have an enormous influence on his life. Annie Magee, he says, was an accomplished Irish dancer with a winning smile, who was to become not only his wife and the mother of their seven children, but also his 'best friend'. 'Annie was a tower of strength for me over the next forty years,' he says.

Annie and her twin brother were the joint-second youngest of Ned and Ethel Magee's nine children. The family lived on west Belfast's Whiterock Road, where Ned Magee and his bride settled when he was demobilised from the British Army. Magee had seen action in the First World War and had lost two fingers. Ethel died at an early age, leaving Ned to bring up the children alone. While he did not speak much to his youngsters about his time in the military, he had long and frank discussions with his IRA volunteer son-in-law.

'When he talked about his days in the British Army,' Cahill says, 'he referred to himself as "one of Redmond's fools".'

(John Redmond, leader of the Irish Parliamentary Party and an advocate of Irish Home Rule, caused a split in the Irish Volunteers, forerunners of the IRA, when he urged them to join the British

Army to fight in the 'Great War'.)

'Ned always said he believed he was going out to fight for the freedom of small nations, including Ireland. He came back very disillusioned,' says Cahill.

Annie, while not an active member of the republican movement, was certainly a sympathiser and showed her support by attending fund-raising functions and other events, such as the annual commemoration service at the site of Wolfe Tone's birth in Bodenstown, County Kildare. On Bodenstown Sunday in 1953, as in other years, Annie Magee came south with friends on a day excursion, to join republicans from all over Ireland in honouring Wolfe Tone.

Normally Cahill would have helped to organise buses from Belfast to Dublin for the Bodenstown commemoration, but he had been unable to do so that particular year because of his accident.

'On Sunday evening I went with a friend to see off the Belfast buses as they left from the Customs House in Dublin. As the last one departed, we headed for the traditional Bodenstown Sunday *céilí* in the Mansion House and were met by four Belfast people. We told them they had missed the last bus. That was the first time I met Annie, who was one of the four. It was her smile that I fell for, and I fell so hard that I skinned both knees,' he says with a smile.

In the following months, the pair often bumped into each other at a *céilí* or *scoraíocht* (impromptu music session), and began 'keeping company' regularly in 1954. Annie was a friend of Marie Maguire, sister of the great Belfast fiddler Seán Maguire, and it was in their home in Dunmore Street, near the Royal Victoria hospital, that the future Mr and Mrs Joe Cahill often met.

But on the Bodenstown Sunday of their first meeting, Annie Magee was experiencing her own problems and romance was far from her mind.

'Our bus had left and we were stranded in Dublin and needed to get to Belfast,' she says. 'We grabbed the first taxi we came across and had the driver chase after the bus until we caught up and flagged it down. The bus was packed and we had to sit on the floor all the way home, but we didn't really mind.'

Within a few days of his first meeting with Annie, Cahill was back in Belfast and on active service. Arms were as scarce as ever, and the IRA was continually carrying out surveillance operations on British Army installations throughout the North. The benefits of a successful raid were twofold: it not only provided good-quality weapons and ammunition – the 'forties men held the British Army's Lee Enfield .303 bolt action rifle in particular esteem – but a 'spectacular' operation ensured maximum publicity and an upsurge in support and recruiting.

Cahill took part in a number of these raids, including one at Palace barracks in Holywood, County Down, in which he played an integral part, and another when he transported weapons captured in an attack on Gough Barracks in Armagh.

'Information about the internal layout and security arrangements at Palace barracks was supplied by two Irishmen who were serving in the British Army. Shortly before they were due to return to civilian life, they contacted an IRA source in Dublin and offered to help set up a raid for a small amount of arms, particularly rifles. I never actually met them, but the information they gave trickled through to us in Belfast. They had been thoroughly checked out in Dublin and were believed to be trustworthy.

'The soldiers had told us exactly how to get into the place. The raid would have to be carried out at night-time. They acquainted us with what sort of sentry duties were in place and how we could avoid them. We arrived at eight o'clock in two cars, which we parked near the back entrance of the barracks while we cut a hole in the wire perimeter fence.

'There were two drivers and four other people on the raid. The drivers stayed with their vehicles while we made our way across a field in the dark. The information we were given was very accurate – we had no bother at all in finding the Nissen hut [a tunnel-shaped, corrugated-iron building with a cement floor] where the weapons were stored.

'When we got near the hut we could observe the sentry on duty. He walked the full length and met the other sentry coming the other way. They stood and talked for quite a while. We were expecting this to happen and we had been told that when the sentries met, they would be together for quite a while. They were totally unsuspecting and totally relaxed.

'The door of the armoury had been left unlocked for us by the two soldiers. We went into the hut and saw a line of rifles in a rack along the wall. The only time I had a doubt during the whole operation was when I saw a chain looped through the trigger guards of the rifles. I examined the chain and it was quite loose. The soldiers had left it in place, but unlocked, so that at first glance the guns looked to be secure. But when we started to lift the rifles away, the chain slipped and there was an awful bloody rattle. Naturally, we thought the sound was a lot louder than it really was. It was magnified to our ears because we were keyed up.'

Cahill and the other three held their breath and waited for a reaction from the sentries. When none came, they began sorting the rifles into four piles. It was, says Cahill, a long way back to the vehicles and the load was heavy. They would only have time for one trip to the armoury, and had to take all thirty weapons at once.

'After a while I thought we were overdoing it, because we had a fair distance to walk to the perimeter and the cars. I suppose on an occasion like that you get extra strength. We loaded the rifles into the two cars without attracting attention and took off, mission accomplished.'

The IRA may have obtained thirty excellent weapons, but Cahill and the other members of Belfast Battalion were deprived of their secondary objective – publicity.

'The strange thing was that the British Army always denied there was a raid on the barracks at Holywood. It was publicised later by the IRA in a statement, which claimed a successful arms raid had been carried out at Palace barracks. However, the British Army denied that any raid had taken place; they would not give us any credit for it.'

Territorial Army (TA) premises were relatively easy prey for foraging republicans, although occasionally the end product of a raid could turn out to be a little unexpected. Cahill led a team which carried out an attack on a TA building on the outskirts of Belfast. The IRA unit broke into the unguarded hut and made off with eight rifles, returning without incident to a safe house in Belfast.

'We were well pleased with our haul, but when we began to examine them, we discovered to our dismay and disappointment that we were in possession of eight training rifles, which were absolutely useless for operations.'

One of the most successful arms raids of this period took place at Gough barracks in Armagh city, in June 1954. During the full-scale operation, nineteen IRA volunteers took over the armoury and guardroom and imprisoned the sentries, before making off with a lorry-load of weapons and ammunition. The operation again severely angered and embarrassed the Stormont government, and netted the IRA 340 rifles, fifty Sten sub-machine guns, a number of Bren light machine guns and some .22 weapons. The haul was taken to an arms dump in County Meath, from where it was distributed to IRA units when the furore had died down.

Cahill was one of those responsible for bringing part of Belfast's share of the weapons back over the border.

'The arms allotted to Belfast and surrounding towns were brought up from the South in two lots. We brought the first consignment up along a small road, at the back of where the border post used to be at Carrickarnon. We had a fair amount of arms in the back of the car.

'We spotted a red light which was sort of waving, and thought maybe it was an RUC roadblock. When we got a bit closer, we discovered it was a woman riding a bicycle with a carrier basket at the front. She flagged us down. She was smuggling stuff – butter or cigarettes or whatever was dearer in the South at the time. She was smuggling it in the other direction and wanted to know whether the road was clear or if there were customs men nearer the border. We were relieved to discover that we had come upon, if not a "fellow" smuggler, then a woman smuggler.'

Some time later, Cahill and a close friend, Joe B O'Hagan, returned south to pick up a second consignment, some of which was to be dropped off in O'Hagan's home town of Lurgan on the way back to the city.

'We were able to use the main road on this occasion, because our scouts had gone ahead and returned to tell us there was no security on the border. There was only myself and Joe B, who was driving, and we had a good number of rifles – between twenty and thirty – lying on the back seat and covered with a couple of rugs. At Drummad Garda station – it's still there to this day – a Garda came out and flagged us down.

'He said he was looking for a big favour from us. He had a friend down from the North visiting him, who needed a lift back north to the Lurgan area. Now, actually, we were going through Lurgan, because we had to drop some off some rifles in Joe B's area. We didn't know what to do. There was no one in the back of the car, so we couldn't very well say we didn't have the space. So the guy climbed in and seated himself on top of our weapons. Our first thoughts were to take him up the road and ditch him somewhere. But the Garda's parting shot as the car was about to move off took the wind out of our sails. He said his friend was a sergeant in the RUC and they were great pals.

'On the way, the sergeant said he lived just outside the town and asked us to drop him off there, which we did. As he was getting out of the car, he thanked us for the lift, but told us we would need to have the vehicle's springs fixed, because they had caused the back seat to be extremely rigid – it was "very hard on the arse".

'He thanked us again and went his way, and we went our way and made our deliveries.'

CHAPTER SIX

The Informer and the '56 Campaign

The Three Macs had seen the IRA through three occurrences of that great curse of the republican movement – the split. The Army Council's intentions regarding the launch of a new campaign was surrounded by a strict wall of secrecy. This was a contributory factor in the resignation of many eager and enthusiastic young volunteers, who left the mainstream republican movement to seek more immediate action. There is no doubt that most of these dissidents would have remained in the IRA if they had suspected what GHQ was planning.

Two other organisations – Saor Uladh (Free Ulster) and Saor Éire (Free Ireland) – were also causing problems for the IRA, by carrying out attacks which occasionally jeopardised mainstream republican operations. But GHQ staff in Dublin were unaware that the IRA's Belfast Battalion was under threat from that other great curse of republicanism – the informer.

To this day, many northern veterans remain bitter that Belfast republicans were totally excluded from the new campaign which, when it began in December 1956, was almost exclusively confined to rural areas of the North. With the passage of time, a belief has grown that the city was left out because of fears that heavy IRA activity there would be likely to bring down the wrath of loyalist extremists, who would launch a fresh series of attacks against the Catholic population. The IRA, the argument goes, would not have been strong enough to protect the nationalist people of the city.

If the threat of a pogrom was the reason for Belfast's isolation, it seems reasonable to assume that senior northern IRA officers would have been asked for their opinion. The city had, after all, received its share of weapons from two successful arms raids in preparation for the forthcoming campaign. But by late 1956, so tight was the clampdown on information that the OC of Belfast first heard of the start of the campaign from the senior RUC officer who arrived to search his home in the early hours of 13 December.

Only occasionally have there been hints at the real reason why Belfast was so strictly isolated by GHQ during the 1956–62 period. Tim Pat Coogan, in his book *The IRA*, touched on the truth when he said: 'Incidents took place which made the Dublin IRA think the RUC had sources of information in Belfast which would prejudice any attempted rising there.'

For two or three years before the launch of the campaign, several senior members of Belfast Battalion staff, Cahill included, were suspicious of the number of operations that had gone wrong or were compromised. It became almost commonplace for an IRA unit to arrive at the scene of a planned operation to find the area saturated with RUC officers. Most of the staff were convinced that an informer was at work.

There were, however, periods when things worked so well that the idea of the informer almost lost currency.

'Certainly,' says Cahill, 'there were occasions when doubt was thrown on the possibility of a traitor in our midst. An informer works in strange ways, whether it is on the direction of certain handlers or not I don't know. Often nothing happens, then all of a sudden things start to go wrong, but there would almost always be something which he could use as a cover.'

According to Cahill, judging by the quality of information being leaked, the informer had to be 'either a member of Battalion staff or someone close to Battalion staff'.

'We had been suspicious for some time prior to the start of the '56 campaign. The idea that we had an informer in the Belfast area, in effect in our midst, went back to around 1953. It was obviously someone who was well up, and had access to what was happening and what was being planned in Belfast.

'In 1953, the year of the coronation in England, a lot of protest operations had been planned for Belfast. The police always anticipated operations by the IRA at times like this, and they arrested people and carried out raids on people's homes, including mine. But even allowing for this, the RUC seemed to know a lot more than they could pick up from surveillance. I had the accident at work around then and was out of action for about three months, but I was told when I returned that the RUC appeared to have information on almost every operation due to be carried out at that time. Because of some things that happened, I am certain that if an inquiry had been held at the time of the coronation, the finger would have pointed directly at the person whom I later became convinced was informing.'

An added bonus for the RUC's Special Branch was the friction generated among staff officers, some of whom believed the OC, Jimmy Steele, was not doing enough to weed out the informer. One of those who felt most strongly about the issue was Belfast Brigade officer Billy McMillen, from the west of the city.

'I remember at one particular staff meeting,' says Cahill, 'there was a heated discussion between McMillen and the OC. McMillen actually resigned from the IRA, taking a few other volunteers with him. They linked up with Saor Uladh for a while. Again, for a time after this, operations that were planned went okay – obviously this was the RUC covering up for their tout. There was a general feeling within the staff that whoever the informer was – and there was no doubt in anyone's mind that there was an informer – he had gone along with Billy McMillen. That sort of shunted people off the question of a tout for a while.'

(McMillen eventually returned to the mainstream republican fold, and was OC Belfast Battalion at the time of the IRA split of 1969–70. He continued as leader of the Official IRA in the city, while another 'forties man, Billy McKee, became the first Belfast commander of the Provisional IRA. Billy McMillen, known affectionately to colleagues as 'the Wee Man', was shot dead in 1975 in a feud between the Official IRA and its offshoot, the Irish National Liberation Army. McMillen, who had married late in life, left a bride of just two months when he was killed.)

Some time after McMillen's defection, operations started going wrong again. By 1956 Cahill had decided to take a hand in rooting out the informer. But first, informer or not, he needed to take a chance on selecting someone to help – someone he would have to be able to trust with his life.

'The more I looked at the problem, the more it appeared to me that the informer was somebody of high rank, somebody on Battalion staff, and it was very worrying. It meant that you could trust no one on the staff. I started investigating people, and the first person I checked out was a pal, because I needed someone to work with. He was the Battalion intelligence officer [IO], a person whose job brought him into possession of a lot of information. I satisfied myself that he was quite clear and no finger of suspicion was pointing at him.

'I arranged a meeting with him, saying I wanted to have a long talk. I told him how worried I was about the situation. He was a dour sort of a boy, and he didn't say yes or no at first. I then said I had taken it upon myself to investigate him, and I was satisfied that he was in the clear. He smiled and said it was very strange, because he had taken it upon himself to check me out and he had found that I was in the clear.

'We set up to work together. An investigation like that is such a serious matter that you have to prod and prod and prod. You have to be one-hundred-and-ten percent sure you are right. The only way to investigate this is by a process of elimination: take every operation that you knew of – find out what happened, who was involved, what went right, what went wrong, who knew about it, and look for a common denominator. After a lengthy investigation, we both came to the conclusion that the finger pointed to just one person.'

Around this time, and despite a heavy workload, Cahill had been seeing more and more of Annie Magee. They had started going out together regularly around 1954 and, along with friends named Rose and Barney, had earned quite a reputation at *céilí* dances with their four-hand reel.

Before setting a date for their wedding, Cahill felt it was time for some honest discussion with his fiancée: 'From the outset I made it plain to her what she was getting into and what the possible consequences were for both of us.'

Annie was undaunted by the black picture painted by Cahill, and the pair were married in St John's Church on the Falls Road on Easter Monday, 2 April 1956. The new Mrs Cahill had an early sample of what married life was to be like for her when Special Branch officers were spotted watching proceedings through the church railings.

'There had been a bit of concern the previous day, Easter Sunday, because I generally carried the tricolour in the commemoration parade up the Falls Road to Milltown cemetery. Some of my friends thought it was tempting fate to risk being arrested the day before Annie and I were to be married. However, there were no hitches; it went off all right and we were married next day. After our reception in Anne's Teashop near the city centre, we headed off on honeymoon for almost two weeks to Dublin, Kerry and Cork. Everywhere we went, the local republicans knew we were on honeymoon and gave us a great time.'

Later that year, a new Belfast Battalion OC, Paddy Doyle from the Pound Loney area of the lower Falls Road, was appointed.

Doyle had been interned in Crumlin Road jail during the war years, but he and Cahill had not met until the early 1950s. He had been close to the Three Macs and was voted onto the Sinn Féin

Ard Comhairle, or executive council, at the 1951 *Ard Fheis*. His appointment as OC Belfast came at around the same time as approximately twenty special GHQ organisers, who were to report periodically in person to the chief of staff, were sent north to train volunteers and collate intelligence. Because Doyle lived in Belfast, GHQ deemed it unnecessary to appoint an organiser there.

Cahill and the IO ran a security check on Doyle before taking him into their confidence. They gave him details of their investigations, but stopped short of identifying their suspect.

'He said he didn't want to know the name of the suspect at that stage, but he wanted us to go back to the start and begin our investigation all over again to see if we came to the same conclusion.'

Down south, preparations for the launch of the new campaign were reaching an advanced stage, although most of the IRA rank and file had no idea when hostilities were due to commence. Paddy Doyle had been summoned to a meeting with senior staff members in October. However, he was unable to attend, and asked Cahill, who was Battalion adjutant and second in command, to represent Belfast. Cahill's friend, the IO, was to accompany him.

'Doyle told us he was aware of what was happening in Dublin and that he wanted us to pay particular attention to what was said at the meeting. He said we were to tell the chief of staff about the suspicions of an informer in Belfast and acquaint him with our investigations so far.'

In Dublin, Tony Magan opened the meeting, but handed over the chairmanship to his director of operations, 'Yankee Seán' Cronin. Cronin, a journalist with the Dublin-based *Evening Press*, had recently returned from the United States, and was believed by a number of senior republicans to be something of a military genius. A former officer in the Irish Army, he was the architect of Operation Harvest, the codename for the new campaign, which aimed to strike at military, police and government targets in the North.

Following the meeting, which was attended by most of the IRA's Battalion OCs from across the country, Cahill and the IO requested a few minutes for a private meeting with the chief of staff. Magan listened with grim intensity as the two Belfast men told him of their suspicions and of their investigations so far.

'Like Doyle, Magan did not want to know the name of our suspect. He gave me the same advice: go back and investigate the matter thoroughly. As soon as we were absolutely sure of the informer's guilt, we were to report back to GHQ staff. But before I left, the chief of staff said he had another job for me. He said he was very perturbed about the possibility of an informer in Belfast, and he was giving me a job which had to be carried out with the utmost speed.

'He told me to get all the arms in the Belfast area removed from the present dumps and secured in dumps under my control. He emphasised that I was to waste no time about it. It was a very tough task he gave me, because I had to do it without raising suspicions, and again I used the IO to assist me.'

Afterwards, Cahill pondered on several points that had been made and questions that had been asked of those present at the meeting. Although no one mentioned the campaign outright, he said he was 'left with the distinct impression that another phase of the armed struggle was about to begin'. He remembers, almost forty-six years later, being unhappy at the IRA's state of unpreparedness for a renewal of the campaign. Just two others at the meeting, however, appeared to be against an immediate resumption and he kept his own counsel.

What he could not have known at that time, however, was that Magan and the Army Council, acting on the information received from Cahill and the IO, had decided not to risk involving Belfast in the new campaign. Even as Cahill and his friend, whom he will not name because he is still alive, travelled back home, their evidence was being discussed. That meeting, Cahill believes, led directly to a change of plans. The campaign would concentrate on targets outside Belfast; the city, with its traitor, would be left strictly alone.

This was a huge tactical shift for the IRA. Belfast city was home to their northern base and had figured largely in republican operations since before the partition of the country. To cut Belfast out of the campaign at the last minute was incomprehensible to volunteers in the city units, and was viewed by some as an insult.

Cahill concentrated on the logistics of securing all of the Battalion's weapons. 'The ploy I used to explain what was happening, as far as Battalion staff were concerned, was that GHQ staff were calling in all arms and they wanted them under their control. It seemed to be all right, people accepted that.'

Much of the work of transporting the weapons from dumps all over Belfast to the west of the city fell to the members of Cumann na mBan, the women's wing of the IRA. Their OC, Bridie O'Neill, worked closely with Cahill on what turned out to be a major operation. She was later to report that her women had several narrow escapes – on one particularly hair-raising occasion a Cumann na mBan unit thought they were about to be captured when they walked into a heavy RUC presence after lifting arms from a dump. By a mixture of skill and luck, the women avoided what they believed had been a trap.

O'Neill, an experienced volunteer, also suspected that an informer was at work. She was convinced she knew the identity of the man and, after her unit's narrow escape, she told Cahill of her misgivings. The man she named was the same person who had been under suspicion for so long.

'When I met her that night she said, "If you don't shoot that bastard, I will shoot him myself." It was another piece of the jigsaw falling into place, another piece of evidence pointing to the guilt of this person. We completed that operation and, to the best of my knowledge, all the arms were transferred to fresh dumps known only to myself and the people involved in the shifting of the weapons.'

Around this time, Paddy Doyle was summoned down south to a meeting with GHQ staff. However, he was to get no further than Belfast's Great Northern railway station in Great Victoria Street, where he was arrested by the RUC as he was about to board the train for Dublin. Doyle, it was discovered later, was captured while in possession of an important document, which only one other person knew he was carrying – the man suspected by Cahill and the IO of being an informer. Doyle received a short sentence for possessing the document, but was interned just as he was due for release, a common occurrence when the IRA was active.

Cahill took over as OC Belfast after Doyle's arrest and, still unaware of GHQ's decision to isolate the city, was confidently expecting to receive orders to begin hostilities in the near future. Unknown to all but a handful of the most senior IRA members, the launch of the campaign, due in November 1956, had been postponed for a month because of the activities of dissident groups on the border.

Annie Cahill was by now pregnant with their first child, which was due in March. When the RUC raided her home at around 6am on 13 December, she thought she was about to lose her husband in an arrest operation. This time, however, the motive of the raiding party was simply to see if Cahill was at home. Similar operations were taking place at the same time in republican homes all over Belfast.

Unknown to Joe and Annie Cahill, a series of carefully coordinated IRA operations had been carried out in every county of the North a few hours earlier. Cahill was puzzled at the raid on his home, and said as much to the senior RUC officer.

'The first I knew of the campaign starting was when the police raided the house I was living in at the time. I asked them why they were raiding and the senior guy said, "Don't give me that shit, Joe." When he realised I didn't know, he told me, as he was leaving, to listen to the seven o'clock BBC radio news. I did, and I got the shock of my life. A number of operations had been carried out by the IRA and I realised then that the campaign had started.'

Cahill and the other Belfast republicans were hurt and mystified at being left out of the action.

'It was not until some time later I was told that, because of our belief that there was an informer in the area, a deliberate decision was taken to ignore Belfast, in case it would jeopardise other areas. Consequently, there was no action in Belfast on the night of 11–12 December 1956.'

Cronin's Operation Harvest had begun. A few days before its launch, teams of southern IRA volunteers had begun travelling north. There they linked up with local republicans, in tactics reminiscent of the 'flying column' days of the War of Independence. Cronin's aim was to attack RUC barracks, military establishments, telephone exchanges and government buildings in strength. He believed that if the enemy was hit hard enough and often enough, they would be forced to withdraw from townlands, villages and even small towns, and the IRA could make areas of the North ungovernable.

In the hours before Cahill's home was raided, a total of 150 IRA members attacked ten targets in all six counties, but not one shot was fired in Belfast. Three bridges were blown up in County Fermanagh and a BBC transmitter destroyed in Derry. The courthouse in Magherafelt, County Derry, was damaged and a TA building in Enniskillen attacked. A hut used by the B Specials in Newry was damaged in an explosion. The following night saw attacks on two RUC barracks in Fermanagh.

The Stormont government reacted swiftly. Within a few days, dozens of border roads were rendered impassable by being either spiked or 'cratered' with explosives. Several bridges were also blown up by British Army engineers. Checkpoints were set up on the remaining seventeen border crossings and each area was patrolled by the RUC, B Specials and the British Army. Legislation was quickly renewed permitting the reintroduction of internment and the imposition of curfews.

In Dublin, John A Costello, taoiseach of the coalition government, threatened to take action against republicans. Costello's Fine Gael party remained in power only with the help of unlikely coalition partners Clann na Poblachta, many of whose members were former members of the IRA who now embraced constitutional politics. Within weeks, government action against the IRA was to have a devastating effect on the coalition.

In Belfast, according to Cahill, bewildered republicans were asking when they would be brought into the action: 'We had been left high and dry. I tried to contact GHQ and was told that someone would be in touch fairly quickly. That did not happen, but what did happen was that internment was reintroduced in the North just a few days later. I was not arrested in that swoop and there was a feeling in Belfast that that was all the interment there was going to be – false thinking, of course, as I was to discover later.'

A lull in activity took place over Christmas, allowing some volunteers to return briefly to their families. Meanwhile, the leadership assessed the situation and took some time to reorganise and regroup.

New Year's Day 1957 was to bring the first republican casualties of the campaign. Seán South, a twenty-seven-year-old Limerick man, and Feargal O'Hanlon, a nineteen-year-old from County Monaghan, were members of an IRA unit which set out to attack an RUC barracks in Brookeborough, County Fermanagh. Again in a return to the tactics of the 1920s, the raiders aimed to gain entry to the barracks by blowing a hole in the wall, and then kill or imprison the occupants and capture their weapons.

Scouts were dropped off on the outskirts of the village to warn of any approaching reinforcements, while the unit's truck stopped directly opposite the barracks. As the men on the lorry provided covering fire, another group carried a bomb across the street and placed it against the wall. When that failed to detonate, the men took a second mine from the truck and, under fire from the building, set it in place. It too was faulty. By now, the RUC defenders were pouring a withering fire in the direction of the IRA vehicle. With the element of surprise gone and several volunteers wounded, the attack was called off.

The truck driver, who like Seán Cronin had returned from the United States to take part in the campaign, had a miraculous escape from death when the RUC men on the upper floor began to concentrate their fire on the vehicle's cab.

Still under heavy fire, the assault party collected the scouts and headed for the border. With their truck damaged and realising the roads ahead would be swamped with RUC and British Army, the unit took to the fields. South and O'Hanlon, the most badly wounded, were by now unconscious. It was decided to carry them to a nearby cow byre, where the pursuing RUC could find them and provide medical attention. As the retreating unit headed over the hill towards the nearby border, they heard prolonged gunfire in close proximity to the cow byre.

The RUC later said that the two IRA men were dead when the pursuers reached the byre. Some republicans maintain that O'Hanlon and South were killed by police as they lay wounded. However, Tim Pat Coogan, in *The IRA*, quotes a member of the IRA unit who believes the gunfire heard by the fleeing republicans was the RUC blasting at the byre as a precaution before attempting entry. Coogan's source maintains that this was normal practice for security forces. He believes the two volunteers were already dead or dying when the RUC arrived.

Dáithí (Dave) Ó Conaill was a member of the unit which

attacked Brookeborough barracks, and narrowly escaped capture despite being wounded. In the 1970s, Cahill became friendly with him while they were both on the Army Council.

'Dave was convinced that South and O'Hanlon were alive when they were left in the byre, but that the RUC were deliberately slow to summon medical aid and the two men bled to death,' says Cahill. 'He told me that as a direct result of that raid, GHQ staff issued an order that never again should a wounded volunteer be left behind to fall into the hands of the enemy.'

In the 1960s, another member of the Brookeborough raiding party revealed that all of the volunteers on the operation had been wounded. The man, who was shot in the leg, described the 'weird sensation' of wading across a river on the way to the border and feeling the freezing cold water running through the bullet hole in his calf.

As a military operation, the Brookeborough raid was a failure, but the image of young men fighting and dying for the liberation of their country caught the public imagination. Feargal O'Hanlon and Seán South were accorded the status of fallen heroes. Thousands flocked from all over Ireland to their funerals and within weeks, it seemed, both men had been honoured by having songs written about their exploits.

Despite unionist claims in early 1957 that the government of the Republic was soft on the IRA, it was taoiseach John A Costello who struck the first telling blow against the organisation. In January, Garda Special Branch surrounded premises where a meeting of GHQ staff was taking place. Most of the IRA leadership was arrested, including chief of staff Tony Magan. They were charged under the Offences Against the State Act and sentenced to six months in prison.

Costello's action, however, led to deep resentment from his coalition partners. Clann na Poblachta leader Seán McBride brought matters to a head in January 1957 by tabling a motion of censure against the government, citing reasons of economic policy and 'the harassment of the IRA'. Costello dissolved the Dáil in February and, in the resulting general election in March, Fianna Fáil swept into power. With no irksome Clann na Poblachta restraint – even Seán McBride, a former IRA chief of staff, lost his seat – de Valera and his new government had a free hand to take on the IRA.

In line with the republican leadership's twin aims of carrying out spectacular operations and garnering popular support, Sinn Féin nominated nineteen candidates for the 1957 Dáil elections on an abstentionist ticket. They won four seats – including one for the brother of Feargal O'Hanlon – with 65,640 votes, the party's highest poll in the South since 1927. These successes helped further bolster republican morale, already fairly high after the May 1955 Westminster results when constitutional northern nationalists had stood aside as republicans contested all twelve Westminster seats. Two IRA men, Phil Clarke and Tom Mitchell – who were serving lengthy sentences in connection with the Omagh raid – were elected, in Fermanagh–south Tyrone and mid-Ulster. A parliamentary fiasco followed. Clarke was thrown out of Westminster, *in absentia*, when his defeated unionist opponent objected. The unionist was subsequently installed in the Fermanagh–south Tyrone seat. The mid-Ulster seat was declared vacant when Tom Mitchell failed to turn up by mid-July, and a by-election was called. Mitchell stood again, and won with an increased majority from an amazing ninety percent turnout, only to be ruled ineligible later. Ironically, his unionist opponent was unseated on an electoral technicality the following year without making his maiden speech.

Cahill's hopes of restoring contact with GHQ staff had been shattered with the arrest of most of the leadership in Dublin in January. The IRA in the North, and in the rest of the country for that matter, was having problems getting in touch with the new staff. Cahill's first contact came through a remarkable Dublin woman – Mrs Boyce, whose son Eamon had led the arms raid on Omagh barracks in October 1954; he had been captured by the RUC and sentenced to ten years.

Mrs Boyce, now regarded by republicans as one of the unsung heroes of her time, was highly respected by Cahill. Just one of her many jobs as an IRA supporter was to act as courier for GHQ.

'This lady brought a communication to me in Belfast, a message requesting me to attend a meeting down south. The only instruction on it was to head to Drogheda on a certain day at a certain time, walk on out the Dublin road in the vicinity of a public house, the Black Bull, and I would be picked up by car.

'I followed the instructions and was in fact overtaken by a car, which must have been parked near the bar. I was picked up and brought to a meeting of senior people in Meath. It was a meeting of whoever was left of GHQ staff, the Army Council and the Executive, and a few other invited people, like myself from Belfast. It was, I suppose, a mini-convention; that's the only way I could describe it. The purpose was to set up a new staff and Army Council.

'Paddy MacLógáin presided over the meeting, and that was the first contact I had with GHQ or with any senior representative of the IRA since October. At that meeting there was a discussion about the effect on the Army of internment in the North and the arrests of the officers in the South, and whether or not the campaign should continue. Some people were of the opinion that it should be halted for the time being, but the consensus was that the campaign should go on and the Army, at top level, be restructured.

'For security reasons, it was decided that MacLógáin, as chief of staff, would set up a department of three people to head the campaign until things regularised themselves and a full staff could be established.'

The new leaders were surprised when Cahill asked why Belfast 'had not been allowed to operate' in the campaign, and again when he revealed that no one in the city had known that hostilities were about to begin. News of his conversation with the previous chief of staff, and a renewed warning about the informer, were also greeted with surprise and in one case with some scepticism.

'One man asked if this was not just Belfast hype. I said no, we were quite confident there was an informer. I was then grilled by a couple of people, who took me to one side and asked how we came to this conclusion. I told them of the investigations that we had carried out.

'In the course of questioning, one asked me how sure could I be. I said I was as sure as I could be without interrogating the person concerned. He then put three questions to me about the suspect.'

Cahill was asked if the informer appeared to be very conscientious; if everything he did appeared to be done well. He was then asked if the man had attempted to *plámás* (Irish: to flatter in a wheedling fashion) him. At this remove, Cahill does not remember the third question. He has not, however, forgotten the chillingly nonchalant advice which followed when he answered all three questions in the affirmative: 'That's the trait of an informer, all right. Shoot him.'

Back home once more, Cahill was pleased to have re-established contact with GHQ and cleared the air over Belfast's isolation. But as far as Belfast Battalion was concerned, the informer had taken a heavy toll. Not only was he responsible for compromising several operations, having a number of senior volunteers arrested, fomenting dissension and causing defections to Saor Uladh, but he had also managed to exclude one of the island's most militantly republican cities from what was intended to be an intensive and high-profile campaign.

The Battalion OC had little time to ponder these points before he too was removed from the scene. Within days of returning home from Dublin, he was to experience again the now-familiar pre-dawn battering on the door, the rush of RUC officers into the house and the short journey from west Belfast to the Crumlin Road jail. To add insult to incarceration, the suspected informer was one of the many other republicans arrested that morning and interned.

'The suspect was never confronted, although at the end of all the inquiries held at the time, the finger pointed to this person. The reason he was not arrested and court-martialled was because everyone involved, including the suspect himself, was arrested and interned. Internment probably saved his life,' says Cahill.

After a decent interval – to allay further suspicion, Cahill believes – the renegade indicated to prison authorities that he was prepared to 'sign out', that is, to put his signature to a written vow not to engage in republican activities. These signees, as they were called somewhat contemptuously by sentenced and interned republicans, were housed in a separate wing, sometimes for several weeks, while their applications were processed by the Stormont Home Affairs Ministry.

Interned republicans in general felt that signing out was unprincipled. Those who did so often bore a stigma, sometimes for several years after their release. Exceptions were made in the cases of men who were forced to take this course for health reasons or because of family circumstances. In a few other cases, internees were ordered by the leadership to sign out because their particular talents were needed on the outside.

In retrospect, Cahill believes he has no reason to change his original opinion that the 1956 campaign failed because of lack of preparation. The IRA leadership, he says, had allowed itself to be rushed into action before it was ready. He is also critical of tactics used when the campaign was underway.

'At the time and looking back now, I believe the '56 campaign was premature. Sufficient preparation had not been put into building up the support of the people and developing the organisation. That campaign was probably launched a year too early and was forced upon the IRA by dissidents such as Saor Éire, who were already carrying out operations. If there had been another twelve months of intensified organisation and building up the Army, it would have had a better chance of success.

'Some of the leadership, who had been arrested just after the campaign began, felt that it should have been called off. They did not expect the reaction from the twenty-six-county government that there was. A lot of senior officers from the South, particularly Headquarters staff, were arrested and charged.'

But now the ill-fated campaign was over for Cahill and many of his colleagues. A further blow to the IRA came in July 1957, following the killing of an RUC officer in south Armagh. Eamon de Valera's Fianna Fáil government in the Republic reacted by reopening the Curragh internment camp and bringing back imprisonment without trial. With hundreds of volunteers – including quite a few of the recently released leadership – imprisoned on both sides of the border, the campaign began to lose momentum.

The RUC and British Army had been caught on the hop several times during the pre-campaign arms raids, and had learned their lesson well. Police and military barracks were now heavily defended, making successful attacks extremely difficult. Republicans now switched tactics and began ambushing RUC officers, B Specials and British soldiers on the heavily patrolled roads. A favourite, but not overly successful, ploy was to blow up an electrical installation or a customs hut at night and wait in ambush for security forces to turn up. Quite often, however, the RUC ignored the bait and waited until daylight before investigating an explosion.

By the end of 1957, by far the most active period of the whole campaign, three RUC officers and seven republicans had been killed. In November, in the largest single incident, four IRA men and a civilian supporter died when a landmine exploded prematurely just south of the border at Edentubber, County Louth. A member of the dissident group Saor Uladh, which had been operating independently of the IRA, was killed by the RUC in mid-1958. A few weeks earlier, Fermanagh's IRA commander died in another premature explosion. Around the same time, an RUC officer was killed by a landmine in south Armagh.

There was a stepping-up of operations in 1958, when Seán Cronin took over as chief of staff. However, once more the southern government drew the sting from the IRA's tail, arresting the entire leadership during a meeting in Dublin in September of that year.

Early in 1959, the Irish government was convinced they had the situation fairly well in hand, and began to release the internees. By March the Curragh camp had been emptied of prisoners and was closed down. Cahill says there was still sporadic republican activity in the North, but there was no doubt that the campaign was in the process of winding down.

'It dragged on and dragged on and eventually fizzled out,' he says. 'It was nothing like the recent campaign – it did not have the same degree of intensity and ferocity. There continued to be odd incidents, but they petered out around '61 and the campaign was officially called off in 1962.'

Looking back on the 1956 campaign, Cahill feels that urban, rather than rural, guerrilla tactics would have been more effective. He is dismissive of Cronin's idea of flying columns, which necessitated dozens of men hiding in dugouts in the woods, living off the land and emerging to strike at the enemy before melting away into the night.

'Digging in and living in the forest, isolated from the people, it's the daftest thing I have ever heard of. No one knew where the units were; they were completely cut off from their comrades and the support of the people.'

Of his return to Crumlin Road prison in January 1957, Cahill says: 'Jail is jail and is never pleasant, but I have to say life as an internee was much preferable to that of a convicted prisoner. We had the run of D Wing. The cell doors were opened in the morning and you were left to your own devices all day. Lock-up was initially at seven o'clock, but was later extended to nine.'

Republican internees were expected to play their part in the running of the wing. Elected Camp staff officers were responsible for the morale and welfare of volunteers and this meant maintaining the same standards of discipline as they observed on the outside.

'We had fairly strict discipline. We kept our own areas and cells clean, did our own cooking and had our own staff in the cookhouse. For part of the time, I was OC cookhouse.'

With several county-class Gaelic football and handball players among the internees, games in the exercise yard were often of a higher standard than club matches in Belfast.

'We also had an entertainment staff who organised plays, concerts and pageants. They were responsible for bringing out hidden talents in many internees. Dixie Cordner, who was also interned, was just one of many fine singers on D Wing.'

It was during one such concert in March 1957 that the *fear an tí* (master of ceremonies) made an announcement congratulating Annie and Joe Cahill on the birth of their first child. In what was for republicans a fairly risqué piece of banter for the period – many were daily communicants before capture – the audience was told that Cahill wished to thank his kind neighbours, 'without whom it would not have been possible'. As far as Cahill and Annie were concerned, there was just one name seriously considered for their son. He was duly christened Thomas, in honour of his father's young friend Tom Williams.

'Irish language classes,' says Cahill, 'were always popular in jail, and gave prisoners a chance to perform at the annual *feis* [festival of

Irish music, dance and poetry]. The *feis* was a big high in the life of an internee.'

Cahill says that chess games also reached an impressive standard, with fierce competition during tournaments for the title of champion of Crumlin Road. Often an education interrupted by active service or going on the run was completed with the help of the internees' library. Minds were sharpened too during sessions of D Wing's debating society.

While politics and the future of their country were often debated, there was one subject which occupied most internees more often than any other – escape. The most serious escape attempt made by internees during the 1957–62 period took place in March 1958 and resulted in several prisoners being badly beaten.

'We discovered that an air shaft ran behind the wall in Proinsias MacAirt's end cell. I believe it ran from the basement boiler room to the roof-space above the third floor. A hole was knocked in the cell wall and the shaft was used as the basis for an escape tunnel. The hole was concealed by disguising it with pictures and postcards.

'It was very attractive to look at,' says Cahill with a wry smile, 'but it was still discovered.'

Work on the tunnel had been going on for some time, and was within three weeks of completion. The disposal of soil had become a big problem. Much of it was taken in prisoners' pockets and distributed around the exercise yard. Other debris was stored in the air shaft. At the same time, internees had managed to obtain an impression of a master key. Cahill's young brother Frank, who had also been interned, had the half-completed key in his possession and was engaged in the painstaking task of filing it into shape.

'All hell broke loose when the screws discovered the hole in the wall while the lads were busy working on the tunnel. The screws rushed to lock the door so that the men could not get out of the cell. Then they ran off for reinforcements. Their intention was to lock everybody in their cells and then grab the lads when they came out of the tunnel. We knew the men would be punished, and tried to get them out before the screws arrived. Frank tried the key but it had not been completed and would not unlock the door. The only alternative was to attempt to break it down.

'Somebody remembered a loose guard rail on the "Threes" [the third-storey landing], and a few guys were upstairs like lightning to rip it off. One end of the rail – it was a cast-iron banister really – had come loose over the years. The lads were able to pull it free, dash back down to the ground floor and use it as a battering ram on the door of MacAirt's cell.

'Whoever engineered the breaking down of the door knew not to waste time battering the lock, but went immediately for the hinges. I have never seen a door being broken in as quickly in my life. It was off the hinges in about twenty seconds and we got the men out. They rushed down to the shower room, had a quick wash and then mingled with everyone else.'

Cahill remembers that the warders were furious. A total lock-up was ordered and a systematic cell-by-cell search was launched. An already tense situation deteriorated further when the RUC reserve was called in to support the warders. These were not, as the name suggests, part-time policemen, but a specially trained quasi-military unit normally used to patrol country areas where the IRA was active.

'There was,' says Cahill, 'no real intention to search. It was just an orgy of destruction. Personal items, handicrafts, family pictures, religious pictures – they were all smashed on the floor and danced on. Prisoners objected to the plundering of their cells and the smashing of their property. It finished up in fisticuffs. The men, naturally, attempted to defend themselves, but were always outnumbered. Quite a few got bad beatings. In fact, they knocked the shit out of us.'

Several prisoners were badly injured, with one man suffering a broken leg and broken ribs. Details of the beatings were published only when two prisoners took a legal action, which subsequently failed.

The lock-up continued for three days, into the St Patrick's Day weekend, with internees allowed out of their cells for a mere one hour of exercise each day. St Patrick's Day that year was on a Monday, and Cahill served at the Mass along with fellow internee Paddy Joe McClean, a schoolteacher from County Tyrone.

McClean had been interned for his association with the political group, Fianna Uladh. The party had not been proscribed at the time of McClean's arrest – the Stormont authorities had to introduce retrospective legislation to make his internment legal.

'The senior prison chaplain, Father McAllister, had come over to the wing for a meeting with our OC,' says Cahill. 'The internees' chaplain, the assistant chaplain who was based in Ardoyne Monastery just up the Crumlin Road, was celebrating Mass for us. He told us he had spent the previous evening with the governor discussing the situation. The governor, he said, was "pretty sore".

'Paddy asked him why the governor should be sore and the priest replied, "Oh, because of the fucking oul' tunnel." Paddy had the same thoughts as myself and immediately said, "Sore? It's us who should be complaining about being sore."

'On the way back to the cell, Paddy seemed very thoughtful, and eventually asked me, "Joe, did I hear the priest right – did he say eff?"'

Cahill spent four years and three months in D Wing. He was one of the last four internees released from Crumlin Road jail in April 1961, leaving through the small wicket-gate set into the prison's massive main gate: 'The other three lads came out just ahead of me – I had the dubious honour of being the last internee to step over the gate.'

✠ ✠ ✠

There were to be two more fatalities in the campaign that year, both policemen. In January, an RUC officer was shot by the IRA in County Fermanagh; in November, another was killed in South Armagh. The second killing resulted in the Irish government reintroducing military courts, and twenty-five republicans were convicted in the Republic before the year was out.

At a meeting of the IRA Army Council in February the next year, it was decided to give the order to dump arms and call off the campaign. The decision was announced publicly on 23 February 1962.

One of the reasons given for the cessation of hostilities was a lack of public support. In their statement the Army Council said: 'The decision to end the resistance campaign has been taken in view of the general situation. Foremost among the factors motivating this course of action has been the attitude of the general public whose minds have been deliberately distracted from the supreme issue facing the Irish people – the unity and freedom of Ireland.'

The '56 campaign had resulted in the deaths of six members of the RUC, eight IRA men and one civilian, killed at Edentubber.

Asked on his eighty-first birthday, 19 May 2001, what had happened to the suspected informer who had caused so much trouble to Belfast republicans, Cahill answered: 'As far as I know, he is still walking the streets today.'

CHAPTER SEVEN
Out of the Ashes ...

The decade of the swinging 'sixties – vibrant years of flower power, the Beatles, protest songs, Muhammad Ali and space travel – was just getting into its stride when Joe Cahill found himself a free man once more.

Across the Atlantic, the people of the United States had elected their first Catholic president – a relatively young, wealthy Irish-American called John FitzGerald Kennedy. The Irish people took the handsome Boston politician to their hearts, and he seemed to reciprocate. It was even suggested that he would solve the 'Irish question' by making Ireland the fifty-first state of the Union!

Kennedy visited Ireland in June 1963, and for years afterwards there were few working-class Irish homes without at least one photograph of JFK and his wife Jackie on the wall.

British politicians worried that Kennedy, the most powerful man in the world, would be influenced in his dealings with Britain by the views of his father Joe Kennedy, a second-generation Irish-American who was reported to dislike England and its people.

In the event, it was another, altogether different, American influence – the civil rights movement – which would inspire northern Irish nationalists. Peaceful protests were staged in the North against widespread electoral gerrymandering and discrimination in employment and public housing. Heavy-handed union-ist reaction to the protests, and the growing politicisation of nationalists, would eventually form the catalyst for a sustained and bloody conflict involving republicans, loyalists and British forces, which would last longer than a quarter of a century and cost more than 3,600 lives.

As Cahill was soon to discover, it was not only political attitudes in the North which were undergoing a sea change. The IRA too was changing, but was headed in a direction which perturbed and unsettled traditional republicans.

Shortly after his release in April 1961, Cahill reported back to the IRA and once more offered his services to the Belfast Battalion. This time, however, there was no warm welcome back into the ranks, no trading of prison stories, no comradely jokes – there was no reaction at all. The modern, trendy, leftist republican movement of the 1960s had no use, it seemed, for an old warhorse like Joe Cahill.

Speaking to other 'forties men, Cahill believed he could recognise a disturbing scenario developing: the IRA was becoming doctrinaire Marxist; the movement had got rid of most of its weapons; republicans had abandoned the tradition of armed struggle; the leadership wanted Sinn Féin members to contest Dáil, Stormont and Westminster elections – and take their seats if elected.

'I discovered, through talking to various people I had known before I went into prison, people I trusted, that there was something wrong within the movement. It was taking the wrong course, the wrong road. There was a complete drift towards the political side of things and the military end was being run down. There was a complete concentration on politics and no effort to build up the IRA.'

Cahill was frequently hearing reports from young volunteers returning home from training camps, complaining that weapons and explosives classes were increasingly being replaced by political discussions and lectures on militant socialism. The attempt to transform the IRA from a revolutionary guerrilla organisation into a far-left political party occurred during what Cahill disparagingly calls 'Goulding Rule', or the 'Goulding Era', a reference to the then chief of staff, Cathal Goulding.

Goulding, a Dublin house-painter, came from a staunch republican family. Along with London-born volunteer Seán MacStiofáin and Derry man Manus Canning, he was captured by British police after taking part in an abortive arms raid on an Officer Training Corps arsenal at Felsted public school in Essex, thirty miles from London. The operation, embarked upon in July 1953, had been planned to provide weapons for the forthcoming campaign, but went awry when the unit's van was stopped by police. MacStiofáin, the leader of the London-based IRA unit, reported later that the vehicle had been loaded with eight Bren light machine guns, a medium machine gun, 109 Lee Enfield .303 rifles, twelve Sten sub-machine guns, a mortar launcher and an anti-tank gun.

At their trial in October 1953, the three were each sentenced to eight years' imprisonment. Canning and MacStiofáin were taken to Wormwood Scrubs prison, while Goulding was sent to another London prison, Pentonville.

Cahill had regarded Goulding as a close friend since they worked together in the early 1950s. Goulding, says Cahill, was an exemplary soldier and would never break or bend the rules, even for a good friend.

'I was in charge of a training camp in the 1950s in the Cooley Mountains in County Louth,' says Cahill. 'It was a great camp, well secluded and well off the beaten track, with a mile-long lane to the entrance. There are certain regulations for the protection of the men and the weapons – particularly the weapons, which had to be securely and safely dumped in case of a raid. We always posted sentries so that we would receive adequate warning.

'We had set up a tent in the camp for the purpose of giving weapons training. I was in the tent lecturing at the time and the first I knew about the raid was when the Garda Special Branch came in and said, "Joe, what sort of scouts are they? They were sleeping when we came up the road." The only weapons they got were those being used for the lecture. The others had been dumped, and were retrieved afterwards.

'An inquiry was ordered into the affair and Cathal Goulding was asked to conduct it. He would not allow himself to be influenced by the fact that we were very close. He told me I would get no favours from him, and I didn't. It was a very, very thorough investigation; he gave me a rough time. The outcome was that as OC of the camp I was exonerated. I had taken all the necessary precautions and the majority of the weapons had been saved. The only weapons lost were those in the tent being used for training.

'That was the type of man that Goulding was. Anything he did, he did well; he had a job to do and he did it well. It did not matter that we were great friends.'

Cahill believes it was during his imprisonment in England that Cathal Goulding received the introduction to Marxism which was, in Cahill's opinion, to have such a far-reaching and ruinous effect on the republican movement.

'I had always the highest regard for Goulding as a soldier,' Cahill recalls. 'I always put him down as a military man. I was shocked when I heard of his involvement in plans to abandon the armed struggle and concentrate on left-wing politics. I knew him before he went to jail in England, and I am convinced that he developed his Marxism in jail through his association with the spy Klaus Fuchs.'

Klaus Emil Julian Fuchs, a German-born physicist, worked for the British government throughout the Second World War, carrying out research into the atomic bomb. In 1950 it was discovered that he was spying for Russia, and had been passing top-grade secret information to the communists since 1943. Fuchs's motives were idealistic rather than profit-making: in his seven years as a spy, he was paid just £100 by the Soviet Union. Klaus Fuchs is reported to have remained aloof from British prisoners during his nine years in jail, but struck up a relationship with Goulding with whom he had many political discussions. The scientist was released in 1959 and immediately left England for Russia where he continued his work in physics.

Goulding should have been freed along with MacStiofáin and Canning in February 1959, but lost two months' remission for attempting to escape and did not return to Ireland until later in the spring. In the meantime, the influence of the Three Macs had waned – all three eventually parted company with the IRA in acrimonious circumstances. Several other veterans of the 1940s and 1950s either resigned or were dismissed around this time.

With the IRA weakened and disorganised following another unsuccessful campaign, Goulding, regarded by many as a safe pair of hands, was persuaded in 1962 to accept the role of chief of staff. However, the road chosen by the new leader was to prove controversial and would be rejected by the majority of traditional republicans, leading eventually to a bitter split in the organisation.

The republican movement, since the days of James Connolly and before, had been home to those who espoused socialist principles of one degree or another, but the majority of IRA volunteers drew the line at embracing all-out Marxism. Many republicans found that the 1916 Proclamation, and the writings of Connolly and others, provided enough 'home-grown' socialism to meet their needs. There were others, particularly in the 1930s and 1940s, who were dyed-in-the-wool communists, but whose overwhelming priority was the reunification of their country rather than the pursuit of an unachievable Utopia.

It took time for the full picture to emerge, but traditionalists gradually became worried as they watched the new chief of staff surround himself with a clique of Marxists and communists of various hues. Goulding believed that physical force had failed and the IRA needed to be guided in a new direction. The people could be won over, he argued, if the organisation abandoned the bullet and the bomb and embarked on a long-term programme of militant socialism, which would include the dropping of the abstentionist policy. Sinn Féin candidates would fight elections for the Dáil, Stormont and Westminster, and take their seats if successful.

One of the Three Macs, Paddy MacLógáin, was found dead in July 1964 with a revolver by his side. Cahill is just one of several veteran republicans who are sceptical of claims that he committed suicide. They maintain that the Armagh man was a victim of a dirty tricks operation carried out by the new breed of Marxist volunteers.

'MacLógáin was a great friend of Pat McCormack from Cushendun in the Glens of Antrim,' says Cahill. 'They had both been in the Irish Republican Brotherhood [the pre-1916 forerunner to the IRA]. It is said that one of the two men proposed Patrick Pearse for membership of the IRB and the other seconded him – that is the sort of influence and background they had. I knew both very well and talked to them often and received a lot of sound advice from them.

'There is controversy as to how Paddy MacLógáin died. He was shot in his own home at Mulhuddart, a few miles from Dublin. It has never been proven, but it has never been denied, that he was shot by those who were destined to become the Official IRA. It is known that he had a disagreement with republicans in the early 'sixties, when he said he deplored the running down of the IRA and the advancement of the political wing to the detriment of the military wing. He also accused the movement of selling off their weapons and he became a target.

'He had tremendous influence with the Irish-Americans – it is believed he was so powerful in the United States that he was able to stop supplies to the IRA of the time. It is said that this is one of the reasons he was eliminated. At his inquest, the coroner said he found it hard to understand how a man of MacLógáin's thinking could take his own life, but there was nothing to prove that he didn't. The inquest was inconclusive.

'I believe his death was staged to look as though it was a suicide. One of the arguments against suicide was that his wife, who was an invalid, was ill in hospital. She was due to be discharged and Paddy was in the process of getting the home ready for her arrival. The night before his death, he had some American visitors over. They were from Clan na Gael [a United States Irish republican support group] and he had a discussion with them. They said afterwards that Paddy MacLógáin had been talking about the next ten years of the republican movement – how it would have to be changed and brought back to what it was. That was not the talk of a man about to take his own life.'

His friendship with Goulding notwithstanding, Cahill was stung at the way he and other 'forties men were first sidelined and then completely ignored. His hurt boiled over into anger and frustration and, after twenty-five years of membership, he felt he had no choice but to tender his resignation and leave the IRA.

'I believed that if I resigned from the movement I could draw attention to what was happening. The opposite was the effect and I became completely isolated. It was a mistake on my part to resign. I realise with hindsight that the only way to bring about change was from within the ranks of the movement. There were a number of people who thought as I did but remained within the movement, for instance, Jimmy Steele and Billy McKee.'

However, McKee and Steele and several other 'forties men were regarded by Dublin as being in the same traditional physical force mould as Cahill, and therefore probably unreformable. Many of these people were dismissed from the movement at the earliest opportunity. After making clear his feelings about the new-style leadership, Steele was ejected from the IRA during a ceremony at the reinterment of two republicans who had been executed in England and whose remains had been released by the British government. McKee, says Cahill, was thrown out after he organised a parade in Belfast which displeased GHQ Staff.

'Jimmy Steele was OC Belfast Battalion at the time. He was removed from his position because of an oration he gave at the funeral and reinterment of Peter Barnes and Patrick McCormack at Mullingar, County Westmeath. Steele said he was worried about the whole situation concerning the IRA – it had been politicised and the military wing was being run down. I fully supported him in making the speech, as did a couple of other people who were involved in helping him to draw up the speech.

'GHQ put him down immediately. The person in charge of the dismissal was Séamus Costello, who was later to become leader of the IRSP [Irish Republican Socialist Party]. I distinctly remember that Costello was annoyed that he was the person selected to convey the news to Jimmy Steele. I suppose as a volunteer he did his duty. I presume he was on GHQ staff at the time.'

Séamus Costello, from County Wicklow, saw action in the '56 campaign. He was to take the Goulding line when the republican movement later split into 'Official' and 'Provisional' wings. When the Officials also split, Costello left to set up the IRSP in 1974. The IRSP's military wing, the socialist republican Irish National Liberation Army, was established the following year. Costello was shot dead in Dublin in 1977, reportedly by Officials, who were said to have blamed him for the death of 'the Wee Man', Billy McMillen.

Cahill had been inactive for around two years after his resignation from the IRA when Steele arrived to rouse him from the torpor of civilian life.

'I did very little after resigning until Jimmy Steele, probably around 1964, called to the house and asked me if I was going to sit on my backside for the rest of my life doing nothing. My reply was that I had never refused to do anything, but what could be done at this stage?

'He said there was work to be done in the National Graves Association. [Steele was chairman of the NGA, which organised commemoration marches and functions and tended republican graves.] He said they intended to erect a memorial in Milltown Cemetery [west Belfast], on the site of the grave reserved for Tom

Williams when his body would be released from the grounds of Crumlin Road jail. The old republican plot in Milltown was full at this stage, and this was a sort of preparation for any other volunteers who might die.

'Steele said he thought it was only right and proper that I should be involved in that type of work. That's where most of my efforts were directed after that. That memorial was unveiled in 1966, and I had the honour of performing the unveiling ceremony.

'I remember saying in my speech words to the effect – and this may have been prophetic if you like – that there was space for a number of graves there; one was reserved for Tom, but in our endeavours to free Ireland, the remaining graves in this plot would not be enough to bury those who would be called upon to make the supreme sacrifice. I never thought when I uttered those words that the sacrifice that has been made since would be so enormous. There had been no hint of a campaign at the time, and the civil rights movement was just about getting off the ground.'

Cahill found that his work with the NGA, as the shrewd Jimmy Steele had intended, kept him in touch with developments within the broader republican movement. On one occasion, as he approached Steele's home on NGA business, he passed a lanky, bespectacled youth who was just leaving.

Steele told Cahill as they watched the boy stride away: 'That's a good lad; he has a good head on his shoulders and will make a fine republican. He should be nurtured and cultivated. His name is Gerry Adams.'

Cahill busied himself with the County Antrim memorial project and the campaign for the reinterment of Tom Williams. He also noted with interest the first rumblings of public discontent and the protests which marked the rise of the civil rights movement in the North.

Nationalist grievances were manifold. Unemployment overall in the North was running at almost ten percent, but was much higher

Above: Shortly after the start of the disastrous Falls curfew in July 1970, when thousands of British soldiers were used to cordon off a large area for thirty-six hours while houses were searched. The curfew was later declared to have been illegal. Photograph: Colman Doyle. **Below:** Some of the hundreds of CS gas canisters which were fired during the Falls curfew. Photograph: Colman Doyle.

Above: Damage was caused to scores of homes during the Falls curfew of July 1970, when troops carried out house-searches for weapons. Photograph: Colman Doyle.
Below: Residents who had been confined to their homes since Friday night are seen walking about freely for the first time on Sunday morning. Photograph: Colman Doyle.

Above: Even in extreme circumstances, people show an amazing capacity to adapt. A Derry lady carries on shopping as British troops prepare to enter a riot situation. Photograph: Colman Doyle.

Right: Máire Drumm, then vice-president of Sinn Féin. A British Army observation post was positioned right opposite her front door in Andersonstown. Mrs Drumm was shot dead by loyalists in Belfast's Mater Hospital, where she was recovering from eye surgery. Photograph: Colman Doyle.

Above left: Ruairí Ó Brádaigh, who walked out of the 1986 Sinn Féin *Ard Fheis*
in protest at the dropping of abstentionism regarding Dáil elections.
He went on to found Republican Sinn Féin. Photograph: Colman Doyle.
Above right: Daithí Ó Conaill, a veteran of the 1956 campaign and former member of IRA
GHQ staff, also parted company with Sinn Féin following the 1986 *Ard Fheis*. Photograph: Colman
Doyle. **Below:** IRA volunteers posing with AK47 assault rifles. Hundreds of these weapons
reached Ireland from Libya, despite setbacks to the IRA such as the capture of the *Claudia*.
Photograph: An Phoblacht.

Above: Youthful rioters learned at an early age to hide their faces to avoid prosecution. Photograph: Colman Doyle.
Below: (from left) Seán MacStiofáin, Rita O'Hare and Joe Cahill, at a press conference in Dublin in 1972, called to publicise the escape of seven republican internees from the British prison ship HMS *Maidstone*. The escapers squeezed through a porthole and swam across the freezing cold River Lagan to the other bank, in loyalist east Belfast. They were spirited across the border and appeared shortly afterwards at this press conference.
Photograph: An Phoblacht.

Anti-internment protests in the 1970s were firmly suppressed by the British Army.
Above: A protestor is arrested, New Lodge Road, Belfast. Photograph: Colman Doyle.
Below: Massed loyalists jeer in the background as a nationalist protestor tries to escape capture, New Lodge Road, Belfast. Photograph: Colman Doyle.

Right: Derry children pray at the blood-stained scene where one of the fourteen Bloody Sunday victims died after British paratroops opened fire on an anti-internment rally, Derry, 30 January 1972.
Photograph: Colman Doyle.

Below left: Martin McGuinness, IRA second in command in Derry city during Bloody Sunday, and now Minister for Education in the Northern Ireland Assembly.
Photograph: Colman Doyle.

Below right: Séamus Twomey, who took over as IRA chief of staff after Cahill was arrested on the *Claudia*. Twomey was himself arrested shortly afterwards and took part in the audacious helicopter escape from Dublin's Mountjoy prison.
Photograph: Colman Doyle.

British troops race to take up firing positions during Operation Motorman, Derry city, 1972. Two people were killed during this operation, which was intended to demolish barricades protecting the nationalist 'no-go' areas. Photograph: Colman Doyle.

in the Catholic community. Skilled jobs and trades in the Belfast shipyards and the city's heavy and light engineering industries were traditionally the preserve of Protestants. Some Catholics were employed by these firms, but generally in a labouring or menial capacity, and they were normally the first to be laid off.

The ingenious system of restricted franchise used in local government elections meant that only rate-payers such as householders and business people could vote. Depending on its rateable value, a limited company was entitled to up to six votes, these to be divided between the directors in addition to their personal vote. A business person and spouse, therefore, received several votes, while whole families living in private rented accommodation were disenfranchised.

Unsurprisingly, council elections, which were operated on the 'first- past-the-post' system, generally returned unionist majorities. Since these councils were responsible for the allocation of public housing, it made good electoral sense to give the bulk of houses – and therefore local government votes – to one's own supporters. The councils were also substantial employers and used the allocation of jobs to garner votes.

Council discrimination was often blatant, with little attempt made to hide injustices. In one case, a nineteen-year-old unmarried Protestant woman, who was secretary of the local unionist association, was allocated a council house in Caledon, County Tyrone, ahead of dozens of Catholic families. This provoked protests, with nationalists squatting in new houses in the area. They were evicted by the RUC, and later fined in the courts.

Among those politicised by the Caledon protest were a couple called Gildernew, whose daughter Michelle, more than thirty years later, was elected as Sinn Féin MP for Fermanagh–south Tyrone, the seat won by republican hunger striker Bobby Sands in 1981.

Maintaining permanent unionist rule in towns and cities with natural nationalist majorities, such as Derry, necessitated a system of boundary-drawing which ensured that a sizeable nationalist ward would return one councillor, while a much smaller unionist ward would perhaps elect two or three.

Republican opponents of this state of affairs were kept in line or removed from the scene for lengthy periods by use of the all-embracing Special Powers Act, enforced by the RUC and the B Specials.

It was against this background that frustrated nationalists began to take to the streets to agitate for jobs, equity in housing allocation and reform of the local government electoral system.

Sir Basil Brooke, who had been prime minister of the Stormont government since 1943, retired on health grounds in 1963. An old-style country squire, land owner and avid Orangeman, Brooke was a founder of the B Specials. His enduring legacy, as far as nationalists were concerned, was the speech in which he admitted he 'would not have a Catholic about the place'. Catholic hopes for electoral reform and a fair deal in housing and employment were raised, albeit moderately, when the seventy-five-year-old unionist hardliner was succeeded by a more liberal colleague, former finance minister Captain Terence O'Neill.

The new premier set about tackling the chronic unemployment, using his international contacts to coax foreign companies to the North. In 1965 O'Neill also took the unprecedented step of inviting his Irish government opposite number, taoiseach Seán Lemass, to Stormont for talks on the possibility of intergovernmental cooperation on areas of mutual benefit. Shortly afterwards, O'Neill made another little piece of history when he accepted Lemass's invitation to Dublin. These cross-border visits led to a series of meetings between the various departments of the Dáil and Stormont governments.

If O'Neill's moderate moves won the approval of some nationalists, they were far from popular with hardline unionists, both inside his own party and out. To the Reverend Ian Paisley, a fire-and-brimstone preacher who had set up his own breakaway branch of the Presbyterian Church, O'Neill's actions smacked of treachery. The prime minister was obviously a traitor, who aimed to hand the six counties back to the Republic and condemn the Protestant people of the North to a miserable existence of priest-ridden Vatican rule. It was not long afterwards that Paisleyites were marching to the slogan, 'O'Neill must go.'

The moderator of the Free Presbyterian Church had already established a reputation as a powerful orator who knew how to work the crowd. In the previous year, 1964, Sinn Féin had placed an Irish tricolour in the window of a disused shop which served as their west Belfast election headquarters. Billy McMillen was the Sinn Féin candidate, standing on an abstentionist ticket. The premises in Divis Street were close to the jobbing house where Cahill was born, and were well within the nationalist Falls Road area. Even the RUC, usually quick to pounce on any display of republicanism, ignored this display of the tricolour. Paisley, however, objected to the presence of the flag and, at a rally in the city's Ulster Hall, whipped up the crowd into a state of indignant fury. If the RUC did not remove the offending rag within two days, Paisley said, he would lead his followers into Divis Street and remove it himself.

The RUC duly obliged the following day, breaking into the premises and capturing the tricolour. Nationalists were furious. By now, a crowd had gathered on the Falls Road to defend the flag and repel Paisley, and their perception was that the RUC had bowed to his threats and carried out the task for him. Rioting followed. Sinn Féin replaced the flag a few days later, and again the RUC, this time in considerable strength, broke into the premises to remove it. Vicious hand-to-hand fighting broke out, with nationalists countering RUC baton charges with hurls, the three-foot-long wooden implements used in the ancient Irish sport of hurling.

Armoured cars and water cannon were brought in to support the police. After almost a week of the worst rioting seen in Belfast in many years, the fighting finally died down. Several leading modern-day republican activists admit to being politicised as youths by the flag incident.

Constitutional nationalists, who had boycotted Stormont for years, returned as the official opposition during the O'Neill years, believing that a new era of liberalism and tolerance was about to dawn. But the nationalists, led by Eddie McAteer, brother of former IRA chief of staff and jail-breaker Hugh McAteer, were quickly disillusioned when they failed to win any concession of significance from the unionist government. Unionists appeared to be doing their best to live up to Cahill's perception that reform of Stormont was impossible.

In spring 1966, loyalists – and RUC intelligence-gathering agencies as it later transpired – were worried that the IRA was planning to carry out large-scale attacks to mark the fiftieth anniversary of the 1916 Easter Rising. Although he was no longer in the IRA, Cahill was in contact with some friends who were, and knew enough about the organisation to know that their fears were unfounded.

'Certainly, commemorative marches were intended, but there was nothing out of the ordinary planned as far as I was concerned,' he says. In the event, the parades passed off peacefully and there was no IRA activity.

An embryo protest movement, organised initially by left-wing students from Belfast's Queen's University, set out to highlight the lack of civil rights, while nationalist politicians pressed the British government to launch a programme of reform in the North. Across the political divide, a more sinister scenario was unfolding. Alarmed loyalists resurrected the Ulster Volunteer Force and a series of firebomb attacks on Catholic homes and businesses followed. June 1966 saw three deaths resulting from the UVF's first few operations in Belfast. John Scullion, a west Belfast Catholic, died two weeks after being shot near his home. Eighteen-year-old Peter Ward, also from west Belfast, was one of four young Catholic friends targeted by the UVF. Ward was killed instantly and two others seriously wounded as they left a bar in a Protestant area. The third fatality was an elderly Protestant lady, who died from burns received during a botched UVF attempt to firebomb the Catholic-owned public house adjoining her home. Later that year, three UVF men were found guilty of murdering Peter Ward and were each sentenced to twenty years' imprisonment.

An extremely volatile situation was to develop over the next three years. The student movement, now titled People's Democracy, continued to hold protest marches and demonstrations, as did the new Northern Ireland Civil Rights Association (NICRA). The idea of using marches to highlight injustice was inspired by the black civil rights movement in the southern United States, and there were indeed parallels. Protests were broken up by the RUC – often brutally, as television footage shows. The image transmitted around the world was of peaceful demonstrators, singing the haunting civil rights anthem 'We Shall Overcome', being batoned. Conversely, the RUC was used to clear streets of protestors so that Orangemen could march unhindered through nationalist neighbourhoods.

April 1969 saw the IRA's first action since the end of the 1956–62 campaign. In Derry city, serious rioting had broken out following a punitive RUC raid into the nationalist Bogside area. As riot police occupied the neighbourhood and the residents prepared for battle, calls went out to nationalists in other towns to help take the pressure off the Bogsiders. A series of protests across the North was hurriedly organised by NICRA and People's Democracy. In Belfast, a handful of young IRA volunteers tried to draw the RUC away from Derry by burning several post offices across the city. Panic and confusion was added to the situation by the unclaimed bombing of water-supply pipelines and an electricity substation. Stormont also attempted to ease tensions in Derry, ordering the RUC from the streets of the Bogside, but the ball was now rolling and rioting continued in Belfast and elsewhere.

Terence O'Neill found himself in an impossible position. Pressurised to introduce even modest reforms, he faced the wrath of his own party hardliners, as well as Paisley's supporters and the increasingly active loyalist paramilitaries.

The almost-defunct IRA was blamed for the spate of explosions which wrecked electricity substations and water mains, causing considerable hardship to the general public. It was subsequently discovered that the bombs were the work of UVF members attempting to topple O'Neill by portraying him as being soft on the IRA.

The end for the hapless Captain O'Neill came in April 1969, when he bowed to the inevitable and agreed that the time had come for 'one man, one vote'. Unionism was not ready for a concession of such magnitude. The announcement caused fury in unionist and loyalist circles and was followed immediately by more UVF explosions. It was a step too far for the hardliners and the unionist prime minister was forced to resign. O'Neill was later to write that it was loyalist bombs which 'blew me out of office'.

Cahill had joined the protest movement and attended several civil rights marches and meetings. He believes that O'Neill was more clever and far-sighted than he was given credit for.

'If even limited reforms had been implemented at an early stage, it is very probable that they would have led to a fall-off in support for the civil rights movement, without doing any great damage to the unionist cause.

'The one person who realised that the nationalist people could be won over with a few reforms was Terence O'Neill; he was shrewd enough to realise that nationalists could be won over with very little at that time. I suppose we should be thankful to people like Ian Paisley and the others who did not want to see any reforms implemented. They were responsible for O'Neill being ousted.

'Quite a few of us saw that the civil rights movement would be allowed to go so far and then the boot would be fully put in. Up until then there were baton charges, people badly beaten up and meetings broken up, but we believed that if the movement ever looked like achieving anything, it would be put down ruthlessly. A lot of us – people like Jimmy Steele, Jimmy Drumm, Billy McKee, the older generation of republicans – could foresee pogroms, burnings, lootings, shootings. Whenever any of us had an opportunity to put these thoughts to the leadership of the republican movement we did so, although we also felt it was a wasted effort. They were not making any preparation to defend the nationalists of the North.'

Each time he encountered a member of the republican leadership, Cahill took the opportunity to put forward his concerns. In England for the National Graves Association's centenary commemoration of the Manchester Martyrs – three republicans who were hanged in England in the nineteenth century – he met Tomás MacGiolla, President of Sinn Féin and one of Cathal Goulding's closest advisors. The commemoration ceremony brought together several members of both the traditionalist and radical Marxist elements of the movement.

'MacGiolla said he would like to have a talk with me, and I replied that there were a number of us present who would like to have a talk with him. He asked why I was not active in the republican movement, so I explained my thoughts and where I believed the movement was going wrong. We also talked about the civil rights campaign in the North and I gave him my theory that you cannot have civil rights without national rights. He replied that the aims of the leadership were the same as mine. He said they would use civil rights to obtain national rights.

'I told him that the leadership had gone completely astray. They had given up the military struggle and were concentrating purely on political issues. I also said that under the system that existed in the North of Ireland – also in the South but particularly in the North – it was impossible then to work politically to achieve the freedom of the country, and that the option of military struggle must remain open to us.'

MacGiolla, Cahill says, reiterated that there was no difference in the thinking of the republican movement and his own.

'I still was not convinced. I remember asking him if he realised what the situation in the North was leading to. I told him that unless defence efforts were put in, the people were going to be slaughtered. I told him it was not possible to obtain civil rights in the North of Ireland because Orangeism would not allow it. He said the leadership realised that and was preparing for it.'

'At the back of my mind, I did not really want to think that the IRA would allow this to happen. I suppose I wanted to believe they were being shrewd in not letting people know what their military plans were. But when we saw people who would have been close to us in their thinking being dismissed or forced to resign, I was asking myself what lay behind it all. Despite all their assurances, all they had said, they really had no plan of defence for the people whatsoever, and no weapons at all.'

On another occasion, Cahill was invited to attend a meeting in the conference rooms above the Continental Café in Castle Street, at the bottom of the Falls Road. Tomás MacGiolla chaired the meeting and was supported by colleague Séamus Costello.

'Why I was invited to the meeting, I don't know, because I was not in the IRA or in Sinn Féin; I was in the National Graves Association. The purpose of the meeting was to sound out people on the ending of the abstentionist policy and there was discussion on republicans taking seats in Leinster House [the Irish parliament]. MacGiolla said it was not a meeting at which decisions could be taken, but he wondered, just out of curiosity, what the vote would be if he asked people their opinion about taking seats in Leinster House. He said, "I am going to ask you to vote, just to see."

'There were around 100 republicans at the meeting, but there were only two people who voted in favour of entering Leinster House and who agreed that it would be a good and acceptable tactic. The two were Frank McGlade and myself. My reason for voting to take seats in Leinster House was because it was the only way of winning the support of people in the South. People who did not support the armed struggle could vote for Sinn Féin, who would be seen to be doing something for the people. I had not fully made up my mind about it, but Frank was fully in favour. The others at the meeting said they would not recognise a partitionist assembly. In another straw poll on entering Westminster, there was 100 percent against. I heard later, and I could scarcely believe it, that when MacGiolla was reporting back to Dublin he claimed that he took a test vote on entering Leinster House and the result was more or less fifty–fifty.'

In the mid- and late 1960s, the republican leadership's apparently naïve attitude towards the deteriorating situation in the North singularly failed to inspire confidence not only in the veterans of past campaigns, but also in the young people who had been politicised by recent events.

Even before O'Neill was forced from office, Cahill says, worried conversations were taking place in nationalist areas all over Belfast. Eventually a group, composed mainly of 'forties men, decided that if the IRA would not or could not defend nationalists from attacks by the forces of unionism, then they would form and train an alternative organisation known as 'auxiliaries' to do the job.

In previous years, IRA auxiliaries were part-time volunteers who, for various reasons – pressure of work, advancing age, infirmity or family circumstances – were unable to devote all their time to the republican movement. Auxiliaries, however, played a valued and essential role, often acting as weapons and explosives instructors, intelligence gatherers, drivers, reconnaissance scouts and even, in well-organised company areas, active service units. The idea of forming an independent auxiliary group in the North was a dangerous one which could have led to severe punishment by GHQ staff, who might well have seen it as a direct challenge to their authority.

'Our only intention was to organise defence groups in the North, so that nationalist people would not be left undefended. This was done completely on our own initiative and without the knowledge of the GHQ of the IRA, because we had no faith in GHQ. Certainly, it could have been dangerous but our only concern was to organise the people for their own defence.'

It was, says Cahill, a mammoth task. Many people placed their trust in the civil rights movement, and refused to believe that a doomsday situation was close at hand which could not be averted by holding protest demonstrations. Across the North, republicans just could not accept that the Dublin leadership was oblivious to the escalating sectarian violence.

'It was difficult for us to convince them of the truth. I do believe that in many cases, company OCs were certain that the IRA in Dublin was making preparations for the defence of nationalist areas. Progress, therefore, was very slow. It was extremely difficult to get the organisation off the ground.'

While the plan to raise a defence auxiliary across the North ran into trouble, and was subsequently overtaken by events, a nucleus in Belfast continued to meet and monitor the deteriorating situation.

✠ ✠ ✠

If Cahill and the other 'forties men had trouble raising a defence group, there was no such problem across the sectarian divide. Loyalists, feeling threatened by the increasingly confident attitude of nationalists, formed the perception that anything gained by Catholics must be at the expense of Protestants. All the agitation and demands for equality, they reasoned, could have only one result if not checked – a united Ireland.

The fiercely loyalist Shankill Road, the heart of the British Empire as residents often claimed, was the first area to organise. The road was connected to the Falls Road by a series of streets of small terraced houses. The Shankill Defence Association was formed around mid-1969, and the idea spread rapidly to other loyalist areas. These groups later banded together under one command to form the Ulster Defence Association (UDA), eventually becoming the largest of the North's loyalist paramilitary groups. The UDA later established a smaller group, the Ulster Freedom Fighters, to carry out assassinations and sectarian attacks.

O'Neill had by now been replaced as prime minister by his cousin, James Chichester-Clark, who appeared unable to bring fresh thinking to the powder-keg situation. Derry civil rights activists asked Chichester-Clark to ban the Apprentice Boys – another loyalist marching institution – from processing along their city's old walled defences, which overlook the Catholic Bogside area. No one in Derry city was in any doubt about the consequences if the Apprentice Boys' march was forced through by the RUC.

The Apprentice Boys are neither apprentices nor boys. The institution, one of a number of exclusively Protestant secret societies whose members may avail of cross-membership, is composed of 'clubs', generally named after a loyal hero of old. Every August, these clubs travel from across the North to converge on Derry, where they hold a march to celebrate the city's deliverance from the army of the Catholic King James II in 1688. The institution derives its name from the young trade and craft apprentices who rushed to close the city's gates in the face of James's advancing forces, thus initiating the Siege of Derry. Many of the city's

Catholics view the march as triumphalist and sectarian. It has frequently led to serious rioting, though in recent times dialogue between marchers and residents has resulted in compromise.

Banning the march would have been tantamount to political suicide for Chichester-Clark, and he allowed it to go ahead. Across the North, people watched in apprehension as the events of 12 August 1969 unfolded with an awful predictability: The march went ahead, protected by the RUC. Stones were thrown by young Bogsiders. The RUC baton-charged, residents defended themselves and, in scenes reminiscent of the French Revolution, threw up barricades. When police attempted to storm the barricades they were repelled with rocks and petrol bombs. Chichester-Clark called up the B Specials to reinforce the exhausted regulars. There was no way the residents were going to allow B men onto their streets, and the fighting intensified. The second siege of Derry was on.

The doomsday scenario painted by Cahill, Steele, McKee and others had arrived. Prolonged rioting was taking place in the nationalist areas of Belfast, Dungannon and several other towns. Incensed Irish government ministers demanded that their taoiseach send troops into the North. (The Irish Army did move close to the border, setting up mobile hospitals for injured northerners and the stream of refugees who fled south.) Ironically, it was the arrival of British troops in Derry which ended the Battle of the Bogside. The RUC and B Specials were withdrawn from around the area and soldiers took over. The Bogsiders breathed a little easier, but in Belfast the worst was still to come.

Shankill Road loyalists had had enough and, on the night of 14–15 August, hundreds of people gathered in the area. Residents later told of seeing neighbours openly wearing gun-belts and pistols, while mingling freely with RUC officers and B Specials. The mood was ugly and rumour was rife, each story more outrageous than the last: the Irish Army was on its way over the border;

Catholics were about to stage an uprising; the Protestant people were going to be wiped out. Adherents of another school of thought reasoned that the Fenians simply needed to be taught a lesson. It was time for action.

The seething mob, with B men armed with Sterling sub-machine guns and Webley revolvers in their midst, streamed down the side streets towards the Falls Road, firing through windows and putting homes to the torch. Terrified Catholics left their belongings, grabbed up screaming children and ran for safety ahead of the crowd.

Cahill was not far from his home in Divis Street when he met an old colleague who was still in the IRA. Surely he could make sense of all this, Cahill thought, but what he heard dismayed and angered him.

'Liam McParland had been appointed by the IRA to look after the area that night. I met him in Divis Street. He had been interned with me in the 1950s. I asked him what was happening and he said, "I don't know, but this is what I have been given," and showed me an anti-personnel grenade. He said that shortly after it was given to him, he discovered it was unarmed and contained no explosive, no fuse, nothing. I can remember the anger in that man's eyes and in his voice. He had been searching for a member of Belfast Battalion staff – any member. He said, "I can't find these people, I don't know where they have gone." This was a member of the IRA talking about his leadership! I am convinced to this day that there was a master plan to run down the IRA and go purely political. The leadership had been warned about the consequences, they were well enough warned.'

As the mob neared the area of the lower Falls Road, it looked as though the whole of nationalist west Belfast was about be razed to the ground. The loyalists reached Divis Street and began burning buildings there. They had actually set up a Union flag near Cahill's home before the first serious efforts were made to repel them.

From the grounds of St Comgall's primary school came the distinctive boom of a .303 rifle, interspersed with staccato bursts of sub-machine gun fire and the crack of pistol shots. Cahill says a little group of 'forties men – those involved in forming the defence auxiliary – had occupied the school with whatever weapons they had managed to scrounge. They found they had six weapons between seven men – the old Lee Enfield .303, four handguns and an elderly Thompson sub-machine gun. The experience of the republican veterans told as they held their ground and began to return fire.

'The school was chosen because it gave a good view of the crowds coming from the Shankill area. It was the auxiliaries who defended Divis Street and actually saved the situation that night,' Cahill says.

The gunfire from the school did indeed turn the crowds and they headed back to the Shankill, leaving a trail of devastation behind. A Protestant man was killed and several others were injured during the encounter. There was, however, little the auxiliaries could do against the RUC Shorland armoured cars which had been brought onto the scene. The Shorlands were each armed with a Browning machine gun – a heavy-calibre, fully automatic weapon which could only be fired in bursts. A nine-year-old boy was killed in his father's bedroom in the high-rise Divis Flats when rounds from a Browning sliced through the walls. A British soldier, a trooper of the Queen's Royal Irish Hussars who was home in Belfast on leave, was also shot dead in the flats by an RUC marksman firing from the nearby police barracks. Further up the Falls Road, the residents' spirited defence of their beloved Clonard Monastery was not enough to prevent the whole of the adjoining Bombay Street from being burned to the ground. A fifteen-year-old Fianna youth, Gerald McAuley, who had been helping to defend the area, was shot dead and became the first republican to be killed in the conflict.

An inquiry headed by British judge Lord Scarman later reported: 'The Catholics fired into the mouth of Dover Street because they saw Protestants and uniformed men erupting into their heartland, Divis Street. They believed that Protestants and police were cooperating to attack them. The tribunal has no doubt that the Protestants in Dover Street saw themselves as helping the police to quell a Catholic insurrection.'

Across the city in Ardoyne, nationalists were forced to gradually withdraw into the heart of the area, as streets on the periphery were burned and B men, RUC officers and loyalists came ever closer. The arms situation in Ardoyne was even worse than that on the Falls. An IRA man who had been shot and wounded in a riot a few days previously commandeered the only available weapon – a malfunctioning shotgun – and hobbled from street corner to street corner, firing a shot each time in the hope of fooling the attackers into thinking there were several defenders. A young Ardoyne woman, to the background of gunfire, breaking glass and screams of sectarian hatred, chose that time to give birth to a healthy baby girl.

Many homes were still burning as dawn broke. Six Catholics and two Protestants were killed or died from their wounds within those horrific forty-eight hours. Hundreds more had been wounded. The British government's Scarman Report into events of July and August revealed that 179 homes and others buildings had been completely destroyed, with another 400 damaged. In Belfast, Scarman found that 1,800 families – 1,500 Catholic and 300 Protestant – had been 'permanently displaced' from their homes. Hundreds of others, mainly women and children, sought succour in the South, in a refugee camp set up by the Irish Army at Gormanstown, County Meath. Newspapers reports told of 'the biggest forced population shift since World War II'.

The IRA in Belfast had been humiliated. Despite many instances of individual bravery, it was clear that the republican movement had been unable to protect the people, or, as Cahill and others insisted, had been *prevented* from protecting the people. The slogan that went up on walls all over the city has now become something of a cliché, but it still brings back bitter memories to Cahill when he speaks of seeing it for the first time: 'IRA = I Ran Away'. The defence of west Belfast, the cradle of northern republicanism, had been left, in the main, to its residents, a schoolboy who gave his life defending his neighbours, a handful of young IRA volunteers and supporters, and a little group of middle-aged or elderly auxiliaries.

Joe Cahill and Jimmy Steele, men who had considered themselves honoured, proud and privileged to be volunteers in the Irish Republican Army, were disappointed but not greatly surprised by the reaction of the nationalist community.

'The name of the IRA was mud. Walking down the Falls Road next day, Steele and I were called deserters and traitors and people spat at us,' Cahill says. 'It hurt, it hurt like hell.'

Barricades were hastily thrown up in most working-class nationalist areas of Belfast that day, 16 August, in an attempt to prevent further incursions. By late afternoon, the British Army was on the Falls Road.

'The Brits were in and people were so relieved that they welcomed them with cups of tea. But they were not there to protect us – they were sent in to protect unionist and British interests, not nationalists. They stood and watched as more nationalist homes were burned and families evicted.

'Immediately after events of 15 August, everybody who had been in the IRA and had been dismissed or resigned or whatever, reported back to the Belfast staff. It was a doomsday situation and we needed to organise defence groups. I remember going to a house in Andersonstown, on 16 August, to report back to the IRA. Even though I had no faith in the organisation, I still believed we could redeem the name of the IRA.

'It was now a matter of survival and first of all we needed weapons. A couple of days after 15 August, three teams of people left Belfast to scour the South for any weapons they could get their hands on. Myself, Jimmy Drumm and Leo Martin were the leaders of the three teams. Whatever contacts we had in the South, whatever people we knew who were in the IRA and had access to arms, we were to contact them and try to get whatever arms we could.'

The teams all headed south initially, but then separated to cover as much of the country as possible in the time available. They were to rendezvous one day later, just south of the border in Dundalk, County Louth, where a van or truck would be waiting to take the fruits of their search to Belfast and elsewhere in the North. Cahill says that transporting the weapons over the border was not expected to be a problem because the roads were clear.

'The British Army was at that time confined to a few nationalist areas, and the RUC were too busy to mount roadblocks.'

'My driver was Danny Burke. We had been travelling for something like twenty-four hours and we had gathered as many weapons as we were likely to get, so we headed for the rendezvous point. We had somewhere in the region of seventy to 100 weapons – a real mixture of shotguns, sporting rifles, .22s and a few .303s. I remember there was one Thompson gun. Just outside Carrickmacross the car ran into a ditch. Danny had fallen asleep. There was no great damage done. I wakened Danny and he said, "Joe, I can go no further." He was totally exhausted.

'I told Danny to try to get an hour's sleep and we would head off again. We got the car out of the ditch and parked a little way up a side road. We had about an hour's sleep. When we woke, Danny still did not feel confident about driving. He asked me if I would have a go. I had not driven for years but I said that if he wanted to put his life in my hands, I would give it a try. So I started to drive and a few hundred yards down the road he said, "Right, drive on, I'm going to have a sleep."'

The vehicle had travelled a short distance when the engine died. Cahill immediately thought the stoppage was due to his rustiness as a driver and that he had made some basic error.

'A minute later, we realised it was not my driving but that the car was out of petrol. It was early morning so we waited until a petrol station opened and filled up, and then headed on towards Dundalk. I had the Thompson in the front with me. I spotted this guy coming towards us. I recognised him as a Garda Special Branch man.

'I told Danny and he said, "Well, they are not getting any of this stuff." I held the Thompson with the butt resting on the floor between my feet. The Branch man came up to the car and I lowered the window. I said, "Obviously you recognise me. We have quite a few weapons in this car and if you dare to put a hand on them – I raised the Thompson – I will blow the head off your shoulders."'

The Garda's reaction amazed Cahill and Burke. According to Cahill, the man produced a parcel which he reached through the car window.

'He said, "I have come over here to give you something," and handed me a Colt .45 and fifty rounds of ammunition. It certainly was an emotive action, and it gives an idea of the feelings stirred up throughout the country by the situation in the North.'

The northerners' anger with GHQ and those on Belfast Battalion who followed the Goulding line of politics only had to be put on the back burner for a few days. There were more pressing issues: temporary barricades needed strengthening; more arms had to be acquired if nationalists were to prevent wholesale loss of life and the destruction of their neighbourhoods; a plan of defence was needed for each area; defenders had to be trained to use small arms and make petrol bombs.

Day-to-day life behind the barricades was a bizarre and surreal existence which, human nature being what it is, quickly became the norm. Male residents were expected to take their turn on the twenty-four-hour sentry rota at the barricades; car-owners left their vehicles unlocked at night to provide shelter for the look-outs; few people had telephones and so another rota was compiled to ensure day-and-night monitoring of RUC and British Army radio transmissions, which gave an indication of events in other areas. Squads were sent out with trucks and lorries to evacuate Catholics living in dangerous areas. Soon a steady stream of refugees was flowing into the relative safety of the streets behind the barricades. They were a pathetic sight. Often a family's whole life was reduced to what could be hurriedly stacked onto the back of a commandeered coal lorry or Transit van. Everyone else, it seemed, spent their time making tea and sandwiches and providing cigarettes for the defenders. Through it all, there were those who literally risked their lives to get to work – it was not unusual to see someone clambering over the barricade at the break of dawn, hoping against hope he would not run into loyalists.

Meanwhile, Cahill and other 'forties men went around the company areas, offering to help set up defence committees and draw up contingency plans – basically to reorganise the local IRA units. They were not always well received.

'I remember on three occasions being sent into different areas to try to organise. We went to Turf Lodge and told the people we were attempting to reorganise the IRA. We were chased; they told us to get out in no uncertain terms. That was how badly people felt about the republican movement. They were completely disillusioned with the IRA after the events of August 1969. The same thing happened in Ardoyne. We went into a house on the Crumlin Road facing the chapel. There were quite a few people there. We were told we were not wanted. And over in the Short Strand in Ballymacarrett, where St Matthew's Parochial Hall had been turned into a defence centre, I asked to speak to the local OC. He knew me but I was not too sure who he was. He asked if we had brought any guns – it was a small and vulnerable area – and I said we had not, we were not there to bring guns. His answer was brief. He said, "Well, fuck off then."

'Gradually, the reorganisation of Belfast got underway and a defence system was got off the ground. There was, of course, a lot happening. The barricades were still in place and there was constant patrolling of the areas. Volunteers were on duty all night long to protect the areas and raise warnings. There were warning systems put in place to alert those who were off duty. It was a very tense time indeed.'

The relationship between the leadership in Dublin and the traditionalists in the North had not improved, and in September the 'forties men decided it was time to act. Representatives of the Belfast IRA units were invited to a meeting in Steele's old stomping ground in north Belfast's North Queen Street area. The gathering agreed that a delegation should be sent to confront Belfast Battalion OC Billy McMillen and his staff, who were believed to be meeting at that moment in a room above a bar in Cyprus Street in west Belfast.

'It was decided then to challenge the existing Battalion staff of the Belfast IRA as to where their loyalties lay, whether to the people or to Dublin. A number of us went over to Cyprus Street, where we had been told a staff meeting was in progress. Billy McKee was the spokesman for our group. Most of their staff were there, but McMillen came in later. There were around eight of us and at least two were armed. There was no running in and producing arms, although Jimmy Sullivan [a Battalion staff officer] claimed afterwards that a gun had been put to his head. It was just not true – not that I remember anyway.

'It started off as a shouting match – Jimmy Sullivan couldn't do anything without shouting. McMillen arrived and it developed into a proper discussion. We told them about the meeting we had just held and that it had been the unanimous decision of the people present that there needed to be changes. We told them we were prepared to split and that all but one of the Belfast units wanted to break from GHQ because we no longer had any faith in them.

'Two main proposals were put to them. We said we wanted the Belfast staff to be enlarged by the co-opting of people of our time. This extended Battalion staff would then give its allegiance to GHQ on condition that they would reorganise and that four named people, including Cathal Goulding, be removed and replaced.

'McMillen and his people said they would put this to Dublin and stress our dissatisfaction, and their dissatisfaction too, because they also were completely annoyed.'

Cahill says there was 'a lot of coming and going between McMillen and GHQ staff', until it was agreed to implement one of the proposals – to co-opt some traditionalists onto Belfast Battalion staff. Cahill was asked to join the staff, but refused.

However, any little trust or good faith that may have been built up was shattered when the 'dissidents', as they were referred to by Dublin, discovered that they were merely being humoured and strung along by GHQ staff. The revelation came when Cahill's group intercepted a communication from GHQ to the Belfast Battalion OC.

'We found out that Billy McMillen had been instructed by Goulding and company to play along with the dissidents and keep General Headquarters staff of the IRA informed of what was happening. In particular, they wanted Billy to find out if we had made any contacts for arms supplies,' says Cahill.

It was the final straw. This example of what was seen as the leadership's duplicity, coming hard on top of the perceived betrayal of the people on 15 August, was too much for the veterans. Since they felt they could not look to Dublin for protection in the event of further attacks, the North would have to go it alone.

'From then on we decided to set up a separate independent Northern Command of the IRA. Between September and December a lot of travelling to different units went on. I went to some of these units myself and talked to them about the idea of a Northern Command and attempted to get their support for it. All this travelling, talking to people and reporting back took quite a bit of time. It was understandable that there was opposition outside Belfast, because we did not have any arms to give them. The country units were still hopeful that GHQ would supply them with weapons. It was a matter of whoever could supply the guns would get the support.

'The final outcome was a decision that, with whatever help we could get from areas outside Belfast, we would go ahead and set up a northern structure of the IRA.'

To this end, a meeting of interested parties was set up and a conference room booked in the International Hotel, a few yards from the rear entrance to Belfast City Hall.

Down south, the politicos and Marxists on GHQ staff were not having it entirely their own way. One or two traditionalists – such as Seán MacStiofáin, who had risen to become IRA director of intelligence and who had great respect for the Belfast republicans – had been making nuisances of themselves at staff and Army Council meetings for some time, demanding that support, and in particular weapons, be supplied to the beleaguered northerners.

The influence of these agitators was reduced significantly when the Army Council, pegged by the IRA Constitution at seven members, was packed with an extra thirteen Goulding supporters. The situation in Dublin came to a head at an Extraordinary Convention of the IRA, where the leadership intended that two controversial resolutions would be forced through. The first motion called on the IRA to enter a coalition of the left, to be called the National Liberation Front. The second, crucially for the traditionalists, proposed the dropping of the policy of parliamentary abstention, which, if also adopted by Sinn Féin, would see republicans standing in elections for the Dáil, Stormont and Westminster.

Cahill maintains that the IRA Convention, held late at night and into the early morning in a little village well out in the countryside, had been packed with Goulding supporters to ensure the desired results.

'Delegates who would have been opposed to the motions were left stranded when their arranged lifts did not materialise. Others were refused admittance at the door, and still others were not informed of the date or venue.'

Despite the opposition of the physical force people, the two motions were passed and the stage was set for the inevitable split. Anticipating the result, the traditionalists had arranged their own meeting, held at a separate, secret location and timed to take place after the close of the Convention. As the mid-December dawn broke, MacStiofáin left the second meeting to be driven to yet another gathering in Belfast.

Cahill's old friend Jack McCabe was among the twenty or so people who attended the meeting in the International Hotel in Belfast to lend support to the new Northern Command, as was the legendary Harry White, known as 'the last volunteer' for his exploits in the 1940s.

Born in Belfast in 1916, Harry White had led a charmed life, having shot his way out of several tight spots and ambushes. On one occasion he managed to escape capture despite being shot twice. He had seen active service in the North, in the Republic and in England and rose to become IRA chief of staff. At one stage in the mid-1940s, while on the run and living under an assumed identity in west Derry, he was the sole representative of GHQ staff outside jail, earning himself the title 'the last volunteer'. White was based in Altaghoney, near the Derry–Tyrone county border, for almost two years, often travelling to Belfast on IRA business and then returning to rural obscurity. He operated a very successful line of communication in and out of Crumlin Road jail. He was eventually captured by the RUC and, quite illegally, handed over to the Free State authorities, where a military court sentenced him to death for the killing of a Garda Special Branch detective during a shoot-out four years earlier. White appealed, and the sentence was commuted to twelve years imprisonment. With the IRA campaign effectively over, the southern government began releasing republican prisoners. In March 1948, after serving eleven months on blanket protest, Harry White was freed from Portlaoise prison.

'Our meeting to organise an independent Northern Command,' Cahill says, 'had been going for around ten or fifteen minutes when Seán MacStiofáin walked in. We knew he had been sympathetic to what we were doing. The more he had to do with Goulding, the more he realised we were right.

'MacStiofáin said it was no longer necessary to set up a Northern Command. There had been a convention during the night, he said, and he had come straight from it. He said there had been a split within the IRA and there was a strong possibility of another convention being held soon by those people who opposed Goulding, the people who had broken away at the overnight convention.'

At the International Hotel meeting it was decided to continue to canvass support from those IRA units who had remained undecided and then organise an Army convention for January. This was described as the reconvening of the pro-Goulding Extraordinary Convention – which was deemed to have been improperly convened – and would be attended by the people who had been excluded from that gathering in December. Cahill said Belfast Battalion staff officers were not invited because they supported the GHQ line. However, it was agreed that four people from Belfast would be invited along as visitors.

'Four were selected, and I was one of that group. This was to be the initial meeting of the setting up of the Provisionals. The meeting was held in January in the midlands and there were, I think, twenty-four people present. The first item on the agenda concerned the Belfast people present: would they be treated as visitors or delegates? After some discussion, it was agreed unanimously that they would be accorded delegate status.

'The Convention lasted for several hours, during which time the two motions carried in December were overturned. In the end it was decided to set up a full Provisional Army Council, to which I was elected. The term "provisional" was used because we intended to reconvene this Convention in six months time and, in the meantime, contact all units of the IRA to find out where their allegiance lay. Those who were sympathetic would be invited along to the reconvened Convention in order to regularise the IRA, and the term "provisional" would be abandoned.'

Another motion was put by Cahill to the convention which, if it had been carried, would have changed the history of the republican movement and put an end to the Irish Republican Army.

Cahill recalls with some amusement that he was among several 'forties men at the January Army Convention who felt that the reorganised movement should take on a new title and drop the name IRA, which they considered to be now associated with ineptitude and criminal neglect of duty.

'One of my big interests at the January Convention was to achieve the dropping of the title and so I proposed a change of name. Many of the delegates agreed with me and felt that the name of the IRA had been sullied. I said, "Look at history – you had the United Irishmen, the Young Irelanders, the Fenians, the IRB, the Irish Citizen Army. When all of these had served their periods of time, no one had any problem changing the name." While I thought the IRA had done a good job up until the 'sixties, it should be laid to rest at that. I was asked if I had a name in mind and I said I had; I would call it the Irish Liberation Movement.

'I was in a minority of one. The general inclination was to retain the name IRA – the title of the Irish Republican Army should be redeemed, cleaned up and brought back. I fully understood that reasoning.'

Before the end of the Convention, a twelve-person Executive was elected. The Executive members then left the room to secretly elect seven volunteers, including Joe Cahill, to the Provisional Army Council. The new chief of staff of the Provisional IRA was Seán MacStiofáin. Billy McKee, by this time, had been appointed OC Belfast Battalion, with Cahill as his second-in-command.

'It was early 1970 and the republican movement was on the road to recovery,' says Cahill. 'It was no surprise when republicans went on to adopt the phoenix as a symbol, because I believe that the Provisional IRA too arose from the ashes – the ashes of Bombay Street and the many other burned-out streets of August 'sixty-nine.'

CHAPTER EIGHT

Father Brown's Mission

The split in the republican movement was completed on Sunday, 11 January 1970, when the proposals to drop the abstentionist policy were put before the Sinn Féin *Ard Fheis* in the Intercontinental Hotel in Dublin.

The previous day, delegates to the two-day annual conference had voted in favour of forming a National Liberation Front. Again there were allegations of malpractice, with supporters of the new Provisional Army Council claiming that the conference hall had been packed with pro-Goulding people who cast votes even though they were not entitled to.

The resolution to take seats in the Dáil, Stormont and Westminster received a simple majority on the Sunday, but not the two-thirds vote necessary for change. Provisional supporters then walked out, refusing to take part in a vote of allegiance to what became known as the Official Army Council. The breakaway group marched to the Kevin Barry Hall in Parnell Square, where a caretaker Sinn Féin Executive was formed, with Ruairí Ó Brádaigh as president.

'The Kevin Barry Hall,' says Cahill, 'had been bought by H Company of the South Dublin Brigade of the IRA and had been used by the republican movement for generations, so it was a natural venue for those who walked out of the *Ard Fheis*.'

Those who remained at the Intercontinental Hotel were initially termed 'Official' republicans, while Cahill's group was known as the 'Provisionals'. At Easter 1970, the Officials earned the new and enduring title of 'Stickies'. Thousands of paper lapel badges depicting the Easter lily, the emblem commemorating republican dead, are sold each year outside churches, door-to-door on housing estates and in bars and clubs frequented by the faithful. Neither organisation wanted their supporters to buy the opposition's version of the emblem. To differentiate, the Provisionals provided a pin with each lily while the Officials used badges with an adhesive back. In Belfast, the Officials quickly became known as the Sticky-backs, while the Provisionals were labelled Pin-heads. The Officials' title was abbreviated to Stickies or Sticks, while the term Pin-head failed to catch on and fell into disuse. However, despite the dropping of the word 'Provisional' at an Army convention in September that year, the breakaways, soon to become the dominant group, are still known – to the mild irritation of senior members – as Provisionals, Provos or Provies.

A new command structure was created in Belfast, with the city now being promoted from battalion to brigade status. Belfast Brigade was composed of three battalion areas, two in west Belfast and the third taking in Ardoyne and New Lodge in the north of the city, Short Strand in the east and the Market–Ormeau Road in the south. Each battalion was subdivided into companies which, depending on strength, were further split into sections. The brigade–battalion–company structure has remained in place ever since.

When Long Kesh prison, near Lisburn, was opened in the early 1970s, initially to house internees and later sentenced prisoners, its hundreds of republican inmates made up the Fourth Battalion. During previous IRA campaigns those arrested and imprisoned automatically forfeited all rank, becoming, in the words of one veteran republican, 'casualties of war'. After 1970, however, jailed republicans remained within the command structure. The Fourth Battalion Camp leadership, therefore, reported to Belfast Brigade, which coordinated matters of discipline, protests, escape attempts and so on, through a clearly-defined line of communication. However, the Belfast leadership soon found the system an administrative nightmare, as they attempted to deal with matters affecting prisoners not just from Belfast, but from almost all thirty-two counties. Shortly afterwards it was deemed more practical for Long Kesh to come under direct control of GHQ.

From January 1970 on, Cahill says, the Provisionals worked ceaselessly to win the backing of the rest of the republican movement.

'Eventually,' says Cahill, 'we had the support of the majority of units across the country. Of course there were areas where there were split decisions – areas like Dublin, Belfast, Cork. Some gave their allegiance to the Officials, some to the Provisional IRA. It was a sad period, but at the same time I felt good about the split. I felt this was the break that was necessary if the Dublin leadership were not prepared to redeem themselves. From then on it was a matter of building, building, building. We acquired a lot more confidence once we had an all-Ireland body. The split was unfortunate but unavoidable.

'We had planned to hold an Army convention in June but, as I recollect, it took a bit longer than that. We wanted to completely rebuild the IRA, and the result was that the convention was not held until September. As with attempts to establish the Auxiliaries, when we went into an area to talk to an existing pre-split IRA unit, their staff questioned us very carefully about our motives. Invariably, they wanted to know if we had arms for them. That was their main concern, that was the bargaining piece. If we could supply arms in the North, they said, we would get their support.

'This was the big problem with the country units – they would not give up their allegiance to the Official IRA until they were certain they would get weapons, until they knew which side their bread was buttered on. It was understandable. Our aim was to find out where they stood. If they supported the Provisional IRA, they were accepted as a unit. If they supported the Official IRA, then we just forgot about them. It was a difficult task; often we would get a half-promise and have to go back. They were very reluctant to change horses in midstream, and would say, "When you can supply arms, get back to us." Despite everything, they were still hopeful that the Official IRA would supply arms.'

✠ ✠ ✠

Cahill recalls that people who had initially welcomed the British Army as saviours in August 1969 were disillusioned when the presence of soldiers failed to stop the nightly attacks on nationalists. Rioting, he says, had become a daily occurrence. Catholics were still being burned out of their homes. Orange marches were still being forced through nationalist neighbourhoods, and the defence of vulnerable areas was left to the IRA and a handful of defence committees. The image of the British Army was not helped by televised pictures of soldiers – albeit unprepared and untrained for a policing role – standing by as nationalists were driven from their homes by loyalists.

A package of reforms introduced by Harold Wilson's British government – including the disbandment of the B Specials, disarming of the RUC and the reform of local government electoral practices – failed to defuse the situation.

'The Specials were replaced by the Ulster Defence Regiment, which was equally unacceptable to republicans and nationalists because it was largely made up of former B Specials. The UDR was regarded as being just as sectarian as their forerunners,' Cahill says.

While nationalists scorned the reforms as 'too little, too late', unionists were furious at what they perceived as a sell-out. The fears and uncertainties of unionists and the complexities of the situation are perhaps illustrated by the death of Constable Victor Arbuckle, the first policeman to be killed since the end of the IRA's '56 campaign. The twenty-nine-year-old father of one was shot dead by the UVF during severe rioting in loyalist west Belfast.

The rioters were protesting against the disarming of the RUC and the disbanding of the B Specials.

✠ ✠ ✠

Thousands of young people were now attempting to join the Provisional IRA. Some were from old established republican families, while others admitted to being '1969 republicans' – young men and women radicalised by the experiences of the civil rights movement and the expulsion of nationalists from their homes. Veterans, however, like Cahill, Steele, McKee and Proinsias MacAirt, while recognising the crucial nature of the IRA's defence role, never lost sight of the movement's primary objective – the establishment of a thirty-two-county Irish republic. Early in 1970, the Provisional Army Council decided to adopt a rolling three-pronged strategy: the IRA would continue in a defence role; harassment and intimidation by security forces would be met with retaliatory attacks; an offensive campaign would be embarked upon once the IRA was in a state of preparedness.

'Defence was the main reason for the Army's existence at the time and there was little obvious evidence of an offensive against the British. Soon, however, some provocative operations were carried out by the IRA, although it was not generally known that they were carried out by republicans.

'A small unit had been selected in early 1970 to take part in sanctioned operations against commercial targets, but the main body of volunteers would not have known about this. The existence of the unit only came to light after one of its members was killed when a bomb went off prematurely at a small electricity transformer in south Belfast,' Cahill says.

Michael Kane, from the New Lodge area of north Belfast, was a member of a three-man IRA bombing team which attempted to blow up the transformer at New Forge Lane in the affluent

Malone area. The thirty-five-year-old died instantly and another man was critically injured when the bomb exploded prematurely. The third man escaped, although he too had been badly wounded in the explosion.

'I was in Prionsias MacAirt's house in Kane Street, west Belfast, when this figure, bedraggled and blood-stained, staggered in. He had made his way on foot across Belfast, from the south side of the city to the west. It was a miracle that he ever made it without collapsing or being arrested. MacAirt took care of him and arranged for transport and medical treatment,' Cahill says.

The badly injured man who was arrested at the scene of the explosion claimed later that he was kicked and beaten by security forces as he lay on the ground bleeding. He recovered from his wounds and was later sentenced to a hefty term in jail. Michael Kane was claimed by the Provisional IRA as a member, and the chief of staff, Seán MacStiofáin, gave the oration at his funeral. While Fianna youth Gerald McAuley is acknowledged as the first republican to be killed in the troubles, Kane is regarded as the first IRA volunteer to die on active service.

'That was the first time,' says Cahill, 'that the public became aware that the IRA was carrying out operations. Up to then it was the loyalists who had been carrying out operations. This came out when they had a man killed in an explosion at a power station in Ballyshannon in Donegal. Almost all the operations at the time were being carried out by loyalists and I think it was a matter of the IRA taking advantage of that situation.

'There was no grand plan about an immediate offensive. Most volunteers were involved in defence work in certain areas – I believe that was the thought uppermost in most people's minds. What happened in August '69 was unbelievable – that it could be allowed to happen and people got away with it.

'The other thing that was happening, of course, was the building up of supplies. We obtained them where we could and continued making contacts to buy weapons.'

These attempts to obtain arms took place amid accusations that the Provisional IRA had come into existence as the result of a secret agreement between dissident northern republicans and representatives of the Irish government. Fianna Fáil government ministers, it was claimed, would supply money and guns for defensive purposes, provided the northerners broke away from the Officials and set up their own organisation.

The alleged approaches, initially made in early and mid-1969, were said to have come from members of TACA – a group of southern businessmen who acted as fund-raisers for Fianna Fáil – at the instigation of Irish government cabinet ministers. Seán MacStiofáin, who was a member of the Goulding-led Army Council before the split, was said to have attended at least one meeting with TACA. MacStiofáin, right up to his death in July 2001, resolutely denied attending any such meeting, claiming the reports were fed to the media by Official republicans in an attempt to discredit the Provisionals. Senior Belfast members of the Provisional IRA, including Joe Cahill, also deny involvement in any agreement with TACA.

'I have no knowledge of that happening at all. I do know that a number of business people got together to donate money for relief work. I had heard of the TACA group, but I never had dealings with them and don't know anyone who had,' says Cahill.

This assertion, and that of other 'forties men, strongly suggests that movement in the North towards a split developed quite independently of any manufactured rift in the South.

'There was a lot of talk going about at that time that Fianna Fáil wanted to set up a northern command of the IRA,' says Cahill. 'To my knowledge, whatever about other areas, they did not contact anyone in Belfast about it. It amounted to nothing. I think a lot of it was pie-in-the-sky stuff. Somebody had the idea that if an armed group, separate from the IRA, could be set up and based purely in the North for defence purposes, well, there would be some sort of assistance for it. Personally, I think it was just a lot of talk, which I know from experience did not amount to anything.'

But as subsequent events were to reveal, Cahill says, there was absolutely no doubt about the existence of a government cabinet subcommittee on the North, set up by taoiseach Jack Lynch. The northern subcommittee, headed by future taoiseach Charles Haughey and Donegal TD Neil Blaney, was provided with funds to be allocated to northern defence committees for the relief of the growing number of refugees.

Meanwhile, Cahill was to receive a donation from an unexpected source, a successful businessman related to a leading Irish politician. The meeting came about as the result of a chance encounter with Máire Drumm, a senior Belfast Sinn Féin member and wife of one of Ireland's 'most-interned' republicans, Jimmy Drumm.

(Mrs Drumm's outspoken and uncompromising republicanism was anathema to British politicians, who publicly promoted her as a hate-figure. Ill-health forced the mother of five to retire from her position as vice-president of Sinn Féin a few years later, at the age of fifty-seven. She was admitted to Belfast's Mater hospital for a cataract-removal operation in October 1976. The Belfast leadership, however, were not happy about Mrs Drumm's safety in the Mater. Cahill was asked to organise her transfer to a hospital over the border. Cahill, who had contacts in Dublin health service circles, arranged for her to be admitted to a hospital at Raheny in Dublin on 28 October. A hitch in the plan meant that her transfer was delayed until the following day. The concerns for her safety proved to be well-founded. Máire Drumm was shot dead in her hospital bed on 28 October by loyalist paramilitaries posing as medical staff.)

'I had the experience of meeting this man in Máire's house shortly after the events of August 1969. I think he had a business in England at the time. It was by pure accident that I met him. I called to Máire's house and she said, "You are the right man in the right place. [The businessman] is very anxious to help out with relief work and would like to do whatever he can. I think you should talk to him."

'A meeting was arranged and I met him in the same house. He knew who I was. I explained that we had erected barricades in the different areas and needed to set up defence units. Money was very scarce, even for such basic necessities as food. There was never any talk of the IRA, just defence units. He said defence was the sort of thing he was interested in helping with. But then he shook his head and said he was meeting me twenty-four hours too late. He had met Cathal Goulding the previous day and given him £10,000. He said if he had met me first, he would have given the money to us. In the event, he gave me £1,000, which he said was all that was left.'

Around this time, support in the South for nationalists led to a number of incidents, including one which dismayed and disgusted northern republicans, severely embarrassed the Irish government and returned periodically to haunt southern politicians over the following thirty years.

Captain James Kelly, an intelligence officer in the Irish Army, was the Dublin government's main link with the North in 1969 and 1970. Kelly's situation reports, compiled from first-hand evidence on his numerous trips north, were made to his superior officer, who passed them directly to defence minister Jim Gibbons. A major objective of Kelly's intelligence reports was to identify nationalists and republicans with whom the Irish Government could do business and lend assistance. Kelly reported that a priority demand of besieged nationalists was guns for defence purposes to prevent wholesale slaughter.

Kelly's reports came at a time when the Dáil had voted £100,000 for the relief of distress in the North. A cabinet subcommittee had been set up to oversee the ongoing crisis. The use to which the voted money was put became a matter of great controversy. Did the 'relief of distress' include guns for defensive purposes? A subsequent Dáil inquiry never got to the bottom of it.

In April 1970, it became known to British and Irish intelligence agencies that a large consignment of weapons was due to be delivered to Dublin Airport. The airport was staked out by Garda Special Branch to await the arrival of the weapons. However, the team on the continent were warned by a senior member of Irish intelligence and the delivery was aborted.

The following month, Liam Cosgrave, leader of the anti-republican opposition Fine Gael party, was tipped off by anonymous Garda sources about the arms deal and threatened to expose government involvement. This was explosive.

There has been much debate over the years on whether Taoiseach Jack Lynch was fully aware of the scale of cooperation between the northerners and a number of his ministers. Captain Kelly has always insisted that this consignment was procured at the behest of, and for delivery to, the Irish government, a claim denied by some at the highest level of government. More than thirty years later, a consensus has developed that Lynch somehow managed to remain ignorant of the affair until briefed by a senior civil servant shortly before Cosgrave's threatened exposé. But at least one of the principals involved in the plan, the northern republican John Kelly, has no doubt that Lynch was 'aware and was kept informed of all events and all the participants of the so-called arms conspiracy.

'The fact is that when Liam Cosgrave, who was in receipt of Special Branch intelligence, confronted Jack Lynch, Jack Lynch sacked Blaney and Haughey and when that didn't satisfy Cosgrave he then had them arrested and charged with conspiracy to illegally import arms.'

In any event, Lynch was forced to go public after being

confronted by Cosgrave. Faced with a scandal of international proportions, the government denied all involvement. Scapegoats
were needed. When Jack Lynch dismissed Charlie Haughey and
Neil Blaney, another minister, Kevin Boland, resigned in protest.

The affair created a sensation, particularly in the South where
Lynch, perceived until then as something of a non-controversial
stopgap taoiseach, suddenly found the grit to sack some of the
most powerful figures in his cabinet.

Shortly afterwards several arrests were made. Captain James
Kelly, Belfast republican John Kelly (no relation), Haughey, Blaney
and Belgian businessman Albert Luykx went on trial, accused of
conspiring to illegally import weapons into Ireland. The accuseds'
defence was that they were acting on behalf of the government.
Blaney was acquitted in July, and the others were also acquitted
when their case was dismissed at a higher court in October.

The arms trial effectively ruined the career of Captain Kelly, by
all accounts an honest man and an exemplary soldier who fully
believed he was carrying out the wishes of his government.

The Public Accounts Committee was established by Lynch to
investigate the destination of the money allocated by the government to help relieve distress in the North. Several witnesses were
summoned before the committee in December 1970. An earlier,
successful importation of arms had allegedly been delivered to
Dublin airport in late 1969. The weapons were reportedly collected by Cathal Goulding, then chief of staff of the IRA. They
were never to reach the North.

'I had heard about the attempt to import guns while it was happening,' Cahill says. 'I met Jim Kelly when he had been sent up
here to see the situation for himself and find out what help was
needed and report back. I took him to be a very sincere person. I
met him only once but I know that other people had regular and
direct contact with him, including John Kelly and Seán Keenan [a
senior Derry republican].'

✠ ✠ ✠

At Stormont, new prime minister James Chichester-Clark found his position becoming increasingly untenable. Caught between implementing reforms ordered by Westminster and appeasing the unionist community with tougher tactics against protesting nationalists, 'Chi-Chi', as he had become known to the newspaper headline writers, was pleasing no one. To add to his woes, the loyalist marching season – always a harbinger of heightened sectarian tensions – was approaching.

And it was indeed an Orange march, through west Belfast's nationalist Ballymurphy area, which was to lead to four days of sustained rioting at the end of March and the first days of April. In what was viewed as a particularly heavy-handed approach, the British Army saturated the streets with CS gas, a totally indiscriminate and pervasive weapon which crept into homes and affected young and old. Residents replied with petrol bombs, leading British commander General Sir Ian Freeland to warn that petrol-bombers could be shot dead. In response, the IRA said they would take retaliatory action if the British carried out their threat. The days of 'tea for the troops' were fast coming to an end.

Towards the end of the rioting Cahill played host to IRA chief of staff Seán MacStiofáin, who had arrived in Ballymurphy to see the situation for himself. After being taken by Cahill on a night-time tour of the republican lookout posts dotted around the housing estate, MacStiofáin reported that he had been very impressed with the alertness of volunteers, who had challenged the pair at every turn.

If it was loyalists who had exposed the weakness of the IRA in August 1969, it was also loyalists – again involved in an Orange Order march – who helped the republican movement to regain its credibility with nationalists.

In June 1970, former chief of staff Hugh McAteer died. Seán MacStiofáin, Dáithí Ó Conaill and Ruairí Ó Brádaigh were among the hundreds of republicans who travelled to Belfast for his funeral. The presence of so many members of the leadership in the city presented a major security headache for the resident units, who were expecting another outbreak of serious sectarian rioting with the approach of the 'mini-Twelfth'. The twelfth of July, or simply 'the Twelfth' as it is known in the North, is the date of the largest annual Orange demonstration, but the mini-Twelfth, a moveable feast generally held around 1 July, also attracts large partisan crowds, with all the attendant dangers for nationalist neighbourhoods. Except in the most unusual circumstances, even the highest-ranking IRA officer must defer to the local com-mander, and so the leaders accepted the suggestion that they should leave the city as soon as was practicable after the funeral.

The mini-Twelfth is an important day for the Orange lodges. Members meet at their outgoing masters' homes, pick up their highly decorative hand-painted lodge banners and, accompanied by marching bands, ceremonially parade around the town. The marchers eventually arrive at the incoming master's residence, where he is presented with the banner. These ceremonies, involving marches through various areas, mean the presence of thousands of Orangemen and band members on Belfast's roads and streets. Quite often Orange marches pass off peacefully but, at times of heightened tension, trouble can always be expected when they parade through a nationalist area against the wishes of the residents.

Cahill recalls that there was an atmosphere of foreboding in Bel-fast in the days preceding the mini-Twelfth, which that year was to take place on Saturday, 27 June. All the city's IRA units and defence groups under republican command were put on standby. But, while Belfast commander Billy McKee, Cahill and Séamus

Twomey (joint vice-OCs) and the rest of Brigade staff knew trouble was coming, no one realised that the IRA was about to face its most severe test since August of the previous year.

'A day or so before the march, I was in the Short Strand over in Ballymacarrett, because a bit of trouble was going on. Brian Faulkner [minister of development in Chichester-Clark's cabinet, and soon to replace him as Stormont prime minister] arrived on the Newtownards Road, opposite the barricade at the bottom of Seaforde Street. He was accompanied by a senior RUC man and he asked to speak to us.'

In 1970 St Matthew's parish, or the Short Strand, in east Belfast's Ballymacarrett district was a small nationalist enclave of around 6,000 souls, living in twenty-two streets of tiny 'two-up, two-down' terraced houses. The area was hemmed in on three sides by loyalist streets, while the River Lagan ran along the fourth side. The parish has been attacked by loyalists on scores of occasions since the late nineteenth century. Perhaps unsurprisingly, many visitors from west and north Belfast claimed to feel claustrophobic when in the Short Strand.

The situation in the city had indeed brought together strange bedfellows – a leading republican who had once been under sentence of death for killing a policeman and an ambitious young unionist politician who made no secret of his desire to be prime minister. Known as the shrewdest and most pragmatic of the Stormont ministers of the era, Faulkner's hardline attitude in the 1950s had earned him the admiration of his colleagues as the 'hammer of the IRA'. The brief meeting between the IRA man and the unionist minister, though unprecedented, went totally unnoticed by the media.

'Faulkner said it was not necessary to erect barricades, and he wanted this one removed,' says Cahill. 'He said nationalists had nothing to fear from the Protestant people of the Newtownards Road. In the background, the loyalists were shouting and chanting slogans. I asked Faulkner how he expected the people of the Short Strand to be confident when such scenes were going on across the road. I asked him why they were not removed. He said, "Get the barricade removed and those people will go away." We held on-the-spot talks with the volunteers in charge of the area and they said they did not trust Faulkner or the RUC, and would not allow the barricade to come down. Faulkner left. He had not gone more than ten minutes when the rioting started again.'

On Saturday 27 June, Cahill says, the tension in the Belfast air could almost be tasted.

'We had held a Brigade meeting to discuss the situation throughout the city, and I told the staff of the incident in the Short Strand. I think that was what decided McKee to go to Ballymacarrett. Each of us had been allocated an area to go to in the event of trouble, to ensure that proper defence systems had been put in place. We considered the Short Strand to be very vulnerable, because it was surrounded by Protestant areas. Of course, the people were quite capable of setting up a system of defence – I knew the area well and knew they had a plan of defence – but we were always afraid that they were going to be slaughtered.'

McKee's decision to travel to Ballymacarrett was to cost him dearly. However, the events of that night were to signal a turning point in the fortunes of the IRA, who were still suffering a lack of credibility since their performance in August 1969.

On the Springfield Road in the west of the city, the Orange march resulted in heavy rioting between the nationalist residents and the RUC and British Army. So incensed were the residents at the march being forced through that the intensity of their attack on the police barracks caused the RUC to abandon the building. On another part of the Springfield Road, a similar scene was played out with soldiers being driven out of their base while Army Land-Rovers were taken out and driven at the soldiers.

In Ardoyne in the north of the city, the Orange parade was also followed by fierce fighting. This time, says Cahill, republicans were determined that there would be no repetition of the devastation visited on the area ten months previously. It soon became clear that the Ardoyne IRA were no longer relying on the single shotgun used the previous August. Now properly organised and better armed, they were determined to reclaim the respect of their support base. Rioting was particularly fierce on the Crumlin Road, in effect the dividing line between Catholic Ardoyne and the Protestant streets a few yards away. The riot soon escalated into a gun battle and three Protestant men were killed.

It was during these incidents and across the city in St Matthew's Parish that Cahill believes the IRA went a long way to wiping out the stain of 'I Ran Away'.

As in other areas, trouble occurred in the east when the local Orange lodges and bands were returning home in the evening. At the Seaforde Street flashpoint, loyalist crowds following the bands made several half-hearted attempts to storm the Short Strand. Stones and bottles were thrown and there were several skirmishes with residents. A tense and uneasy peace fell over the neighbourhood as the band music and the chanting of the crowd faded into the distance. No one, however, believed for a moment that the area was going to escape so lightly.

The IRA's B Company of the Third Battalion was backed up in the Short Strand by a residents' defence group called the Catholic Defence League (CDL), which took its name from the 'defence leagues' formed to protect nationalist areas of Belfast in the pogroms of the early 1900s. Belfast Brigade staff intended that groups like the CDL should play a totally defensive role, to be employed only in dire emergency.

Billy McKee was not long in the area before he decided that a 'dire emergency' was indeed upon them. The plan of defence was put into operation. Following the experience of the people of Ballymurphy in March, pails of water were left at each street corner.

These were to be used by residents to soak handkerchiefs to cover the nose and mouth in the event of soldiers using CS gas. Arms and ammunition were distributed and volunteers told to stand by.

Just before midnight, the area was besieged by hundreds of angry loyalists. Attempts were made to burn down St Matthew's church, on the edge of the parish. The hail of petrol bombs and rocks soon gave way to the rattle of gunfire, the prelude to a firefight which lasted until dawn and claimed the lives of two Protestants and a Catholic. The leader of the Belfast IRA also came close to death when he was hit by a burst of machine gun fire.

'Much of the shooting was centred in and around the church grounds,' says Cahill. 'It was there that McKee was badly wounded and a local man, Henry McIlhone, received injuries from which he died a couple of days later. There were British soldiers in the area that night, but they stood by and let the attack on the Short Strand happen.'

A senior British Army officer later agreed that troops were present, but said there were insufficient numbers to force the loyalists back from the parish and its church. Moreover, the isolation felt by the Short Strand residents was made complete when soldiers blocked the two bridges on the periphery of the area, sealing off any help that could be expected from the west of the city. An elderly resident claimed the few soldiers present in the vicinity seemed inept and confused. An eyewitness to the early events of the night, the man said that a Ferret armoured car on the nearby Newtownards Road knocked over a massive granite pillar at St Matthew's gate as the driver reversed to escape from a hostile loyalist crowd. The same vehicle, commanded by a young cavalry lieutenant, screeched into Seaforde Street, flames leaping from its turret after it was targeted by loyalist petrol bombers. A couple of nationalist bystanders, feeling sorry for the soldiers, used the emergency buckets of water to douse the flames. In one of the ironies of conflict, one of these men was shot dead by soldiers just over a year later as he stood on the corner of the street where he lived, just twenty metres from the spot where the Ferret incident took place.

The night sky glowed red from the flames of burning buildings on the periphery of the Short Strand area, where loyalists had managed to get close enough to use their petrol bombs effectively. St Matthew's sexton and his large family, who lived in a neat little house in the church grounds on the Newtownards Road, had a narrow escape. The family finally and reluctantly took the advice of the local IRA commander, who had told them that the building could not be defended. Minutes after fleeing their home, a barrage of petrol bombs turned it into a roaring inferno. By morning it was just one of the many smoking piles of rubble littering the city.

'There is no doubt about it, we were taxed,' Cahill says. 'There had been attempted invasions of several areas in Belfast that night – not only Ballymacarrett, but North Queen Street and Ardoyne as well – and we were stretched. Naturally, we were extremely concerned that the OC of Belfast Brigade had been shot and came close to death, but the IRA had proved in their actions across the city that they were now capable of defending the people.'

If the British Army was now being regarded with suspicion by nationalists, its alienation was completed a few days later, through events in the west of the city.

Cahill was among several senior republicans who believed that the Stormont government, known to be angered and alarmed by the scale of recent gun battles, would want to strike back, swiftly and emphatically. Acting either on good intelligence work or information supplied by an informer, soldiers raided a house in Balkan Street in the lower Falls, a strong Official IRA area, on Friday, 3 July. The house was the site of an Officials' arms dump and the raiding party discovered twelve assorted handguns and a sub-machine gun, along with some explosives and ammunition. The trauma of the previous year's attack, when the area was virtually defenceless, was fresh in the minds of the people and a hostile crowd formed. Residents remain adamant to this day that the search party could have departed with the captured weapons and the situation would have been defused. A riot situation developed, they insist, only after troops employed very heavy-handed tactics. The British commander, Lieutenant-General Sir Ian Freeland, was well prepared for a reaction, and reinforcements rapidly arrived. In a ploy widely perceived as an attempt to draw republicans into a full-scale battle, the area was bombarded with CS gas canisters while the troops withdrew a short distance. The Officials took up the challenge and there were exchanges of gunfire.

'When we saw what was happening,' says Cahill, 'myself and MacAirt went down to see what we could do. It was obvious by this time that a big British operation was about to take place, and we knew the Stickies had a fair amount of weapons in the area. The British had already announced that they would conduct a house-to-house search. We were sent down to make arrangements for the arms to be taken out of the area with a guarantee to the Officials that they would be given back later. It was an offer of help and it was refused. We had dumps ready elsewhere and people ready to take the arms out. The Stickies said they were quite confident that their own dumps in the area would suffice. They lost a lot of stuff through not accepting the offer. They said afterwards they preferred that it went to the Brits rather than to the Provisionals.'

Freeland had decided to take out the IRA – he appeared not to distinguish between Provisionals and Officials – once and for all in the lower Falls area. Three thousand troops, supported by armoured vehicles, surrounded the neighbourhood as the British GOC announced a curfew to facilitate a house-to-house search. The lower Falls was to be cleared of every weapon, defensive or offensive.

Nightmarish scenes followed. Amid the pall of CS gas hanging over the district, doors were kicked in, floors ripped up and holes smashed in walls by troops searching for arms. Residents were forbidden to leave their homes as a helicopter circled overhead, its public address system blaring out details of the curfew (which, incidentally, was later declared to have been illegal).

Units of the Provisional IRA's Second Battalion's D Company (the 'Dogs' or 'Doggies' as they subsequently became known) took part in resistance, until they were pulled out to avoid becoming surrounded and trapped. The Provisional Belfast Brigade staff ordered units to launch diversionary attacks across the city in a bid to draw off troops and ease the pressure on the people of the lower Falls. Freeland was not taken in; he kept up his stranglehold on the area. Over 100 weapons were captured, most of which, according to Cahill, were the property of Officials.

The British Army afterwards admitted to having fired around 15,000 rounds, but no Provisional or Official IRA members or troops were killed. However, three civilian men were shot dead and another crushed to death by an armoured personnel carrier.

The thinking of the military high command after the events of 27 June was summed up by Colonel Mike Dewar in his book *The British Army in Northern Ireland*: 'Not surprisingly General Freeland was not prepared to let the IRA get away with it. He decided a show of force was needed and that the Falls had to be brought back under control. At 8.20pm on 3 July the Army went in. The IRA opened fire on the Black Watch and the Life Guards, the latter unit having just got off the ferry from Liverpool. The Army returned fire and used CS gas and imposed a curfew at 10pm which was not lifted until 9am on 5 July.'

For thirty-five hours, between Friday night and Sunday morning, the entire area was held incommunicado. People ran out of food and were still not permitted to go to the shops, despite appeals from churchmen and human rights groups. Nationalists were particularly incensed at reports that mothers were having trouble obtaining baby food for their children. Further insult was added when residents were held at gunpoint as two unionist Stormont government ministers, accompanied by British officers, were driven around on a tour of the district, somewhat in the style of conquering heroes, apparently to view the vanquished.

'Something had to be done, and quickly,' says Cahill. 'That was when the idea of a hunger march came up. I always admired Máire Drumm for organising, almost single-handed, thousands of women in a very short time to march from all over west Belfast down the Falls Road, to bring food into the area, particularly milk and baby food.'

Television pictures of the day showed many hundreds of nervous but determined women, often with children at their sides, pushing prams and buggies loaded with milk, bread and baby food, as they brushed past the armed cordon and marched into the heart of the beleaguered area. But, according to Cahill, Máire Drumm's 'march of mothers' still had work to do.

'The same prams used to carry in food were used to take out a considerable number of weapons, handed over by people who were in danger of being caught in possession. The women brought the food in and brought the guns out.'

General Freeland announced that his troops had recovered thirty rifles, twenty-four shotguns, fifty-two handguns, 20,000 rounds of ammunition, a quantity of gelignite and some incendiary bombs.

While Freeland insisted that the curfew and searches were a military success, there is little doubt that, politically, it was a disaster. The adversarial attitude evident in the operation in the lower Falls in July destroyed any remaining shred of trust the Catholic population may have had in the troops. Feelings against the military were running at an all-time high, and again there was an upsurge in the number of young people attempting to join the IRA. Belfast Brigade had many more potential recruits than they could handle. Their support base becoming stronger with each passing week, the

Provisionals became bolder and increased the range and scale of offensive operations. In the following weeks, two RUC officers were killed in a booby-trap explosion in the County Armagh border village of Crossmaglen, a bank in Belfast's High Street and a number of electricity stations throughout the North were bombed and attacks were carried out on the homes of judges.

In less than a year, the situation had changed dramatically. In August 1969 the IRA had been accused of running away and failing to defend nationalists. Between then and 1970 the traditionalists had split from the Dublin leadership and organised themselves into a cohesive force. They had trained and armed themselves and set up plans of defence for vulnerable nationalist neighbourhoods. Defence units had been formed to help implement the plans. In Ardoyne, Crumlin Road and the Short Strand, the Provisionals had come out ahead of the Officials by proving themselves capable of defending Catholic districts. And while the imposition of the Falls curfew had caused considerable hardship and suffering, it also played an important part in radicalising and politicising national-ists. The outcome was that there were now many in the Catholic ghettos who believed their community was effectively involved in a war against loyalists and the British Army.

The long-term political effects of the curfew were the subject of debate for years afterwards. The respected *Sunday Times* Insight team, in their book *Ulster*, noted: 'The curfew did convert what was perhaps only an increasingly sullen Catholic acceptance of the Army into outright communal hostility.' And in his *History of Ulster*, Jonathan Bardon wrote: 'The incident did more than any other in 1970 to bring recruits to both factions of the IRA.'

✠ ✠ ✠

It was around this time that Cahill lost his friend and mentor, Jimmy Steele. Steele died on 9 August 1970, the day after his sixty-third birthday and just five weeks after his comrade and fellow escaper Hugh McAteer.

'Steele was a natural leader and had always held a leadership position in the IRA or in Sinn Féin. He was the type of man you could go to with any problem and he would sort it out. His life was dedicated to the freedom of Ireland and to the republican movement and if there was any way that he could assist or help, well, there was no better man than Steele. But he could be cantankerous at times and would fall out with you over simple things, tiny little things. Then that would pass and all would be well again.

'He would never hold spite, although on occasion he had good reason to because there were some very bitter, and in my view, unjust, things said about him. His commitment and dedication, I believe, were unmatchable. He was a great man for the pen and was continually writing. Any time I called into the house to see him I would find him with a manuscript of some type beside him which he had been working on. He was always jotting down something, was always involved in republican publications. It was Steele who realised the importance of establishing our own newspaper after the split, and he became the first editor of the *Republican News*,' says Cahill.

Such was the esteem in which Jimmy Steele was held that the firing party at his funeral in Milltown cemetery was composed of senior members of Belfast Brigade. The funeral was observed and captured on camera by undercover RUC officers, who noted: 'Shots were fired at the funeral of an IRA member, James Steele, at Milltown cemetery and Cahill was identified from photographs as part of this firing party.'

✠ ✠ ✠

If republicans felt the Irish government had let down the people of the North with the arms importation fiasco earlier in the year, they knew of a rich source of support and cash on which they could always rely – Irish America. Cahill and Leo Martin, a well-known Belfast republican who had been targeted by loyalists several times, were asked to make the trip to the United States.

Sympathisers in the States had been confused by events in Ireland. Reports that the IRA had 'gone commie' did not go down well with America's traditional republican supporters, and no one knew very much about the newly established Provisionals. It was the job of Cahill and Martin to enlist the aid of the faithful and reassure them that the IRA was back on course.

Cahill did not know it then, but the success of that first trip in November 1970 – his only *legal* visit until the IRA ceasefire in 1994 – was to establish him as Irish republicanism's unofficial ambassador to the Irish diaspora in the United States. This was just what the Americans needed: a no-nonsense, down-to-earth Belfast republican of the physical-force tradition who could speak with the authority of the Army Council.

'On that first visit, I was able to move about freely, because I had no problem obtaining a visa. I actually told the United States Consulate in Belfast that I had been in prison for political, not criminal, reasons, and it was accepted. The trip was very successful. Leo Martin and I carried out an extensive tour, fund-raising and organising branches of Irish Northern Aid, starting off in New York and doing the whole east coast, the mid-West, Chicago and from there over to the west coast to San Francisco.

'I still remember the meeting where Irish Northern Aid was mentioned for the first time. There was a small group of people who were active in the republican movement. These were immigrants who had gone to America and had always remained loyal to the republican movement. In New York they were known as the Thursday Night Committee, because that's when they met,' says Cahill.

The two republicans also met several dignitaries, including the mayor of Chicago, Richard Daly, whom Cahill found to be 'very supportive'.

'In San Francisco we met a lot of trade union people. One man who had a lot of influence out there was Dan McCormack, originally from Coalisland in County Tyrone. He was the man who was standing by in Coalisland in 1916, ready to mobilise. Coalisland was the gathering point for the North and they were waiting for the word when they got the countermanding order. He was part of that contingent meant to go down south. Until the day he died, he was an uncompromising republican and he was Mr Irish Republican in San Francisco. He was highly respected and he had the contacts.'

McCormack had been one of hundreds of northerners who assembled at Coalisland in 1916, awaiting the order to march southwest to Connemara to link up with the force commanded by republican leader Liam Mellowes. Mellowes was to lead the Rising from Galway and then, reinforced by the northerners, head for Athlone in the centre of Ireland, where it had been arranged that Irish troops in the town's British Army barracks would mutiny. Armed with artillery from the barracks and strengthened by the mutineers, Mellowes' column was then to march on Dublin. The plan came to nought when an order to stand down was sent out to Irish Volunteer units across the country – with the exception of Dublin city, where the Volunteers and the Citizen Army took over the General Post Office and several other buildings and fought off British forces for a week. Nora Connolly O'Brien, daughter of Citizen Army leader James Connolly, acted as courier between North and South in the days prior to the Rising. In Coalisland, she reported viewing a 'big barn which was filled with weapons', intended to be used by Dan McCormack and his comrades.

Far from treating Cahill and Martin's visit to San Francisco as an undercover mission, McCormack had organised a fife and drum band to welcome the Belfast men on their arrival at the city's international airport. It was a Sunday afternoon, and Cahill had a pleasant surprise when he asked one of his hosts where he could find evening Mass being celebrated in San Francisco. 'I don't know. You will have to ask a Catholic, because I'm a Protestant,' the man replied. This same man was later jailed in the United States on charges connected with supplying arms to the IRA.

During their stay, Cahill recalls, he and Leo Martin were asked to attend a 'fairly big' gathering of a group known as the Knights of the Round Table.

'The meeting was held in their premises which was located, I think, in the Mission area. The lights were dimmed except on the stage where we were sitting, which was brightly lit. There was a question-and-answer session. One guy in the audience said that he wanted a question answered first by me and then by Leo Martin. He asked me if I was in the IRA. I had no hesitation in telling him I was. It went down well with the audience, because the place erupted. This guy, who had a northern Irish accent, asked Leo the same question. Martin said he had been in the Fianna and it was through meeting me that he transferred to the IRA. When I asked the man if he had been trying to trip us up, he identified himself as a republican from Magherafelt in County Derry and said he had been interned in the 1940s.

'Afterwards I asked him why he had asked us that particular question. He said he felt the meeting was getting nowhere and he wanted to bring it alive, which he most certainly did.'

Irish-America's republican supporters throughout the country took Cahill to their hearts and he was given the somewhat incongruous *nom de guerre* Father Joe Brown. On subsequent visits, when he slipped illegally into the States, support groups across the country knew to organise a clandestine meeting when they received the message: 'Father Brown's in town.'

On one occasion when 'Father Brown' was addressing a meeting in a private house, a giant American insisted on standing outside. Cahill repeatedly asked him to come in and take part in the discussion but the man demurred, eventually holding open his coat to reveal a holstered revolver and indicating that he considered himself on guard duty for the night. 'Nobody gonna take this meeting by surprise,' he told Cahill, who discovered shortly afterwards that the sympathiser was a serving police officer of Irish descent.

The establishment of Irish Northern Aid (Noraid) on that initial visit began to benefit the republican cause almost immediately. The group was to send vital financial assistance for republican prisoners and their families, and offer unswerving support to the movement throughout the highs and lows of a quarter-century.

There were, of course, other supporters who wished to send more than dollars to Ireland, and their contributions were gratefully received by the IRA. Following Cahill and Martin's initial contact with the Americans, a steady stream of small arms began to find their way to the North. According to Cahill, these weapons consignments were 'nothing spectacular', but nonetheless vital to the early development of the reformed IRA.

Soon IRA members were being summoned to gun lectures in kitchens and living rooms across the North, to be trained in a wide variety of weapons, old and modern. Volunteers were expected to be familiar with perhaps a dozen different guns, leading to claims that IRA weapons training was superior to that of British soldiers of the period, who were taught to use one rifle and one handgun. The 'small consignments from the States' included hunting rifles, Second World War assault rifles, Thompson sub-machine guns and a wide range of revolvers and semi-automatic pistols. Later, as the network of contacts grew and the IRA's international operations became more sophisticated, American connections were to provide much larger shipments of modern weapons, such as the Armalite.

'Some of the people we met in the States,' says Cahill, 'would have been involved in sending arms to the IRA – small amounts of arms, but they still did send arms. During 1970 they sent quite a few small consignments. They had their own ways of getting them into Ireland. They kept that very tight, which was a great thing, I didn't know and didn't want to know how they were doing it, but to me it was a great thing. They weren't bombastic or boasting about their work.

'Now, they were also supplying arms to another group in Ireland, a small group. The reason they were sending arms to this group was because one of the people involved with them was responsible for what we called "the line", or the method of transporting the weapons. When this was arranged first and this guy was approached, he had no problem with cooperating, but he asked that a percentage of the arms be given to the remnants of his group in Ireland.

'He said he had a commitment to these people who he claimed were interested in the defence of the people of the North. The people he was dealing with in America had no problem with sending weapons to his group. He asked for a quarter of the first consignment. That should have been him satisfied, but it did not work out that way. In talking with people responsible for procuring the arms, we discovered that he had asked for a further share in the next consignment.

'I told them they had honoured their part of the bargain and they shouldn't cooperate with him any further; they should have him cut out of the line. I told them my biggest concern was that there was no control over his people. I asked the main supporter how would he feel if one of the bullets he sent to Ireland was used by this group in a feud to shoot a volunteer dead. He said, "Right, that's it, I see your point of view, any arms we are sending will go to the IRA."

'I have to say that these people were sincere – they were the remnants of the old Clan na Gael – and wanted to be absolutely sure that the Provisionals were also sincere and were not going to let the nationalist people down. They actually came over to Ireland to check things out. They sent people over here to investigate the Official IRA and the Provisional IRA and they had no problem after they talked to people that their support was going to the proper place.'

(By autumn of 1970, the Provisional IRA had held their second Army convention, which voted to drop the term 'provisional'. The group was increasingly being regarded as the mainstream element of the republican movement. From this point on in the text, the term IRA will apply to the Provisionals, while their opponents will be termed Officials or the Official IRA.)

The IRA was now just twelve months away from one of its most active periods of the latter half of the twentieth century. In February 1971, on a night of confusion, vicious sectarian rioting and heavy gun battles, mainly in north Belfast, the British Army was to lose its first soldier and the IRA another volunteer. Jim Saunders, a member of the Third Battalion's F Company, was shot by an Army sniper who was covering soldiers attempting to dismantle barricades in the area. Gunner Robert Curtis of the Royal Artillery died when a burst of Thompson machine gun fire was aimed in his direction. A civilian, Bernard Watt, was shot dead by soldiers in controversial circumstances a mile away in Ardoyne. Barney Watt was said to be a member of Sinn Féin, but was not in the IRA. There were distasteful scenes at his funeral, when mourners were attacked by loyalists who grabbed the tricolour from the coffin and ran off with it.

Following the death of Gunner Curtis, Stormont prime minister Chichester-Clark appeared on television to declare: 'Northern Ireland is at war with the IRA Provisionals.' The challenge was accepted with enthusiasm by an increasingly confident IRA.

The IRA, however, was soon to find itself fighting on two fronts. As the number of attacks mounted, there was a sharp deterioration in the relationship between the Provisionals and Officials.

Simmering hostility and mutual distrust came to a head and, inevitably, resulted in a shooting war.

Several Official areas had now gone over to the Provisional IRA, but the lower Falls remained a 'Sticky' stronghold. An incident which the IRA claimed involved the beating-up of a Fianna boy led to a series of events in early March which ended in the death of a highly respected volunteer and the wounding of another – Cahill's brother, Tom.

Two members of D Company, who had been sent to investigate the beating of the youth, were themselves abducted by the Officials and badly beaten. Tensions in the city rose even further following claims that the volunteers had been tortured and had their fingers broken with pistol butts while being held in separate public houses. An attempt to burn down the two bars where the men had been held led to a gun battle in the Official stronghold of Leeson Street. One pub had been set on fire and an active service unit was on the way to burn the second when they were intercepted by Officials. No one was injured in the resulting firefight. Mediators eventually got the two sides to agree to discuss their differences.

Later that night, D Company's OC, Charlie Hughes, was in a house in Cyprus Street with Proinsias MacAirt. As MacAirt prepared to leave, Hughes stopped him and went outside to check that the coast was clear. Hughes' caution was an indication of the tension in the area, despite the earlier agreement that both sides would attempt to calm the situation. The twenty-six-year-old IRA lieutenant had only taken a few steps when he was caught in a burst of gunfire. He fell to the pavement, mortally wounded.

'MacAirt told us afterwards that Charlie had died in his arms,' says Cahill.

Many IRA members wanted revenge for the death of this popular republican, who had become something of a folk hero through his exploits with D Company. Reason, however, prevailed.

Mediators were again called in and a truce was arranged between the two groups. Just hours later, however, the city was once more brought to the brink of a bloody republican feud.

Tom Cahill, who had followed his oldest brother into the IRA, was carrying out deliveries on his milk round when he was attacked by Officials. The younger Cahill had an automatic pistol in his van, but had the gun and the magazine concealed separately. Cahill, caught unawares, was shot several times in the face and body. Bleeding heavily and close to death, he was rushed to hospital.

The Officials were reported to have apologised immediately after the shooting of Tom Cahill, claiming he had been attacked by one of their units which had not received news of the truce. The apology did little to mollify rank-and-file IRA members and once more the leadership came under heavy pressure to strike back.

Billy McKee, officer commanding Belfast Brigade, called an emergency staff meeting to discuss the latest incident. The veteran McKee deemed that his number two, Joe Cahill, was too close to the situation and asked him to wait in another room. It would not be fair on Cahill, McKee said, to expect him to take part in a discussion concerning possible reaction to the shooting of his brother.

'Apparently, after some discussion,' Cahill recalls, 'the staff were evenly split on whether to launch a counter-attack on the Sticks. I was called in to give the casting vote. I said that obviously I was concerned about the attack on my brother, but pointed out that what was happening in the city was a diversion from our overall purpose. We should concentrate on the task we were established to carry out and, to that end, we should try to end the feud without any further loss of life. No action was taken.'

That particular episode was now over, but the hostility between the two groups was to erupt periodically into violence in the years that followed.

Tom Cahill underwent emergency surgery, which doubtless

saved his life, but surgeons felt it was too dangerous to carry out a further operation to remove a bullet which had lodged near his spine. Cahill recovered from the attack, but remained partially paralysed for the rest of his life. While in hospital, he was charged with possession of the firearm and ammunition. He was later sentenced to two years in jail.

(Despite his state of health, Tom Cahill remained active in the republican movement. He was arrested several times over the years and questioned at Castlereagh interrogation centre in east Belfast, where suspects could be held for up to seven days without access to a lawyer. Detectives in Castlereagh had an extremely high success rate in obtaining confessions.

In the mid- to late 1980s, Tom Cahill was arrested once more and taken to Castlereagh. After each interrogation session he was returned to his cell. As he was later to tell his family, one day while awaiting the return of the uniformed RUC officers who would take him to the detectives' interrogation room, he 'felt or sensed' liquid of some type trickling down his spine. Sitting up on his bunk, he reached round to check on his old wound. As his fingers probed the scar tissue, one of the bullets which had ripped into his body in 1971 dropped into the palm of his hand.

'Tom was released on that occasion, but strangely enough, after the bullet incident in Castlereagh, his health began to deteriorate even more and he never did make a full recovery. He was never the same man since,' Joe Cahill says. Tom Cahill died surrounded by his family in early 2001, after a long and lingering illness.)

✠ ✠ ✠

With unionists demanding a return to the 'peaceful injustice' of the pre-civil rights days, and nationalists seeking the implementation of an equality agenda – for example, no 'one-man, one-vote' elections had yet taken place, the scene was set for continued unrest. Chichester-Clark was coming under heavy pressure to deal with the increasingly active IRA. Unionist hardliners were demanding the introduction of a raft of repressive measures, including the return of internment without trial and a dramatic increase in troops levels. His government had already been given a vote of no confidence by the Orange Order's Belfast County Grand Lodge and by January 1971 the Ulster Unionist Council, his party's ruling body, was calling for his resignation. The hapless Chi-Chi flew to London in a last-ditch bid to get Conservative prime minister Edward Heath to agree to send thousands more soldiers to the north. Heath, acting on the advice of his military advisors, refused. Chichester-Clark held out until 20 March, when he finally threw in the towel.

His replacement as leader of the Unionist Party and prime minister was made of much sterner stuff. Brian Faulkner, a businessman, was regarded as a brighter and more astute politician than his predecessors, the cousins Terence O'Neill and James Chichester-Clark. He believed he was the natural successor to Lord Brookeborough, and had been hurt when the party selected O'Neill in 1963. The hurt had been compounded in 1969 when he was again ignored and Chichester-Clark was chosen to succeed O'Neill. Faulkner believed he had been passed over for the leadership because he was not a member of the unionist landed gentry, who somewhat disdainfully regarded him as a product of the merchant class.

Brian Faulkner was convinced that he could do a better job of combating republicanism than O'Neill and Chichester-Clark, and was also confident that he could get Heath to agree to the reintroduction of internment. The new Stormont prime minister believed in the effectiveness of detention without trial. As minister of home affairs in Brookeborough's government in the 1950s, he had signed hundreds of detention orders – including that of one Joseph Cahill.

CHAPTER NINE
Operation Demetrius

New prime minister Brian Faulkner was deeply concerned after reading intelligence reports on the Easter Rising celebrations held by republicans across the North in April 1971.

The biggest turnout, as usual, was in Belfast on Easter Sunday, when republicans traditionally made their way to Beechmount Avenue, in the Falls area. Here they assembled behind marching bands and colour parties bearing a collection of flags, including the Irish national tricolour, the Starry Plough (emblem of the Citizen Army) and the insignia of Ireland's four provinces.

This year, however, there were two parades. The Provisionals and the Officials both left from Beechmount, but separately and with a prudent time gap. The Provisional parade was first to move off on the two-mile march. The parade route took them within yards of Andersonstown RUC barracks, then swung left into Milltown Cemetery and went downhill to the republican plot.

What worried Faulkner and his security advisors was the size of the first parade. With more than 7,000 marchers, it was double that of the Official gathering. The Official IRA was still carrying out some aggressive operations at this time, but its leadership remained determined to take the political path and their commitment to violence was waning. A year later, after a disastrous attack on a military barracks in England, the Officials were to call a ceasefire.

Supporters of the physical force tradition, however, were standing up to be counted. The show of strength at the Easter commemoration parade clearly reflected approval for the growing number of gun and bomb attacks in Belfast.

'More and more nationalists and republicans,' Cahill comments, 'were coming to the conclusion that reform of the system by peaceful means was impossible.'

An anxious Faulkner was coming to the same conclusion. He had been elected party leader and prime minister on the understanding that he would take a firm stance against those who were intent on destroying the state of Northern Ireland. The escalating IRA campaign had to be stopped. Internment had broken republican resolve before, he reasoned, and this time would be no different. A major swoop would remove most of the leadership and the bulk of volunteers. The IRA would then be in defensive mode, and would find it difficult to maintain momentum. Individuals could be arrested in mopping-up operations. All he had to do was convince the British government that internment was vital. Faulkner reasoned, correctly as it transpired, that British prime minister Ted Heath would be loath to risk further instability by losing another Stormont leader so quickly.

Events were moving at a breathtaking pace. There were almost 140 bomb attacks on business premises in the three months following Faulkner's accession to the leadership of the Unionist party. Also during this time, a soldier was shot dead to the south of Belfast city centre, an IRA man was killed in a gun battle with soldiers on the north side and a paratrooper was blown up in an attack on an RUC barracks in the west.

Faulkner relaxed the rules of engagement for security forces, announcing that anyone acting suspiciously was liable to be fired on. Soon afterwards, two youths were shot dead in Derry by troops operating under the new 'fire with effect' rules. Army claims that the pair were IRA volunteers were rejected by republicans and indeed the general Derry nationalist community. The incident led to members of the newly-founded Social and Democratic Labour Party walking out of Stormont, after their demand for an inquiry into the deaths was turned down.

The face of Belfast was changing almost weekly. The business community became anxious, then despairing, as the IRA's 'economic bombing' campaign began to bite. Visitors to the city centre, an increasingly rare species, would often find that their intended destination – a bank, department store or office building – had been 'car-parked' – republican slang for creating vacant lots by bombing buildings.

A politician's disparaging reference to 'mad bombers' was picked up by the media. Almost immediately it was seized upon by young IRA members, who claimed it for themselves. Soon the slogan 'Up the Mad Bombers' was being painted on gable walls and shouted out defiantly in courtrooms. In July alone, the IRA carried out ninety-one bomb attacks, including detonating ten devices along the route of the main Orange parade in Belfast in the early hours of 12 July. Tensions rose further later that day, with the killing of a soldier in the city. The following day, an IRA man who had been arrested after being wounded in a gun battle with troops was rescued from the Royal Victoria hospital, despite the close attentions of armed guards. Faulkner was determined to react to the escalation of republican violence.

Nationalist areas were rife with rumours of internment, and Cahill and MacStiofáin knew that these were more than mere rumours. Belfast Brigade had been receiving information from a sympathiser working in the nerve centre of Faulkner's administration, the offices of the Ministry of Home Affairs. The IRA leaders were being kept abreast of developments in Faulkner's efforts to convince Heath that internment would be a fatal strike against the IRA.

British government cabinet papers of the day, released in January 2002 under the thirty-year disclosure rule, report that the general officer commanding Northern Ireland, Lieutenant-General Sir Harry Tuzo, had advised Heath against introducing internment. It would be, in Tuzo's opinion, 'counterproductive'. Heath, however, knowing that Faulkner was under pressure from his party's hardliners and was in danger of being dumped, eventually agreed to the unionist leader's request. If Faulkner, Northern Ireland's third prime minister in two years, was to fall, it would almost certainly mean that Westminster would have to impose direct rule and consequently accept total responsibility for the situation.

Heath's decision to go along with internment was to prove one of the most disastrous moves of the Troubles.

'We knew from our source inside Stormont,' says Cahill, 'that Heath had already given the OK for Faulkner to bring in internment. Senior IRA members were instructed in late July not to sleep at home.'

In the last few days of July, hundreds of soldiers took part in a huge raid-and-arrest mission which republicans believed was a rehearsal for the actual internment operation. Many of those arrested in the dawn raids were members of the Official IRA. In any event, the Provisionals escaped relatively unscathed.

It was a different story in the first week of August. Cahill continues: 'Towards the weekend our person at the office of the minister of home affairs told us that internment would be introduced within forty-eight hours. Seán MacStiofáin, who was then chief of staff, travelled with me around the North to the different company areas, giving the general order that no volunteers were to sleep in their own houses.'

Most of those who received the warning did indeed take heed, and those who did not paid a price. At 4.30am on Monday, 9 August, a huge coordinated arrest mission, codenamed Operation Demetrius, was launched. Thousands of troops swept into nationalist areas in cities, towns and villages. Noisy engines in the military's cumbersome 'pigs', as the armoured personnel carriers were known, were switched off well away from the homes of suspects and the vehicles coasted silently to the door.

There was no standing on ceremony. Soldiers had been hyped up to believe they were arresting dangerous activists and could possibly face armed resistance. Doors were sledge-hammered open or knocked off their hinges as the troops took advantage of the surprise element. Many detainees later reported that they believed their homes had been invaded by loyalists. In most cases startled family members, awakened by the sound of shattering glass and splintering wood, ran downstairs to find their living rooms swarming with soldiers. Husbands, sons and brothers were dragged in various states of undress from their homes and deposited in the back of the pigs.

The story of one Belfast man, arrested with his semi-invalid father and schoolboy brother, is typical. Following his release, the man told a human rights inquiry that after being thrown into the pig, they had been driven through a loyalist area before eventually being taken to Girdwood Army barracks in north Belfast:

'The circumstances of our arrest and detention were terrifying. I had recently been reading books about the Holocaust and the Nazis' extermination of the Jews, and when we were being driven through loyalist territory, I thought we were being taken there to be killed. It came into my mind that this was the Final Solution for Catholics.'

This trio was among dozens of detainees who were beaten, degraded and physically and mentally abused at Girdwood and other barracks. The three were released, separately, over the following three days. Others, selected for special treatment, were not to be so lucky.

The Special Branch had intended to arrest 452 men on 9 August, but the final tally that morning was 342. Interrogation revealed that many of those being held were elderly republicans who no longer posed a threat to the state. Others were civil rights campaigners or members of the student-based People's Democracy. A blind man, a chronic asthmatic and a man with a serious heart condition were among those arrested. There were also many cases of mistaken identity.

'There was one old man arrested who had not been active since the Rising in 1916. He must have been the only person lifted that day who was pleased. He was delighted to be still considered a threat to the state,' says Cahill.

Within two days police were forced to release 105 detainees. These men, and many of those interned, were later judged in the courts to have been wrongfully arrested and received compensation.

'Internment failed,' says Cahill, 'because our instruction to stay away from home was carried out. There were one or two people who did stay in their homes and were arrested. Most of the people arrested were ordinary citizens and some, for example, were involved in defence committees. Some volunteers were arrested, but very few. Two, or at the very most three, were senior figures.

'What they [the security forces] were working on were old RUC intelligence files, which they later admitted were far out of date. A lot of the people arrested had been ex-internees and ex-prisoners, people who had not been active for many years.'

Cahill says his own case highlights the dearth of up-to-date information then in the possession of Special Branch. A member of the Army Council and OC of Belfast Brigade, he could have expected to be amongst the first to be targeted for internment.

'I changed house in 1970 from Divis Street and moved to the Whiterock area, and they just did not have a clue where I lived. I suppose, though, it would have been fairly difficult for the Branch and British to gather intelligence, because the no-go areas were in operation at the time.'

'No-go areas' were those districts where makeshift barricades had been set up by residents at the entrances to roads and streets as a defensive measure. They were so called because security forces did not patrol there. These areas developed into havens for the IRA and, to a lesser extent in Protestant areas, the UDA and UVF. The idea of nationalist districts where the Queen's writ did not run was anathema to unionists, who were constantly pressing the British government to tear down the barricades and re-establish a presence there.

Those arrested in and around Belfast were taken initially to Girdwood Army barracks. Here they were herded into a gymnasium and ordered to sit on the floor. Periodically throughout the night, groups were taken outside and, regardless of physical condition, obliged to race around a football pitch, encouraged by military policemen and their attack dogs. Other unfortunates were seated in a helicopter with their backs to the entrance while the machine's engine was revved up for several minutes. Convinced they were hundreds of feet in the air, the terrified men were thrown out, only to discover that they had been hovering six or seven feet above the ground.

Girdwood adjoins Crumlin Road jail and eventually the detainees were chased and beaten, a few at a time, through a newly excavated hole in the wall and along an 'obstacle course in a ditch', into the prison grounds. Many of the detainees, especially those without footwear, sustained injuries from the broken beer bottles and thorny branches littering the route.

Most of these men were either interned in Crumlin Road jail or on the prison ship *Maidstone,* which had been docked in Belfast Lough to await the completion of the internment camp at Long Kesh, twelve miles from the city. A few, however, were singled out for special treatment.

If the GOC Northern Ireland, General Tuzo, was lukewarm about internment, other senior British Army officers connected to military intelligence agencies appeared to welcome the opportunity to research and refine new methods of extracting information from suspects.

The 'hooded men', as they came to be known, were to be used as subjects in an experiment involving a form of interrogation new to the North. These twelve men were suspected by the Special

Branch of being senior IRA members, and were therefore believed to be in possession of valuable information. Thirty years later, some of the men claim they are still not sure where they were held after being hooded and handcuffed and taken from Crumlin Road prison by helicopter.

One of those selected to undergo the new interrogation techniques was Cahill's fellow altar-server, Paddy Joe McClean, the man who had been so shocked to hear a priest say the 'eff' word. McClean, a civil rights activist who espoused non-violent principles, is generally acknowledged to have been subjected to some of the worst treatment meted out to the hooded men.

Palace barracks, the military camp at Holywood, County Down, where Cahill had carried out an arms raid years before, was one of a number of sites used as interrogation centres in August 1971 and afterwards. It is now believed, however, that the men selected to undergo special interrogation were ferried by helicopter to Ballykelly, a large Army base in County Derry. It was only when some of the men were released that details of the technique known as sensory deprivation came to light.

Once inside a large room at Ballykelly, the men were separated. Still hooded, they were stripped naked and dressed in oversized boiler suits. Each man was then spreadeagled against the wall in the search position, legs wide apart, leaning forward at an acute angle with his full body weight resting on his fingertips. The drawstring on the hood was pulled fairly tightly around each man's neck, making breathing difficult.

The prisoners had already become somewhat disorientated on the flight from the jail. Their confusion was compounded when they were subjected to a continuous 'white noise', a sound similar to the hissing sound made by an untuned radio or television, turned up painfully loud. Very quickly the search position became painful and prisoners fell to the ground. Unseen guards punched and kicked the men back into position. Any attempts to move or remove the hood were similarly treated. No prisoner was allowed to sleep.

Limited amounts of food and water were administered by an apparently disembodied hand, with the bottom of the hood being raised to nose level for a few seconds. It later emerged that the food contained little nutrition and had been selected with the deliberate aim of lowering the prisoners' blood sugar levels, helping to weaken their resolve during questioning.

The bizarre experiment began to take its toll. With the blood draining from constantly upraised arms, exhaustion from lack of sleep, the artificial darkness of the hood and the incessant hissing of the white noise, several men began to experience mental problems.

One man reported suffering a hallucination in which he imagined that his dead child was floating through the air towards him. When he attempted to hold out his arms to embrace her, he fell and was beaten. A prisoner who had reached this stage was deemed ready for interrogation. These sensory deprivation techniques went on for eight days.

The Irish government took up the cases of those who suffered sensory deprivation and lodged a complaint with the European Commission for Human Rights, which concluded that Britain was guilty of torturing the prisoners. Later the European Court of Human Rights found that Britain's treatment of the detainees had been 'inhuman and degrading', but fell short of torture.

Meanwhile, the ferocity of nationalist reaction to the reintroduction of internment took the government by surprise. Belfast erupted as news of the arrests spread across the city. In the east at Short Strand, a transport company's premises and a paint store were set on fire. The gates of the local bus depot were smashed open and vehicles were taken out, driven across the entrances to the area and set on fire to create blazing barricades. Soldiers, among them crack assault troops of the Parachute Regiment, were rushed to the scene. They were repelled with barrage after barrage of bricks, rocks and petrol bombs and faced with a determination they had not met before on the streets of the city. The rising smoke in the east acted as a signal to the north and west, and soon the sound of smashing petrol bombs and the thud of brick on armoured plating gave way to the rattle of gunfire across much of the city.

Faulkner's gamble had failed. Far from quelling violence, the one-sided nature of internment had angered even those nationalists who did not support the IRA. The detainees were all Catholics, with the exception of three Protestants – one a member of People's Democracy and the others Official republican sympathisers. Nationalists and republicans were convinced that the troops had been brought in not to act as peace-makers, but to shore up the wobbly unionist regime at Stormont.

At times it must have seemed to the Heath administration that the whole nationalist population of the North had taken to the streets in protest. Internment was to herald one of the most violent periods in the history of the state. In the seventy-two hours following Operation Demetrius, twenty-two people, including a Catholic priest, were killed.

'Heath and Faulkner,' says Cahill, 'were claiming they had smashed the republican movement, but we knew that was not true. Most of our people had heeded the warning and the number of republicans arrested was relatively few.'

On 13 August, Cahill was invited to represent the republican movement at a press conference organised by independent Stormont MP Paddy Kennedy and members of the local Citizens' Defence Committee. The venue was St Peter's school in Britton's Parade, in the Whiterock Road area of nationalist west Belfast. Despite the district being heavily patrolled by security forces, Cahill slipped into the school without event.

'The press conference started out as a drab sort of thing,' says

Cahill. 'It was not originally called to talk about internment. It was to tell what was happening and what nationalists were up against.'

The bespectacled middle-aged man in the cloth cap, seated second from the left in the five-member platform panel, did not immediately attract the attention of the Irish, British and international print and broadcast journalists. Television and newspaper cameras and the attention of the reporters were, in the main, focussed on the panel chairman, the articulate young Republican Labour politician Paddy Kennedy. The others on the platform were John Kelly, the republican acquitted of involvement in importing arms into the Republic the previous year, and Belfast city councillors Eugene McKenna and John Flanagan.

'Brian Faulkner had been on television news programmes saying how successful internment had been and that it spelled the end of the republican movement,' remembers Cahill. 'Things really came to life when one of the press asked about the number of people arrested; if internment had been a severe blow to the IRA; was it the finish of the IRA, that sort of thing.

'The man in the chair, Paddy Kennedy, said, "I can't answer that. The best thing you can do is ask the OC of Belfast yourself," and pointed towards me. The place just erupted then.

'I was able to give facts and figures and actually, because of the warnings, there were very few volunteers arrested that morning. Only about thirty republicans, very few of them members of the leadership, were among the 340 or so arrested. Two volunteers had been killed in the aftermath.'

The reaction to the press conference was little short of sensational, and provided a major propaganda coup for the IRA. Here was the commander of the Belfast Brigade, the IRA's most active component, calmly being interviewed by the world's press and claiming to give the lie to Stormont and Westminster claims that his organisation had been shattered by internment. Paddy Kennedy's throwaway line, 'ask the OC of Belfast,' had transformed

Cahill's casual agreement to attend the press conference into an act of defiance towards the British and an act of reassurance to republican supporters at home and abroad.

As the story was flashed to newspaper, radio and television newsrooms around the world, its significance was being quietly assessed by twenty-nine-year-old Libyan leader Colonel Muammar Gaddafi.

Cahill's new home was quite close to the press conference venue, but it was decided that he would be safer staying in the maze of terraced side streets in the nearby Beechmount area. The guide who took him from St Peter's school across the fields to Beechmount was Gerry Adams, the young man pointed out to him years before by Jimmy Steele.

The day's excitement was not over yet. Later that night, Cahill decided to build on the impact of the press conference by giving a face-to-face interview to Vincent Browne, the northern editor of the Dublin-based *Irish Press*, who had good contacts in the republican movement at the time. Again it was Adams, this time accompanied by a friend, who arrived at Beechmount to guide Cahill back to the Whiterock area for the meeting with Browne.

'We were crossing the football pitch in the dark when gunfire broke out,' says Cahill. 'I knew there were volunteers on the alert for soldiers and loyalist attacks on the area, but this firing was directed at us. It was close and we had to dive to the ground. Eventually we got to our destination. A while afterwards a young guy burst in, full of pride and claiming he had broken up a loyalist attack and "shot three fucking Orangies [loyalists]".'

The British government had fared badly in the publicity battle surrounding the internment debacle. World opinion had swung against them, and the audacity of Cahill in addressing the press conference had further stung security chiefs. Cahill's name was now at the top of the wanted list. His photograph and any personal details known about him were posted in every police barracks and every Army operations room in the North.

In the days following the onset of detention without trial, gun battles between the IRA and the security forces became a daily occurrence, and bombings were commonplace. Loyalist paramilitaries also stepped up their campaign against Catholics. This intensified level of violence was reflected in the casualty figures. In the months between January and August, thirty-one people died. From 9 August to the end of the year, 149 were killed. The four years of internment were to prove the bloodiest period of the troubles. In 1972 alone, 497 people were killed.

'There is no doubt about the intensity of violence following the introduction of internment,' Cahill says. 'A reporter at the press conference had said to me the IRA would not be able to keep up that level of activity. I said I did not expect volunteers to maintain that level of activity, but told him that after three or four days we would return to guerrilla tactics, and that happened.

'I admired the discipline, courage and determination the volunteers of that time showed. The British Army ran amok, went completely mad, and the IRA had to retaliate as hard as they could. It's fair to say that while it is the policy of the IRA to avoid civilian casualties, because of the intensity of the war at that particular time we had to accept that there would be civilian casualties. But certainly they would never be deliberately targeted, not by republicans at any rate.'

✠ ✠ ✠

Shortly after the press conference, the chief of staff, Seán MacStiofáin, asked Cahill to come to Dublin, where his experience was needed at leadership level. The Belfast man was reluctant to leave, feeling that his place at that time was in his own city. He realised, however, that he had become a marked man and his arrest would hand the propaganda initiative back to the British.

He had been keeping a low profile since 1970, but was now, as he puts it, 'fully on the run'. The veteran republican crossed the border many times in the course of the IRA campaign, and it was to be fully thirty years before the security situation and the hectic pace of his lifestyle permitted him and his wife to return to something approaching a settled life in their native city.

'In Dublin, they told me what their plans were and what part they wanted me to play. It transpired that they wanted me to go to America,' he recalls.

The coast-to-coast speaking tour was to take place as soon as possible, and was aimed at briefing American supporters and building on British discomfiture over the internment issue.

'We held a series of meetings to arrange the American trip. It was to be a publicity drive following the furore over the press conference, which had received a lot of attention in the States. Shortly before leaving I did two newspaper interviews, one for the *Sunday Press* and the other for the *Sunday Independent*. The stories were not meant to be published until the Sunday after I had landed in America. I'm not too clear as to the actual days, but the stories were published before they were due. This is what started the Brits blocking me from America. They started screaming their heads off.'

He flew out on 1 September, but was to get no further than New York's Kennedy airport, where he was arrested. Cahill said the resulting publicity provided the republican movement with more newspaper column inches and radio and television airtime than the speaking tour could possibly have done. The British government, alerted to Cahill's travel arrangements by the premature publication of the newspaper interviews, immediately pressed the United States administration to prevent him entering the country, on the grounds that he was a convicted murderer. Banner headlines in practically every British newspaper demanded his deportation. The pressure had the desired effect – Cahill's multiple-visit visa, which he had obtained for his earlier trip to the US, was cancelled while he was in mid-air on his way across the Atlantic.

'I remember when we landed and I was about to come off the plane at Kennedy, I was approached by a member of the Aer Lingus staff, one of the hostesses who was probably based in New York. She said I was wanted in the office and she would take me directly there. I thought this was normal procedure.

'There was a man behind the desk in the office, whom I understood afterwards to be immigration personnel. He asked for my passport; I handed it over, not suspecting that anything was afoot or wrong. He said he was holding on to the passport because the immigration people wanted to see me. Immediately I handed over the passport the guy looked at it and rubber-stamped the word "void" over the visa. He took me to a back office, where several people were waiting – immigration and FBI people. I was told I was being held for illegally entering the United States. I immediately challenged this, but they weren't interested.

'There was no great questioning or anything. I just sat around until I was taken to the Immigration Service's detention centre in Manhattan.'

There then began a week-long series of legal moves and appeals against his deportation. Although he was being held under lock and key, Cahill only needed to indicate his acceptance of the deportation order and he would have been put on a plane for Ireland almost immediately. His lawyer Frank Durkan, though, was intent on exhausting every avenue in an attempt to save the speaking tour. Durkan vowed to take the case all the way to the Supreme Court, but to Cahill that would have meant precious time spent in detention when he could be working for the republican cause back home.

'The weather was beautiful and I was initially allowed out on the roof of the detention centre, but that was stopped after a young

man appeared at a window in a nearby skyscraper and shouted over to me. I waved back and he took a photograph which was widely published. That again infuriated the British press and they all carried stories about sunbathing terrorists.'

Few of the other forty-to-fifty detainees spoke English and Cahill would have been bored had it not been for the constant stream of legal visitors, friends and well-wishers who telephoned or came to see him.

'But not all republican supporters wanted to see me released. A friend of mine, Jack McCarthy, was a trade union organiser in New York. He rang me in the detention centre and said, "I hope they keep you in there for a year. The longer they keep you in, the better. You are worth a million dollars in publicity to us every day you are there."'

Eventually, with applications for parole and bail turned down, it was decided that the legal battle was in real danger of becoming unproductively prolonged. Seven days after the IRA man's arrival in New York, Durkan and government lawyer Vincent Schiano met for a one-hour private discussion before the afternoon session of the appeal hearing. Both men then approached the presiding officer to request an immediate decision. The government lawyer said he was prepared to reduce the grounds for exclusion from the murder conviction to a claim that Cahill 'lacked a valid visa'. Cahill says the lawyer conveniently overlooked the fact that his visa was valid when he left Ireland, but had been declared invalid by the time he landed in New York.

The presiding officer, Special Inquiry Officer Francis Lyons, then ruled that Cahill be deported. Two hours later, he was taken by immigration officials from the detention centre to the offices of Aer Lingus on Fifth Avenue, to be booked on a flight home. New York police were not pleased at the throng of reporters and photographers who disrupted Fifth Avenue rush-hour traffic in a bid to get close to the republican.

Cahill said little to the press, but Durkan told journalists that it was the Belfast republican's own decision not to carry on with the appeal.

'The realities of the situation were that Joe is needed in Ireland. His choice was, he felt he should be there,' the lawyer said.

Cahill's homecoming drew as much publicity as his arrival in New York. An enterprising newspaper photographer booked himself on to the same flight and was rewarded with some fine pictures. It was no surprise to Cahill that among the first to greet him at Dublin airport were members of the Republic's police force, the Garda Siochána.

'I was immediately arrested getting off the plane and taken to the Bridewell Garda station, where I was held on suspicion of being a member of an illegal organisation. I was held for quite a while – a few hours – but not questioned at all. A crowd of supporters had gathered outside the Bridewell and I heard them chanting, "Release Joe Cahill." It was good-heartening. As I was being released, a garda said to me, "There's a big mob out there, go out and quieten them." Another said, "Come on, Joe, we will get you out of here as soon as possible."

'When I went out onto the street, a tremendous cheer went up. I was grabbed by a couple of people, who said they had a car to take me away. We had a bit of bother getting through the crowd, but eventually we got to the car and I was taken to a safe billet in Dublin.'

A meeting of the leadership followed and, says Cahill, there was a short discussion on 'the happenings in America'. Deportation from the United States had ensured that Cahill's name was still very much in the headlines and the republican leadership decided to use the publicity to keep up the pressure on the British government.

'It was decided that the most useful role for me would be to attend a series of meetings in the twenty-six counties, taking in

Tralee in County Kerry, Cork city and Letterkenny in Donegal.'

Cahill was well received in County Kerry and his meeting in Tralee attracted a large crowd. In County Clare he was met by Martin White of Sinn Féin, and they called to see a friend, Denis McInerney from Ennis.

'We all went to Lisdoonvarna for a meal. We were sitting in a restaurant when Denis and Martin told me that they recognised some Special Branch men sitting at a table across the room. The Branch men came over to our table and shook hands and said they were glad to see me. One said they were not there to watch us but were just out for a meal. Before they left, they each made a donation of five pounds to Sinn Féin. That was a fair bit of money in the early 'seventies.

'Martin White then talked about holding a meeting in Lisdoonvarna that night, in the hall where Sinn Féin held their functions. I told him it was not practicable to expect people to go to a meeting which was only being organised at nine o'clock. Martin laughed and told me I would be speaking at midnight. We turned up at twelve o'clock and the hall was packed to overflowing. We had to rig up amplifiers so that the people outside could hear.

'But it was in Letterkenny in County Donegal that we had a really massive crowd. Neil Blaney [the TD and former Irish government minister acquitted of arms importation charges] also spoke from the platform. He told me the meeting had attracted one of the biggest crowds ever seen in Donegal. He said he thought his political meetings were the biggest, but this one was even bigger.

'He told the meeting he was delighted to associate himself with me and he gave his full support to the IRA in the North. He said that if I was not welcome in some parts of the twenty-six counties or the six counties, there would always be a big welcome for me in Donegal.'

Cahill's publicity drive, considered highly successful by the leadership, was to have greater impact than the Belfast man imagined. For it was around this time, Cahill reports, that Muammar Gaddafi's roving ambassador began making contact, through intermediaries, with the IRA man.

But as the year drew to an end and Cahill and the other members of the Army Council reflected on the next stage of the campaign, they couldn't have known that the introduction of internment and its violent consequences would soon be overtaken by dramatic events.

CHAPTER TEN
'A Terrible Anger'

Nationalist rage and frustration over internment had abated little by the new year and an additional slogan, 'Release the Internees,' was added to the banners carried at protest marches.

January 1972 saw fresh evidence of the British government's tough new stance during an anti-internment march to a hastily built detention camp at the remote Magilligan Strand in County Derry. The camp, more than eighty miles from Belfast, had been built to house detainees from the northwest. March organisers were later to claim they had chosen to hold the demonstration on the beach at Magilligan to avoid the possibility of young hotheads clashing with soldiers.

Fighting broke out, however, and soldiers of the Parachute Regiment were accused of heavy-handed tactics when they confronted the protestors and blocked them from the vicinity of the camp. The encounter did little to assuage nationalist anger. But it was another, larger anti-internment demonstration a week later which was to mark the lowest point in relations between the British government and nationalist Ireland for many years.

Joe Cahill was at a meeting of senior republican personnel at a venue outside Dublin on the last Sunday in January. Like most northerners and virtually all republicans during the Troubles, he had become a near-addict of news bulletins. 'It was not unusual for the radio to be kept on during the course of a meeting at that time, because things were happening, day and daily,' he says.

As the meeting progressed, bulletins began to tell of trouble at the big anti-internment march in Derry. Cahill says that by the end of the meeting, newscasters were reporting that several people had been shot dead and many more injured.

'I have a recollection that after the meeting I was travelling back to Dublin with Dave [Daithí] Ó Conaill, who was driving, and we were listening to the car radio. As we were driving along, the numbers mounted. We heard at first there was one dead, two dead, three dead, four dead. Then the death toll reached, I think, seven. It was coming up to six o'clock so we decided to stop at a bar in Ashbourne to catch the television news on RTÉ. The news carried on-the-spot footage. It had the same effect on both of us – we both felt a terrible anger. It was just unbelievable, there were so many deaths. It was a terrible shock when we learned that thirteen had died.'

The television footage was indeed also 'unbelievable' for viewers throughout the country. Following the shootings, which occurred within a sixteen-minute period, stunned Derry people could be seen tending to the dead and dying. It seemed that no matter where the cameras panned, they picked up images of little groups of men and women kneeling, crying and praying by the side of a prone figure lying in a pool of blood. Some of the victims, it transpired, had been shot while going to the aid of the wounded. One of the most poignant, emotive and enduring scenes showed Father Edward Daly, later to become Bishop Daly, accompanying a group of men as they carried the lifeless body of a neighbour to an ambulance. The television camera focussed on the priest, who was obviously still fearful for the safety of his flock. Walking half-crouched and wary, he could be seen waving a blood-stained handkerchief in a cautious and sad little gesture of truce in the direction of menacing paratroopers.

The number of victims of British Army action on what became known as Bloody Sunday rose to fourteen when another man died from his injuries in June. Seventeen others had been wounded. Paratroopers said afterwards that they fired only at gunmen who had attacked them first. No weapons, however, were found on or near the dead.

Cahill remembers that as he and Ó Conaill looked up at the

Above: An IRA volunteer takes aim with her AR18 assault rifle on a west Belfast street corner. This woman was one of a handful who broke away from Cumann na mBan to join the IRA, because they wanted to play a more active role in the campaign. The small group created a precedent, and from then on women played a full part in all departments of the IRA, including active service units.
Photograph: Colman Doyle.

Right: An under-car booby-trap bomb. The magnets held the device in place, and a mercury-tilt switch was activated when the vehicle began to move.
Photograph: Pacemaker.

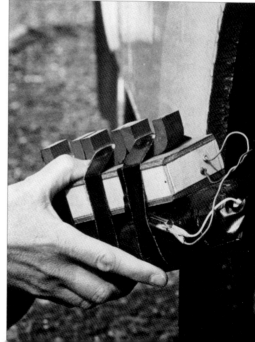

Above: The funeral of veteran republican Jack McCabe, killed in December 1971 while preparing a bomb. Cahill (on the right) helps to fold the tricolour which was presented to McCabe's widow. Photograph: Colman Doyle.
Below left: Muammar Gaddafi, who at the age of twenty-seven led a coup to topple the elderly King Idris of Libya. Photograph: An Phoblacht.
Below right: Sculptor Yann Goulet fled to Ireland after being sentenced to death by both the French government and the German occupying forces during the Second World War. Goulet acted as go-between when Colonel Gaddafi sent his ambassador to contact Joe Cahill. Photograph: Colman Doyle.

Right: Kevin Mallon (with Thompson sub-machine gun) and Brendan Hughes getting into position for an attack on a British Army patrol near Aughnacloy, County Tyrone. Mallon, along with Séamus Twomey and Joe B O'Hagan, escaped by helicopter from Mountjoy jail, Dublin, in October 1973. Shortly after being recaptured, he was one of the nineteen who blasted their way out of Portlaoise prison in August 1974.
Photograph: Colman Doyle.
Below: The funeral of Michael Gaughan as it passed through Dublin, 8 June 1974. Gaughan died on hunger strike in Parkhurst jail, Isle of Wight, in June 1974.
Photograph: Colman Doyle.

Above: Riot police and British soldiers break up an anti-H Blocks protest in Belfast's Ballymurphy area in the late 1970s. Photograph: An Phoblacht.
Below: An RUC man fires a plastic bullet, or baton round, during disturbances in west Belfast in the late 1970s. Photograph: An Phoblacht.

Above: Gerry Adams and Alex Maskey on the campaign trail in west Belfast before the Assembly elections in October 1982. The party, standing on an abstentionist ticket, took five seats with over ten percent of the vote. Photograph: An Phoblacht.

Right: An IRA volunteer taking part in an exercise at a training camp in the Irish Republic. His weapon, an AR18 assault rifle, was one of hundreds smuggled into Ireland from the United States. Photograph: Colman Doyle.

Above: A bomb disposal robot sent to examine a suspect device in Henry Street, Dublin, April 1985. *Photograph: An Phoblacht.*
Left: The result of a republican car bomb, Enniskillen, 5 May 1983. A UDR man suffered serious leg and abdominal injuries in this attack. *Photograph: An Phoblacht.*

Above left: Joe Cahill displays his deportation order from the US
on his arrival at Dublin Airport, 2 July 1984. Photograph: An Phoblacht.
Above right: Cahill's photograph from his fake passport, used to gain illegal entry to the US.
He is wearing spectacles, which he did not need at that time,
and a wig bought in a Dublin department store.
Below: Cahill passes on a little advice to Gerry Adams at the historic 1986 Sinn Féin
Ard Fheis. From left: Martin McGuinness, Cahill, Adams and Danny Morrison.
Photograph: Derek Speirs/Report.

IRA volunteers mingle with the crowd at an anti-internment rally, Belfast, August 1980. Photograph: Derek Speirs/Report.

scenes on the bar's television screen, the Cork man turned to him and said that perhaps good could come out of the terrible slaughter in Derry that day.

'Dave said something like, "This sort of thing will continue to happen until we get the British out of Ireland. But maybe this will bring the whole thing to a head. It will enrage the people of the South and maybe bring about a united effort to get the British out."'

Thirty years later, Cahill still regrets what he sees as a lost opportunity to harness and direct the anger of the Irish people towards rendering the British government's position untenable:

'We were not strong enough at that time to react politically. It has been said often that if we had been in a strong position politically, then we could have taken over the country. The feeling throughout the land was unbelievable. I have never seen such a wave of revulsion against British rule in Ireland. I have never witnessed the like of it before or since.

'I saw sights in Dublin which were really fantastic. The workers of Dublin Corporation, for instance, coming out on a wet day with their yellow waterproof clothing on, it was like an army of people parading down O'Connell Street. No matter where you went in Dublin that day, the day the protest was called, people were walking, marching and chanting in protest.

'And no matter where you went throughout Ireland, you could see the workers coming out onto the streets showing their anger at what had happened. It was amazing. The reports coming into the Sinn Féin offices, the newspapers, television footage, all told of protests and parades held all over the country. Every village in the south of Ireland held a protest. It lasted for three days. There was a terrible anger everywhere. On the day of the funerals all businesses closed down – hotels, stores, everything closed down.

'It proved to me that if we had had political clout, if we had the strength then that we have today, we could have done fantastic things. If we had had a couple of TDs at that stage and a stronger Sinn Féin, strong in different areas, we could have seized the opportunity. We could have given strong leadership, encouraged the people and directed their protest towards the British and British rule in Ireland.'

But there were, Cahill believes, certain events which tempered the anger of the people of the South and drew the sting from their protests:

'With hindsight, and hindsight is a great thing, I think there were two incidents which took the steam out of the protests as far as we were concerned. One was the national day of mourning called by Jack Lynch and the other was the protest at the British embassy.

'I often thought the shrewdest man around that day was Jack Lynch. Lynch was often referred to as a very mild sort of man, but I thought he was a very shrewd man. He saw the dangers of what that day could lead to and I think he was actually afraid at the scale and size of the protests. He defused the situation by calling a day of mourning for the day of the funerals. The perception was that here was Jack Lynch actually doing something, but that – and recalling the Irish ambassador back from London – was all he was prepared to do.'

Three days after the Bloody Sunday killings, Joe Cahill witnessed one particularly vigorous protest, which he recalls with some relish. The incident came at the climax to a protest march which was due to end outside the British embassy in Dublin's fashionable Merrion Square. A section of the 35,000-strong crowd, including several men carrying a mock coffin, managed to get close to the embassy's front entrance. Gardaí, however, had no real concerns about the safety of the building, which was now empty and behind apparently secure fortified doors.

'I was present at the protest at the embassy and I still get a great kick out of it,' says Cahill. 'There was quite a gathering of people outside the building, and quite a gathering of Gardaí. I was standing on the opposite side of the street from the embassy. The Gardaí had cordoned off the street.

'There was an attempt to break down the embassy door with a sledgehammer. There seemed to be a general feeling – I don't know where it came from – that the embassy was going to be burned down or wrecked. A number of senior Gardaí were standing beside me. One said, "I wish to God that whatever is going to happen would happen till I get away home."'

Cahill noted that the police were still not unduly worried when the sledgehammer was produced and the door attacked.

He recalls a Garda officer crossing the road to where he was standing to say: 'They can forget that, boys. Those efforts are futile because the door is reinforced. We don't want to have to arrest anybody here tonight.'

It was at this point, Cahill says, that spectators, demonstrators and police began to realise that those at the embassy doors were not involved in any token protest, but were determined to gain entry to the building.

'There was a small explosion just at the front door. I assume it was part of the plan to open the door. The next thing was that the coffin was carried in and shortly after that the building went up in flames, to the cheers of everybody around – including, I might add, quite a number of the Gardaí.'

The mock coffin, which had seemed so appropriate while being carried through the streets of Dublin, had served another purpose – as a container for the explosives used to blow open the doors and the incendiary bombs which were ignited inside the building with such devastating effect. Vehicles from the Dublin Fire Brigade were quickly on the scene, and probably could have saved the embassy from total destruction had it not been for the intervention of the demonstrators.

'Some firemen got fairly near to the building and rolled out their hoses, but the hoses were rendered ineffective. People cut their hoses to ribbons. People just would not allow them to fight the fire,' says Cahill.

The Irish government paid the British Conservative government £1 million in compensation for the destruction of the embassy. However, in light of Cahill's assertion that the incident acted as a pressure valve for the nation's anger, it was probably viewed by southern political leaders as money well spent.

The political repercussions of Bloody Sunday were to reverberate for many years. An inquiry was ordered by the British government shortly after the killings, but its findings did little to ease Derry's agony. Relatives of the victims were left feeling bitter, angry and betrayed at what they perceived as a whitewash and a cynical attempt at vindicating the senior Army officers and political leaders who had ordered the operation. A series of independent investigations over the years have strongly suggested that the inquiry was indeed flawed and hopelessly biased in favour of the authorities.

In March 2000, following years of campaigning by relatives and human rights groups, a second official inquiry into the events, the Bloody Sunday Tribunal, opened in Derry city. It was expected to last three years. Ted Heath, British prime minister at the time of the shootings, found himself three decades later being grilled by the media about his role in the Bloody Sunday affair, following the publication of secret government papers released under the thirty-year disclosure rule.

There were, however, other, more immediate consequences of the killings. Heath and his cabinet, stung by the international opprobrium being directed at Britain and conveniently overlooking their own role in the Bloody Sunday operation, decided that Faulkner's government could no longer be trusted with responsibility for law and order in Northern Ireland. When Heath announced the transfer of security powers to London, the

Faulkner government refused to accept the decision and at the end of March the British prime minister suspended Stormont, initially for one year. Direct rule from London was imposed as a temporary measure but became a fixture, despite a series of experiments in power-sharing government over the next thirty years. Northern Ireland's one-party-rule system, however, never recovered and was effectively ended by the events of late January 1972.

Brian Faulkner, Stormont prime minister in 1972, died in a riding accident in 1977. In late May 2002, his former principal private secretary, Dr Robert Ramsey, was called to give evidence to the Bloody Sunday Tribunal.

Ramsey recalled that he had telephoned Faulkner to inform him of the happenings in Derry. Faulkner, said Ramsey, was appalled at the loss of life and questioned the British Army's version of events.

'When I told him on the telephone that the first reports were that the Army had returned fire against terrorists, he replied that he could not believe that all, or even most, of the victims had been terrorists,' Ramsey said.

Faulkner's disbelief was reflected in another comment during the same conversation: 'When were a dozen gunmen ever killed in a crowd situation, and with no civilian casualties?'

Ramsey said that Faulkner then went on to predict the political implications of the massacre: 'This is London's disaster, but they will use it against us.'

But Faulkner's private comments were in stark contrast to his public statement just hours after the shootings. 'Those who organised this march,' he told reporters, 'must bear a terrible responsibility for having urged people to lawlessness and for having provided the IRA with the opportunity of again bringing death to our streets.'

Just weeks later the Stormont Parliament was closed down by

Heath's government and direct rule was imposed.

The IRA, meanwhile, was continuing with its devastating car bomb campaign, which had been intensified at the beginning of the year. It was a year of strange contrasts, with unprecedented levels of violence and death running parallel with overt and, in Cahill's case, covert peace-making efforts.

'Around this time, a propaganda war began. The people had to be given some hope, and there were different slogans thought up each year. 1972 was dubbed the "year of victory". The following year it was, "In 'seventy-three, we will be free," and so on. I don't know how they meant to achieve that, but there was a different propaganda line, a war cry, every year,' says Cahill.

But, he recounts, even as the conflict in the North raged on, contacts were being developed on a number of levels between representatives of republicanism, unionism, the churches and the British and Irish governments. These contacts, initially tentative and almost always deniable, led to a series of meetings between strange bedfellows: republicans held meetings with northern Protestant churchmen, a point of contact which continued for the duration of the troubles and with which both sides appeared to be reasonably comfortable. Often a feeling of mutual respect, if not friendship, grew from these talks. Unionists also met British government representatives to discuss the possibility of negotiations with republicans; and unofficial agents of both governments talked secretly to anyone they thought might be useful in bringing about a ceasefire.

Cahill was involved in a number of meetings aimed at ending the conflict. However, his first experiences of negotiating with the British at a high level were to prove disappointing and unproductive.

The behind-the-scenes contacts between the republican leadership and the British resulted in the IRA calling a unilateral seventy-two-hour ceasefire in March 1972. John O'Connell, a

Dublin doctor who was also a Labour party member of the Irish parliament, was in contact with British Labour party leader and former prime minister Harold Wilson. Wilson had lost the 1970 general election to Edward Heath's Conservative party, but was to regain power in 1974. He was leader of the opposition when he made it known to Dr O'Connell that he was keen to explore the possibility of a ceasefire which could enable preliminary peace talks to take place.

Cahill says Wilson, through his own contacts, asked Dr O'Connell to set up a meeting with senior republicans in Dublin during the three-day ceasefire. Even at that early stage of the campaign, Cahill recalls, there was no great belief among the republican leadership that Britain could be driven out of Ireland by force of arms alone.

Tactics for the forthcoming meeting were the subject of an Army Council meeting chaired by chief of staff Seán MacStiofáin. In retrospect, the stance adapted by the IRA may seem to have been uncompromising and to have left little room for manoeuvre, but Cahill maintains it was a true reflection of the republican mood at the time. The three-man IRA delegation was told to demand that Britain recognise the right of the people of Ireland to self-determination, that they should declare a date for British withdrawal from the North, with British troops confined to barracks pending that withdrawal, and should proclaim an amnesty for political prisoners.

'We wanted a general date from them, a statement of intent to withdraw. Withdrawal was never a fixed date. Generally the term used was "within the lifetime of the present parliament" or "within a generation". But it was always realised that we would have to sit down and talk these things out.

'It was never visualised that the British would just pack up and go. In fact I remember discussing with different people the break-up of the British empire. Wherever they left, they left chaos behind, and we did not want to see that happen in Ireland. The phrase we used was always "a phased and orderly withdrawal", to ensure that mayhem was not left behind. I don't think I ever met anybody who said, "We have the ability to drive them into the sea."

'Things are possible now that would not have been possible ten, twenty, thirty years ago. There was a time when the IRA was almost beaten, practically on their knees. But no one doubted that they would come back again and intensify their efforts. The point is, thirty years ago we were not allowed to work politically to achieve our aims. That is the difference today. The system did not allow it. Thirty years ago I would not have dreamed of entering Stormont.'

Harold Wilson, says Cahill, had travelled to Ireland for the meeting, using as cover a series of talks with the leaders of Ireland's three main political parties and an interview with the national television service, RTÉ. The Labour leader let it be known that he and Merlyn Rees, his spokesman on Northern Ireland, had been invited to the home of fellow Labour politician Dr John O'Connell for a drink when he had concluded his business. Wilson accepted the invitation and said he would visit the doctor's home between finishing the television interview and flying home to London.

Cahill and the other republican representatives, Daithí Ó Conaill and John Kelly, were all on GHQ staff, on the run from northern security forces, under close observation in the South and liable to arrest at any moment. Cahill recalls 'wondering about the extent of Wilson's security', as they waited for the English politician to arrive at Dr John O'Connell's large house, near Heuston railway station on Dublin's southside. Chief of staff Seán MacStiofáin did not attend the meeting, explaining that he did not want to leave Wilson open to accusations of meeting the head of the IRA without his government's knowledge.

'I remember,' says Cahill, 'we had been concerned with the

feasibility of setting up the meeting, to see if Wilson would have an escort of Special Branch with him and that sort of thing. We went into the house first, naturally, and he arrived some time afterwards with Merlyn Rees and two other guys, one of whom was his press man.

'Wilson was in opposition at this time and his main interest was to get the ceasefire renewed – it was just about to end. I remember saying, how the hell did he get in without Special Branch? The doctor said it had been easy enough and explained about the tele-vision interview and the invitation to come back for a drink. There was, as it turned out, no bother with Special Branch.

'We met in the sitting room and it was informal. No names were used. There were no introductions. Wilson referred to us as "friends of friends". The first thing that John O'Connell did was bring out the glasses and a bottle of whiskey. We didn't drink. Wilson seemed to be disappointed that none of us took a drink; he was sort of surprised at this. Tea and biscuits were brought in then.'

The IRA delegation did not know it then, but Wilson had asked his Northern Ireland spokesman to enter O'Connell's home first and to perform the introductions in some fashion that would avoid the necessity of handshakes. Rees was to reveal later that he man-aged this by standing in front of Wilson, his press officer Joe Haines and secretary Tony Field and making a casual back-hand movement while intoning their names. Wilson then promptly moved out of handshake distance to the end of the table and across from the republicans.

'I can't remember,' says Cahill, 'what the initial thrust of the thing was, but we had gone along on a listening brief to see what he would say and what his interest was. There was no question of negotiation. Everything was to be brought back [to the Army Council].

'Wilson was interested in a ceasefire. He pointed out that no talks could take place unless there was a ceasefire. He said we needed to have peace to have talks. The atmosphere was quite cordial and quite friendly, although Rees struck me as being a nervous sort of person and appeared to be jittery, ill at ease. Wilson would speak, we would reply and then Rees asked a question or two to clarify our answers.'

There had been a tacit agreement that news of the meeting would not be leaked to the media by either side but, before leaving, Wilson told the republicans he intended to issue a covering statement.

'There was talk that the whole thing would be strictly confidential – no publicity about it, before or after,' Cahill says. 'We always respected confidentiality in these things and never publicised them. But Wilson said before the meeting ended that he would have to make a statement about the meeting. We told him that was up to him. He said he would wait until he got back to England and he did.

'There was damn all came out of it. It was just a talking shop, really. The meeting lasted around four hours and ended about midnight. After we talked to him, he headed off. He left the house first; we remained for some time afterwards.'

But whatever about Cahill's view that 'damn all came out of it', Wilson must have seen some benefit in talking to the republicans because, four months later, he suggested another meeting. This time, however, he wanted to speak to the Irishmen on his home ground.

Cahill's second meeting with the Labour leader came after another, lengthier IRA ceasefire had been engineered to facilitate covert talks between republican leaders and Conservative government minister William Whitelaw. Whitelaw, the first secretary of state for Northern Ireland, had been appointed by Ted Heath to take over the running of the North when the Stormont parliament was mothballed.

Following a series of clandestine contacts between republicans and the British, an open-ended truce was called for 26 June 1972, to enable exploratory peace talks to take place. The IRA agreed to halt all offensive operations and British troops were to cease activities in nationalist areas. A telephone hotline would be set up to permit ready contact between the republican leadership and a representative of the government. Whitelaw, bravely risking the wrath of unionists and fellow Conservatives, agreed to a secret meeting in England with republican representatives. The Irish delegation, headed by Seán MacStiofáin, was flown to England on 7 July for discussions at the London home of Paul Channon, Whitelaw's junior minister at the Northern Ireland Office. Accompanying MacStiofáin were Cork man Daithí Ó Conaill, and Ivor Bell and Séamus Twomey, both from Belfast. Myles Shevlin, a Dublin lawyer with a republican background, was asked along to act as legal advisor and note-taker. The final two members of the group were Derry man Martin McGuinness and Gerry Adams from west Belfast. Adams was released from internment in Long Kesh to take part in the discussions. These last two were in later years to assume leadership of the republican movement.

The London meeting was totally unproductive and the Irishmen were flown home the same day. There were those in the republican delegation who came away convinced that the talks had been an attempt to dupe the IRA and get the measure of some of its most senior figures. The consequences of all of this on the conflict were far-reaching. Republicans believed that the British could be brought to the negotiating table, while the British dug in behind a counter-insurgency strategy, convinced they could win.

Two days after the Whitelaw meeting, the truce, less than two weeks old, broke down in acrimonious circumstances. IRA volunteers were helping to rehouse Catholic refugees in homes which had been abandoned by Protestants on the Lenadoon estate in west Belfast. A British officer at the scene told republicans he had been ordered not to permit the houses to be occupied. A stand-off developed and trouble flared when a Saracen armoured troop carrier rammed a lorry loaded with the belongings of a Catholic family who had been burned out of their previous home. Rubber bullets, or baton rounds, were fired by the soldiers and shots were exchanged shortly afterwards.

As soon as news of the resumption of violence reached Wilson, he and Merlyn Rees visited a dejected Whitelaw in his London flat. Rees said Whitelaw raised no objection when Wilson revealed his intention to meet the IRA leadership again in an attempt to have the ceasefire restored. Prime minister Ted Heath was also informed, but sent a note to Wilson warning that the Labour leader was on his own and that his actions could not be construed as representing the government.

Nine days and forty-two deaths after the collapse of the truce, the leader of the British opposition had once again persuaded Dr John O'Connell to set up a meeting with the IRA. The meeting was to take place in Wilson's country retreat, at Great Missenden in Buckinghamshire. Cahill was the only member of the original delegation to take part in the second talks with Wilson. He was accompanied by fellow northerner and GHQ staff member Tom O'Donnell, and the lawyer Myles Shevlin.

O'Donnell, a veteran republican from the Short Strand in east Belfast, was a quiet, serious forty-year-old who had been in the IRA since he was eighteen. Like Cahill, he had been interned shortly after the start of the '56 campaign. When the Troubles broke out in the 1960s, he abandoned a promising building business to concentrate on his republican activities. An enigmatic figure, he was always careful about his personal security and managed to keep a low profile even though he rose to high rank in the IRA. While Merlyn Rees knew Cahill and had heard of Shevlin, in his report of the meeting he described O'Donnell as 'another Belfast man whom I did not recognise', an omission which would have pleased the Short Strand man. Seven months after meeting Wilson and Rees, O'Donnell was injured in a car crash. He remained in a coma until his death in May 1973.

The IRA team's brief was to play hardball and make the same demands – a date for British withdrawal and so on – as they had at the first meeting with Wilson. It was essentially the same case that the larger republican delegation had presented to Whitelaw a few days previously.

'This second meeting,' Cahill says, 'took place in Wilson's residence, a country cottage. We flew out from Weston airport, a private airport near the Baldonnell military airfield just outside Dublin. They sent a plane over to pick us up – not a big plane, it's a grass runway we are talking about – and we went to England in that.'

Cahill recalls landing at an RAF airfield, which he believes was 'not far from Harold Wilson's home'.

'There were lots of RAF and military personnel and civilians around when we landed. You got the feeling the people in plain clothes were spooks – MI5. We were driven from the airport to Wilson's house; it took around thirty minutes. When we arrived at the house, he was there to greet us. He was very friendly. At this stage names were used.'

It did not enter his mind, Cahill says, that the British would resort to an act of treachery while they had the IRA's second-in-command and an important GHQ officer in their keeping. Wilson was trusted with their welfare, if not with the ability to broker a peace deal.

'We had been fully briefed by the chief of staff after discussions with GHQ. The IRA tactics would be to take a hard line until we found out what he wanted.'

It soon became obvious that what Wilson wanted was another, prolonged ceasefire. He also chided Cahill and O'Donnell about the leadership landing secretary of state Whitelaw in hot water by revealing details of his secret meeting with the other republican delegation.

The IRA had indeed leaked news of the meeting when the ceasefire had broken down, and Whitelaw was forced to make a statement in the House of Commons. The leak, however, was deemed by the IRA leadership to have been well justified. Republicans considered that all bets were off when the truce broke down. Their perception was that Whitelaw had demonstrated bad faith in refusing to help save the ceasefire even though he had been kept fully briefed about the deteriorating situation at Lenadoon. Daithí Ó Conaill had used the hotline on a number of occasions to warn his British contact, a highly experienced MI6 official called Frank Steele, that the truce was being strained to breaking point. On the British side, however, the feeling was that the government had shown considerable latitude in agreeing truce terms and holding secret talks with republicans. In return, they felt they had been presented with a set of demands which were impossible to meet. To give in to republicans at Lenadoon, it appeared to the British leadership, would be interpreted as a sign of weakness rather than willingness to compromise.

Given this background, and the fact that Cahill and O'Donnell were back with an unchanged agenda, the Wilson talks seemed doomed to failure before they began.

'Wilson said that, as opposition leader, he was unable to give the undertakings we wanted. He again asked about the possibility of a ceasefire. We told him that a ceasefire for us was not possible. We told him that the British would have to indicate that they were getting out. That was our bottom line. We did not expect anything to come out of it, but I think Wilson was very disappointed. Again that meeting did not amount to anything. We stayed just a few hours, then went straight back to the plane and home again. I think Wilson said afterwards that he did not get anywhere and, as far as he was concerned, that was his last effort

– he would not talk again to the IRA.'

Cahill says several approaches were made to the IRA around that time by people attempting to initiate peace talks. These were mostly politicians, clergymen, civil servants or government representatives. Occasionally, he says, a request for discussions would come from a more unlikely source.

'Whilst we would explore every approach that was made, we neither ran down nor stepped up the campaign. We always hoped there would be a breakthrough through some of these approaches, but it certainly did not work out that way.

'One of the most surprising mediators was Dame Ruth Railton. She was married to Cecil King, who would have been what is now called a "press baron". She had several meetings with Dave [Daithí] Ó Conaill and myself. She had a big innings [a great deal of influence] with the British prime minister, Edward Heath. This was through classical music. He was into that in a big way and so was she.'

Heath was an enthusiastic and talented organist, who had conducted a number of world-class orchestras over the years. He shared a love of music with Dame Ruth, who was a founder member of the National Youth Orchestra of Great Britain and the National Junior Music School. It was not unusual for Dame Ruth to lunch with Heath or visit him at the House of Commons, and there was little doubt that he valued her opinion on matters other than music.

Her husband, Cecil King, was a man of tremendous political power. In the 1960s he had been chairman of the International Publishing Corporation, which controlled a string of newspapers and magazines, including the *Daily Mirror*, the *Sunday Mirror*, the *Sun* and *People*. Among other appointments, he had also been made a part-time director of the Bank of England.

As the head of a publishing empire, with a direct line to those at the heart of the financial world, King was consulted by the decision-takers and opinion-formers of the day – the leading bankers and industrialists, top trade unionists and the nobility. His views were sought by cabinet members and prime ministers. Harold Wilson, before being replaced as prime minister by Heath, would invite King to his offices in the House of Commons to discuss cabinet changes, industrial relations, the state of the pound or the war in Vietnam.

King's diaries for the years 1965 to 1974 illustrate a man whose finger remained firmly on the pulse of his nation, even though he had retired from the cut and thrust of big business. The former media magnate seemed perpetually engaged in a round of cosy chats with his contacts over lunch or dinner, clearly relishing the power conferred on him through his role as master intelligence-gatherer and disseminator.

Dame Ruth Railton, who Cahill describes as a charming and intelligent woman, fitted in easily with her husband's lifestyle as a power-broker. She often acted as proxy for him, on occasion making the initial approach to a contact and cultivating a friendship before introducing her husband. Dame Ruth also occasionally acted as an unofficial representative of her friend Ted Heath.

King began to pay more attention to Ireland as the situation in the North continued to deteriorate. He was intrigued by the Reverend Ian Paisley, founder and leader of the Democratic Unionist Party and moderator of the Free Presbyterian Church. King felt that Paisley was receiving a bad press – that he did not deserve to be demonised in his role as defender of Northern Ireland against those working for the removal of the Irish border. Dame Ruth made the initial contact with Paisley and before long he was invited to lunch with Cecil King. The men quickly became friends, with King saying in his diary that he would occasionally pick up Paisley at the airport and give him a lift to the House of Commons. Of their first lunch, King wrote: 'He is a nice man – I am sure he is not the thug suggested by ministers and others.'

The Kings became frequent visitors to Ireland, to the Republic in particular, and bought a house just outside Dublin. In 1972 Dame Ruth contacted Cahill and he, after consulting others in the leadership, began a series of meetings with her.

'I met her along with Dave Ó Conaill. She seemed to be a very sincere person and there was no doubt of her influence with Heath. Dave and myself had gone to her house several times quite openly.'

Cahill was still meeting Dame Ruth when he was one of three prominent republicans arrested in early June under the Offences Against the State Act, the Republic's equivalent of the North's Special Powers legislation. He was charged with membership of the IRA and with inciting people to join an unlawful organisation. Cahill's case related to a public meeting in October 1971 in Killarney, County Kerry, one of the venues where he spoke following his deportation from the United States.

'I immediately went on hunger strike. That was IRA policy at the time. All members of the leadership were to refuse food as soon as they were arrested. The idea was to force the authorities to release us rather than risk the consequences of a public uproar if they had let us die.'

The gamble appeared to pay off. Three weeks later his case came before the non-jury Special Criminal Court in Dublin, where a weak, unsteady and underweight Cahill had one charge dropped and was acquitted on the other.

Cahill says Dame Ruth was very concerned at his appearance and state of health when she first saw him after his release.

'She gave me some body-building medication. She offered to get me any medical care that I needed. She was that type of person.'

At another meeting, he says, her impeccable credentials were evident when she was able to make instant contact with the British government at the highest level.

'On one occasion we asked her some question which she could

not answer. She said, "Hold it until I make a phone call," and she called Heath on his direct line from her house. Whatever the British point of view, her interest was to get the war stopped and get a ceasefire. She was certainly very close to Heath.

'Again in hindsight, it may have been a sounding-out by Heath, trying to obtain political intelligence, but I don't think Dame Ruth would have been involved in that knowingly.'

✠ ✠ ✠

Up north, a deadly game of brinkmanship had developed between British Army ammunitions technical officers (ATOs or bomb disposal experts) and IRA engineers, the people responsible for devising and constructing weapons and bombs. The IRA had at this stage moved well beyond its stated aims of defence and retaliation, and was now fully on the offensive. Booby traps, roadside bombs and ambushes were the preferred tactics in rural and suburban areas, but it was in the city streets that the IRA found the banks, insurance offices, manufacturing firms, luxury hotels and department stores, all prestigious targets for their 'spectaculars' in the war on the economy.

The main weapon used in that period was the simple but lethally effective car bomb, which the IRA used to flatten large areas of Belfast. The streets of the city at times resounded to the boom of explosives with the regularity of a busy quarry.

As the manufacturers of the car bomb became more proficient, so too did the ATOs. Initially, the IRA bomb squads set their timers to give a comparatively lengthy warning period, allowing security forces to evacuate the target area before detonation. But when ATOs succeeded in defusing several devices, the IRA replied by reducing the warning period. This was meant to give enough time to clear the area of civilians, but not long enough for the ATOs to carry out the thorough examination needed before attempting to defuse a bomb.

A plethora of hoax bomb warnings – some from republicans, some from disgruntled workers – added to the confusion and, for several hours at a time, often achieved the IRA's objective of bringing commerce to a standstill. The telephoned warnings, evacuations of shoppers and workers, and the race to defuse the bombs became almost a daily routine.

Then, on Friday, 21 July 1972, it all went horribly wrong.

In what was meant to be one of their biggest coordinated attacks up to then, Belfast IRA units planted twenty bombs in a variety of locations across the city. Warnings were given for all the devices, which detonated within a seventy-five-minute period. But soldiers and police were overstretched, and had difficulty coping with so many warnings. At two locations – Oxford Street bus station and Cavehill Road – the devices exploded before the areas could be cleared. Nine people were killed and 130 others injured. The book *Lost Lives* records: 'In many places there was panic and pandemonium as shoppers and others heard bombs going off all over the city. The carnage, with some people blown to pieces, was such that the number of dead was unclear for some time, newspapers at first reporting that eleven people had been killed.'

The date of the tragedy was referred to as Bloody Friday by a government official, who compared it to Bloody Sunday. The name stuck.

The IRA leadership, according to Cahill, were aghast at the catastrophe and ordered an immediate ban on the use of car bombs until further notice.

'The car bomb was a useful weapon, but it was very indiscriminate. You had not enough control over it. The proof of that was when the IRA decided to abandon the use of car bombs. At the start, one warning was given, then two warnings. In the end it was necessary to give three warnings. Even with three warnings, it was too indiscriminate, or things still went wrong. After that it was decided to give it up. The danger of loss of civilian life was too great. The weapon became counterproductive and it was actually banned. Every effort was made to avoid civilian loss, but it was a deadly weapon,' Cahill says.

Northern secretary William Whitelaw was also horrified at the deaths. He was to reveal years later that, following the abortive 7 July talks, he had intended to have the British Army bulldoze the barricades and reoccupy the no-go areas in Derry. Part of his incentive for this was the threat by loyalist paramilitaries that they would smash the nationalist no-go areas themselves if the government delayed. Whitelaw said planning was already fairly well advanced for Operation Motorman (the military code name for the invasion of these areas). Bloody Friday and the propaganda setback suffered by the IRA gave him the opportunity to give the order for immediate commencement.

The operation commenced in the early hours of Monday, 31 July, and involved thousands of troops backed up by light and heavy armour, as well as sailors and marines from a warship berthed in the River Foyle. Motorman had been widely anticipated by republicans and the IRA decided against any set-piece defence of the target areas. Classic guerrilla tactics were to be followed. Volunteers were ordered not to resist the troops, but to blend back into their communities. From Derry city's Creggan and Bogside areas, many republican activists slipped over the border into Donegal to await developments. There were two fatalities, as the massive military bulldozers tore the barricades apart. A nineteen-year-old IRA man died after being wounded in unclear circumstances, and a sixteen-year-old unarmed boy was shot dead by soldiers. Several people were arrested on charges of possessing weapons, but the expected widespread fighting did not take place.

Motorman, one of the biggest military operations mounted by the British in years, went better than both sides expected. Senior Army officers were pleased at achieving their objective with little resistance. Republicans, apart from the Derry deaths, escaped relatively lightly, and there were no mass arrests.

✠ ✠ ✠

The final months of 1972 were particularly busy for Cahill. In addition to his duties as deputy chief of staff, he was becoming more and more deeply involved in the IRA's Libyan connection. While MacStiofáin concentrated on obtaining arms from continental Europe, the Belfast man was intent on pursuing the offer of weaponry from the Libyan government.

In November 1972, Seán MacStiofáin annoyed the Dublin government with an interview on RTÉ. Cahill recalls driving the chief of staff towards Malahide when MacStiofáin asked to be dropped off, because he wanted to walk the rest of the distance towards his destination. MacStiofáin was not to complete that fateful journey. Shortly after leaving Cahill, he was picked up by Gardaí. Charged with IRA membership on the basis of the radio interview and on the word of a Special Branch officer, he was sentenced to six months' imprisonment.

In line with standard practice of the time, he immediately went on hunger strike in protest at his arrest. But the strong-headed Englishman exceeded his remit by also embarking on a thirst strike. A protestor refusing food but taking liquids could survive for several weeks before his life was in danger. Those on hunger and thirst strike seldom lasted beyond twelve days.

By upping the ante, MacStiofáin hoped to bring the matter to a head quickly and alarm the authorities into dropping charges and releasing him at an early date. His tactics, however, did not receive the total approval of the leadership, who frowned on what was perceived as an unsanctioned move and a complication.

Whatever about internal feelings, Cahill says, there was widespread public anger at MacStiofáin's arrest. This intensified as the danger to his life increased, and particularly after he was moved from Mountjoy prison to the Mater hospital.

'There was a hell of a feeling throughout the country after he was lifted, so we gave serious consideration to a proposal brought forward by a young person working at the hospital. The source believed that it was possible to rescue MacStiofáin from the hospital. Naturally, everybody realised the value of this if it could be brought off. A couple of people were selected to organise it. A few plans were set afoot and thoroughly looked at.

'There were such massive crowds on the streets protesting. I don't think they [security forces] anticipated an escape and there was a feeling that there was not that much security on him, so the plan was simply to go in and lift him.'

Cahill says that around ten people were involved in the escape attempt. MacStiofáin would be in a weakened state, so he would be physically carried from his hospital bed by republicans disguised as orderlies and priests. A vehicle was waiting outside to whisk him away to a safe house, where he would receive medical treatment.

MacStiofáin himself remembered very little of the incident. In his memoirs he reports being in a semi-coma, only hazily aware of being moved around in the midst of much commotion and noise.

Cahill, who was not directly involved in the episode, says he is still unsure of the sequence of events. 'The attempt was made to lift MacStiofáin out, but whatever went wrong, I have no idea. I do know that a shot was fired in the hospital, which was disastrous of course, and the attempt failed then,' he says.

MacStiofáin was rushed to a military hospital, where he was guarded by armed soldiers. This period in prison was to result in a falling-out between the former chief of staff and his colleagues on GHQ staff. His hunger and thirst strike was marked by accusations that he took a number of showers every day in order to swallow a little water. MacStiofáin stoutly denied the stories, claiming that while he had access to a bath, there was no shower in the unit where he was being held.

After several mediation attempts by clergy, he ended his protest. Cahill says MacStiofáin's relationship with the leadership had been irrevocably damaged. He was never accepted back into the IRA. Although no longer a member of the organisation he once commanded, he remained, in his own words, 'an unrepentant republican separatist'.

In December a report by a leading British jurist was to lead to the introduction of a controversial piece of legislation, which was to bedevil the republican movement for the following twenty-five years. Lord Diplock had been invited to set up a commission to look at 'more effective means of combating terrorism'. The awkwardly-titled 'Report of the Commission to Consider Legal Procedures to Deal with Terrorist Activities in Northern Ireland' was duly included in the 1973 Emergency Powers Act. The arrest procedure was simplified, to the extent that a suspect could now be locked away on the word of a soldier. In cases of weapons possession, the concept of guilty until proved innocent was turned on its head, with the onus on the suspect to prove that he or she was innocent. Confessions were automatically considered admissible unless the suspect could prove that the statement had been extracted under torture. The Diplock courts, as they became known, also differed from normal courts of law in another respect: juries were dispensed with, verdicts being reached by a single judge. It was an effective system and took its toll on the IRA. In the twelve months following April 1973, almost 1,300 people were sentenced under the new law.

The final weeks of 1972 saw Cahill confirmed in the post of chief of staff. The year had proven to be the bloodiest and most violent of the Irish Troubles, with 497 people killed. The IRA lost seventy-four members and was responsible for 235 deaths. Casualty figures were never to reach the same terrifying heights again.

A few weeks into 1973, the new chief of staff began finalising preparations for a trip abroad which, if it went well, would provide the IRA with as much arms, ammunition and explosives as it needed. In late February Joe Cahill, now approaching his fifty-third birthday, set off on his long-delayed and fateful journey to Libya.

CHAPTER ELEVEN
The *Claudia* Affair

Muammar Gaddafi, born in Libya's northern Sirtica region in 1942, was a zealous young man, proud of his Arab heritage and with the fire of republicanism burning fiercely in his heart. At the age of twenty-seven, he led a group of young army officers in a coup which toppled the country's monarchy while the elderly King Idris was abroad.

The following year, 1970, Gaddafi became chairman of the Revolutionary Command Council. He began implementing his policies of Arab nationalism and Islamic socialism, in an effort to improve the lot of the people of what was to become the Popular Socialist Libyan Arab Jamahiriha.

Believing that he had seen his country safely on the right path, Gaddafi looked around for other causes to espouse. Joe Cahill's nerve in appearing at the Belfast press conference while on the run, and his high international media profile following his deportation from the United States, drew the admiration of the new Libyan leader.

Cahill, immersed in helping to arm, train and reorganise the IRA, knew nothing of Gaddafi's enthusiasm for the Irish republican cause until he was approached by an unlikely intermediary.

'The first thing I knew about Gaddafi's interest,' Cahill says, 'was when a man – a Breton national, a sculptor who lived in Bray – approached me. He in turn had been approached by someone from Libya who said his people were very anxious to contact me because they wanted to help the IRA. The Libyan wanted to know if it was possible to set up a meeting with me.'

The go-between was Yann Goulet, an artist who had settled in Ireland after the Second World War and went on to become a highly respected sculptor. Goulet was immediately attracted to

Irish republicanism and this was reflected in his work. The piece of which he was proudest was the Glory memorial in the staunchly republican County Armagh village of Crossmaglen. Goulet took great delight in the fact that his work, dedicated to the memory of local republican dead, was erected in the middle of the night in the village square, just yards from the heavily fortified British Army–RUC base.

A leading member of the separatist movement in Brittany during the Second World War, he had had many narrow escapes in the struggle against the German forces occupying France. Goulet was eventually imprisoned and went on hunger strike. On his release, his activities again led to him being hunted by both Germans and French. Condemned to death in his absence, Goulet fled France for Ireland.

Goulet was recognised as a sculptor of some importance in Ireland and won his first major commission in 1950, when he was asked to design a memorial to the Old IRA's Dublin Brigade at the capital's Customs House. However, Goulet never lost interest in the struggle for an independent Brittany, confiding to close friends that he had been involved in a brief Front de Liberation de la Bretagne campaign, which fizzled out after a series of bombings in 1967.

In 1971, although by now a well established figure on the Irish art scene, he did not hesitate when asked by Gaddafi's roving ambassador – an equally colourful figure, who had served in the Algerian government under President Ahmed Ben Bella – to relay a series of messages to the IRA.

Cahill, who was keen to equip the IRA with the best weapons available, had been taking chances since he was a boy in Na Fianna Éireann. Deciding he had nothing to lose, except, as he says, his life or his freedom, he immediately agreed with Goulet's suggestion that he meet the Arab.

'Naturally, I told the go-between that I would be happy to meet the Libyans' representative. However, nothing really happened until December 1971, when this roving ambassador for Gaddafi arrived. I can't remember his name, but I believe he had been a member of the old Ben Bella government. After the fall of that government, he was appointed by Gaddafi to work for him and that work took him to Ireland and throughout the world.

'Jack McCabe, the IRA's quartermaster general, and I eventually met him and we talked through an interpreter. The emissary told us that Gaddafi was very interested in the Irish question, would like to help and would like to meet me and whoever else came with me. Seán MacStiofáin was chief of staff and I reported back to him.

'Actually, at that time – late 1971, early 1972 – the IRA was working on another method of getting arms into Ireland. They were attempting to bring arms in through, I think, Holland. MacStiofáin was working on this other method and, although he was interested in the Libyan offer – on the basis that we should not put all our eggs in the one basket, the Libyans seemed to be left hanging in the air.'

✠ ✠ ✠

It was during this period that Cahill's now legendary capacity for survival was to be tested again. Hunted by the British Army and the RUC in the North, he arranged for his wife and children to travel to Dublin for a family reunion over Christmas. The Belfast man and his close friend Jack McCabe, a lifelong County Cavan republican, had been working together making the explosive 'black mix', the main ingredient in the massive fertiliser-based bombs then being used by the IRA north of the border.

The men used a garage in the Ballymun area, on the northern outskirts of Dublin city, to fill the orders, which came regularly from northern active service units. The black mix was then smuggled north, where the addition of a small amount of commercial explosive and a detonator was enough to convert it into a cheap but highly effective weapon of destruction.

McCabe was a veteran of the IRA's bombing campaign in England before the Second World War and served several years in prison there. He continually refused to give an undertaking to stay out of England as a condition of release and, as a result, was one of the last republicans to be freed. A traditional republican, he was totally opposed to the politics of the republican leadership in the late 1960s and, along with Cahill, helped to reorganise the republican movement into what became known as the Provisional IRA.

Described by colleagues as a warm and generous man, McCabe immediately offered the use of his Dublin home to the Cahill family for their Christmas visit while he and his wife stayed elsewhere. The reunion was to be an eventful one. To ensure Cahill as complete a respite as possible, McCabe said he would deal with any IRA business while keeping Cahill's whereabouts 'on a strictly need-to-know basis' for a few days.

Shortly after his family arrived, and despite McCabe's best efforts, Cahill was forced to interrupt his break – Gaddafi's representative was in Dublin and wanted to see him. Cahill had not seen his family in months, but the meeting with the Arab was too important to miss.

Cahill and McCabe had a 'very good' meeting with the roving ambassador, during which they were told that Gaddafi was extremely interested in meeting Cahill. The Belfast man then returned to his family in McCabe's house. Meanwhile, another request for a consignment of black mix had arrived from Belfast. It was a small amount – 'twenty pounds or so,' McCabe told Cahill – and not worth a further interruption in the Cahill family's visit.

The quartermaster general refused Cahill's offer of help, saying he would have no trouble filling the order on his own. Besides, as McCabe pointed out, the Belfast man had spent very little time with his family so far.

It was to be Jack McCabe's last task for the IRA. The mixture ignited when McCabe's shovel came into contact with the concrete floor of the garage and created a spark. Engulfed in flames, McCabe is said to have rushed outside and shouted a warning to playing children, telling them to 'get away'.

Cahill heard of the explosion on a midnight news bulletin and rushed to McCabe's family.

'It was Jack himself who told us what went wrong. I heard that he kept calling for me. Knowing he was dying, he told Paddy Ryan [another IRA man] to let me know that he had made the fatal mistake of not doing the mixing on the usual eight-foot-by-four-foot sheet of plywood. He wanted to make sure that no one else ever made the same mistake.

'I helped make arrangements for his funeral. Jack was a Cavan man and wanted to be buried in his home county. Word came as we travelled to Cavan that there was a very heavy Garda presence in the cemetery. The cortège was stopped en route and a couple of people approached Jack's remains and fired a volley of shots over the coffin. But as it turned out, there was a huge crowd at the cemetery, thousands of people, and the Gardaí were pushed back for a second volley to be fired. Jack is the only man I know who was honoured twice in that way.'

✠ ✠ ✠

After his friend was buried, Cahill was itching to get the Libyan operation off the ground, but found it difficult to fit the trip in with his other duties. As the months passed, a number of republican leaders made the journey to Libya, but Gaddafi insisted on dealing with Cahill, whom he respected and believed he could trust.

Cahill, now chief of staff of the IRA, made his influence felt quickly when, at either the first or second Army Council meeting following his appointment, it was decided that the IRA would carry its war to England. MacStiofáin had often come under pressure from his colleagues to attack targets in England, but had urged restraint, arguing that such a strategy should only be adopted as a last resort.

MacStiofáin's main objection to direct attacks on England had concerned the difficulties and logistics of carrying on a sustained campaign there. Such a campaign, he had reasoned, should be held in reserve in case a time came when the IRA found it impossible to operate in the North. Other members of the Army Council, particularly those from the North, respected his opinion but had made no secret of their belief that the way to hurt the British most would be to carry out a series of 'spectacular' attacks, preferably in London.

MacStiofáin had made just one exception to his ruling, when he sanctioned the formation of a special unit to carry out an assassination attempt on the life of the British Army's Brigadier Frank Kitson in his own home. Kitson was seen as a particularly apt target, because he was widely believed to have been the brains behind the 'psy-ops' (psychological operations) counterinsurgency campaign. The activities of these operatives ranged from the mental and physical ill-treatment of captured suspects during the introduction of internment to the establishment of clandestine undercover military groups which 'kept the pot boiling' by killing innocent nationalist civilians.

MacStiofáin's arrest removed any opposition to extending the campaign across the Irish Sea. A special Overseas Unit was set up under the command of a senior volunteer, who was appointed 'OC England'. The unit's staff had a free hand, within a strict set of criteria laid down by the Army Council, in selecting military and economic targets for attack. The OC England's brief was broad, recommending the bombing of prestigious industrial, commercial and military targets as well as any 'spectaculars' which would command international attention. The brief, Cahill says, also included an order that all possible steps be taken to avoid loss of civilian life. However, despite this order, many people were killed and back in Ireland a great deal of time was taken up with inquiries into operations that went wrong.

✠ ✠ ✠

It was around this time that contact was re-established with Libya through the sculptor. Word came back that Cahill should make every effort to get to Tripoli. There followed a delay of several unproductive weeks, before Colonel Gaddafi sent a message reiterating his interest in meeting Cahill specifically. The message ended with the intriguing promise that if the IRA chief could somehow manage to get to Libya, 'everything would be possible'.

Once the IRA Army Council decided it was worth the risk of allowing Cahill out of the country, the republican machine swung into operation. As one team began to make arrangements for the four-man IRA group to travel incognito to Libya, another set about providing passports.

These were genuine documents, obtained either by deceit or supplied by sympathisers and doctored by an IRA specialist. The donor's photograph – at that time it was glued to the document – was peeled off and substituted with a picture of the republican. The official state stamp was forged simply by placing a specially prepared Irish coin bearing a harp on the document and hitting it with a hammer.

Cahill flew to France in a small private plane, which took off from County Cork. His companion on the tiny four-seater was a legitimate businessman and republican sympathiser who made the trip to France regularly and was so-well known that he did not have to go through customs. This suited the Belfast man admirably, although the weather did not:

'On the way over, the plane was bobbing up and down like a yo-yo. I am not normally troubled by flying, but this trip was a nightmare. It didn't help when the pilot told us to put on our life jackets – not the seat belts, mind you, but life jackets.'

At another small airport in France they were picked up and taken by car to Paris, where Cahill met up with members of the earlier delegation. With three others, he then set off on the road to Rome. From Rome the group flew to Tripoli, where they were met by officials of the Libyan government.

'We were treated like foreign dignitaries and were taken by Mercedes to a villa, complete with cook and staff to look after us. Colonel Gaddafi was not in the capital at the time; we spent five or six days waiting for him to return,' Cahill says.

The republicans were treated with kindness and courtesy and their wait, in the main, was uneventful.

'Quite unlike a later trip to Libya, when there was one incident which caused us considerable alarm and consternation. We were again treated well and, while we waited for Gaddafi, we spent some time listening to a Libyan radio station which broadcast in English every day. One particular day we were scheduled to have a meeting with Libyan officials, who told us they would pick us up at eight o'clock that night. All that day, every hour or so, the station broadcast an announcement to the effect that an important Irish guest had arrived and would be interviewed live on the radio that night.

'We were intrigued as to who this guest could be, and we told each other there was no possibility the Libyans would ever contemplate doing a dirty-joe [Belfast slang for an act of betrayal] on us. It would have been foolish in the extreme and would have jeopardised the whole operation if I had been asked to go on the air live.'

The Irishmen were further concerned when their hosts did not arrive at the villa at the specified time. Cahill remembers: 'I said to the others, "Surely to Christ they are not going to go public with this." We listened to the programme, wondering if the operation was about to go down the tubes. There was huge relief when the important guest was finally introduced. It was the journalist and broadcaster Tim Pat Coogan, who was then editor of the *Irish Press*. He had come to Tripoli for an interview with Gaddafi and had been asked to take part in the radio discussion.

'On that first trip we were eventually taken to a military barracks for the meeting with Colonel Gaddaffi. I have to say I was impressed with his grasp of the situation in Ireland and his friendliness.

'He was not aloof in any way, but was a very down-to-earth guy, easy to talk to. He spoke through an interpreter. He had perfect English, but would not use it. He had an awful hatred of England – we never really got down to discussing why. It was obvious that he had perfect English because his answers came back before the interpreter had finished translating. The interpreter later confirmed to us that Gaddafi had good English. Gaddafi said he did not understand why we did not speak in Irish, and why did we speak in English, the language of our enemies.

'He was quite open about his reasons for wanting us in Libya. He said he wanted to help us because he believed in the cause of the IRA and that Ireland had a right to freedom. He could not understand why the twenty-six-county government had not done anything about the reunification of Ireland. He seemed to have a great knowledge of the whole thing. He said he would be glad to help in any way that he could.

'I said we would be glad to accept help from him, but there could be no strings attached. I made that very, very clear, but subsequently we found there was never any question of strings being attached to his offer. My impression was that the man was very genuine. Libyans had obtained their freedom and they wanted to help other countries which were struggling for their freedom. He did tell me that he was interested in other liberation movements throughout the world. He said he believed the IRA were sincere, they were genuine, they were dedicated people who were committed to bringing about the reunification of their country.'

Gaddafi then asked the Irishmen to present their 'shopping list'. Cahill gave the Arab leader a list of what he believed was needed to make an impact on the British – short-arms, assault rifles, general-purpose machine guns and explosives. There was no request for rocket launchers at that stage, because the British Army was not yet using helicopters as extensively as they did in later years.

Part of the delay in getting Cahill to Libya was caused by difficulties in finding a safe means of transporting the arms back to Ireland. The delegation which had gone out before Cahill to spearhead the operation eventually tasked a German IRA volunteer to organise transport in the event of the meeting between Cahill and Gaddafi being productive. According to Cahill, it was this man, known to the others simply as 'the German', who organised the leasing of the *Claudia*.

'I have no idea what the finer details were that lay behind the acquiring of the ship. What I do know is that we left it entirely up to the German. Our people had met the Libyans before I went out, and it was decided that a boat should be moored outside Libyan territorial waters and the stuff could be transferred at sea. After I had met Gaddafi, we arranged that a radio signal from the *Claudia*, by this time just outside the limits, would let us know when to give the Libyans the go-ahead to head out to sea with the arms.

'When the people on board the *Claudia* could not make contact, they headed into Tripoli, which they should never have done. It was never intended that the boat would go into Tripoli. That was to be the safeguard for the Libyans, but the ship arrived in the harbour and there was a bit of a panic. The Libyans were fair enough. They said they would load the ship where it was. However, for reasons which I did not discover until years later, they did not supply all they said they were going to supply.'

The Irishmen were somewhat disappointed, but decided that what was on offer was much better than nothing. While the Libyans had slashed the cargo to about one-eighth of the original, the IRA would still have five tons of pistols, rifles, ammunition and a small amount – 'a couple of hundredweight' – of explosives. The Irishmen were present while Libyan soldiers loaded the weapons onto the ship under cover of night, but they did not see much of the operation.

Cahill discovered the reason for the reduced shipment when, undaunted by his arrest and conviction for the *Claudia* episode, he accepted an invitation from Gaddafi to return to Libya in 1975:

'On my second visit to Tripoli, almost three years later, I met Gaddafi again and he explained that they had initially been very worried about the ship. He said they had checked out the *Claudia* and discovered that it had a notorious international reputation and had been involved in smuggling operations – cigarettes and stuff like that. Not wanting to tell us to hump off, the Libyans decided to take a chance and give us a certain amount of stuff, even though they knew there was a chance it would be lost. If it got through, well and good. To us, that was an indication of their sincerity in their dealings with republicans.'

Although Cahill, a non-swimmer, hated the sea, it had been decided that the safest way back to Ireland for him and two of his colleagues would be on the *Claudia*. As a child on holiday in the Glens of Antrim, Cahill had caught cramp while bathing in the Irish Sea at Glenarm and had had to be fished out. And when the *Claudia* was to run into foul weather in the Bay of Biscay, he could not help remembering the stories told by his elderly relatives of an uncle, a merchant seaman, who had perished in the same waters.

But his quarters were clean and tidy, and the food was good enough. When the weather behaved, he enjoyed the company of his colleagues and the boat's crew, getting on particularly well with the master, Hans-Ludwig Fleugel, and his brother, the first mate. To take his mind off the sea, there was always the thought that the arms consignment under his feet would make a significant difference to IRA units in the North, who were under heavy pressure from the Army, police and legal system.

The Irishmen were alarmed momentarily when the captain revealed that he had spotted a submarine as the *Claudia* cruised through the Mediterranean. Cahill, his instincts honed by years of clandestine operations, immediately suspected that their movements were being followed by the Royal Navy.

Fleugel, however, assuaged his fears by telling the men that the submarine was unlikely to be British. The Russian government, he said, often sent submarines to the area for intelligence-gathering purposes.

'We did not pay a lot of attention to it after that and were quite confident we were going to make it to Ireland,' Cahill recalls. A few days later, 17 March, the Irish national saint's day, Cahill says, was one of his best days in years.

'On St Patrick's Day, we felt good, out in the sun on the deck as we sailed through the Mediterranean watching the tuna. It was a happy Saint Patrick's Day for me.'

But the fine weather was not to last and conditions deteriorated badly when the coaster left Portugal behind and entered the waters of the Bay of Biscay. The storm raged on and at one stage, as they neared Ireland, the *Claudia*'s master was forced to divert from his course and run for the shelter of the Welsh coast.

Eventually arriving off the Waterford coast towards the end of March, the republicans were further frustrated when they were forced to put out to sea again for twenty-four hours because the cargo could not be unloaded in such heavy weather. Equally frustrated were anxious IRA volunteers gathered at Helvick Head, where they had arranged for a fishing launch to meet the *Claudia* and guide her into the little harbour.

'The communication problems which had dogged us in Libya returned and we were unable to make radio contact with our people on the shore at Helvick,' Cahill says.

On 29 March, the *Claudia* was spotted by the watchers in the harbour and the launch was despatched to meet her. It was not only the republicans on shore who waited for the vessel, however. Three ships of the Irish Naval Service – two minesweepers, the *Gráinne* and the *Fola*, and a fishery protection vessel, the *Deirdre* – had kept a stealthy watch on the gun-smuggling operation. Cahill's instincts about the submarine in the Mediterranean had been correct and its commander's running reports on the *Claudia*'s progress since it left Libyan territorial waters had ensured a hot reception for the Irishmen.

'The people who came out on the fishing launch,' Cahill says, 'knew nothing about the Garda and naval operation. They informed us that everything on shore was perfect, everything was ready for the dispersal of the cargo. There was not even a sign of a customs man, they said. But the Gardaí had kept their operation so tight that no one noticed they had dozens of soldiers and police all around the place. One of the boys on the launch stayed with us and one of our people from the boat left on the launch to begin the operation on the shore. We were still quite happy that all was in order and the operation would be a success.

'Myself, Garvey and Murphy were talking when the captain came in and said there were some people who wanted to talk to us. Before he could say any more, a gun was stuck to my head and I was told not to move. It was quite a shock. The crew and the captain said they did not even see them approaching the boat.

'I told the young fellow with the gun to wise up and take the weapon away from my head. He did so after I told him I was unarmed. They were actually quite civil after that.'

Meanwhile, another drama unfolded when the *Gráinne* and the *Fola* were ordered to intercept the launch before it reached shore. Apparently ignoring commands to stop, the launch was racing at its best speed for the harbour when the minesweepers opened fire with tracer rounds. Naval gunnery officers later told of aiming ahead of and around the launch, but, despite the intimidating water spouts raised by the rounds, the helmsman refused to heave to. It was only when a high-speed rubber dinghy from one of the ships sped alongside the launch, and a further two shots were fired at close range, that the vessel eventually came to a halt.

Sharp-eyed Irish sailors, however, had spotted something being thrown overboard from the launch. After the arrest of Cahill and his colleagues, a government diver was sent down to search for the mystery object, but found nothing.

'The object thrown overboard,' says Cahill, 'was a sealed box containing between £40,000 and £50,000, in sterling, I think. It had been given to the boys on the launch to take ashore separately. A few days later, with us in jail and things a bit quieter in Helvick, the IRA sent down their own diver and he recovered the box and the money.'

So sudden and unexpected was the appearance of the boarding party that the republicans had no chance to carry out a pre-arranged plan to scuttle the ship if there was a danger of the weapons being captured. Enough explosives had been provided to rip open the *Claudia*'s hull, but they were not in a state of preparedness when the Irish navy struck. Alternatively, if there had been time and enough clear water, the IRA team had planned to run for the open sea and the safety of international waters. The *Claudia* experience was a costly lesson for the IRA. Volunteers accompanying every arms shipment from then on were ordered to have mines prepared which could be used to sink their vessel at short notice.

On 21 May 1973, Joe Cahill was sentenced to three years' penal servitude for his part in the *Claudia* gunrunning operation. Denis McInerney, from County Clare, and Seán Garvey, from Kerry, each received a two-year sentence. Donal Whelan and Gerald Murphy, both from County Waterford, received suspended sentences of two years. Whelan was also suspended for seven years from his job as headmaster of a Waterford vocational school. The crew of the *Claudia* were exonerated after Cahill claimed total responsibility for the operation.

The sentences were short by later standards, but were in line with the punishments being handed down in the Republic in that era. If caught in the North, the men could have expected much heavier sentences.

Cahill recalls with a hint of a smile: 'Donal Whelan's job was continually advertised, but no one ever applied. When the seven years were up, there was only one application and that was from Donal Whelan and he was reinstated.'

During the trial, the court heard that the *Claudia*'s cargo hold and life boats contained 250 rifles, 246 bayonets, 850 rifle magazines, 243 pistols, more than 20,000 rounds of ammunition, 100 anti-tank mines, 500 high-explosive grenades, gelignite and TNT explosives, primers, cortex fuse, electric fuse and material for making booby traps.

Told by the judge there was no doubt that he was the ringleader of the operation, Cahill replied: 'You do me an honour.'

Later, in a speech from the dock, Cahill said: 'All my life I have believed passionately in the freedom of my country. I believe it is the God-given right of the people of Ireland to determine their own destinies without foreign interference and, in pursuit of these aims and ideals, it is my proud privilege as a soldier of the Irish Republican Army, just as I believe it is the duty of every Irish person, to serve or assist the IRA in driving the British occupation forces from our shores.

'If I am guilty of any crime, it is that I did not succeed in getting the contents of the *Claudia* into the hands of the freedom fighters in this country. And I believe that national treachery was committed off Helvick when the Free State forces conspired with our British enemies to deprive our freedom fighters of the weapons of war.'

Cahill says he did not allow the capture of the arms shipment and his arrest to depress him. He admits, however, that as he lay in his prison cell on the first night of his sentence, he consoled himself with thoughts of a previously undisclosed arms-smuggling operation which met with considerably more success.

Again Cahill was in charge of the operation and again it involved a consignment of Libyan arms.

Two Canadian mercenaries, a pilot and co-pilot who had the use of a small aircraft, were hired to collect cargo comprising one ton of weapons and explosives from Tripoli and take them to southern Ireland.

'This operation took place about six months before the *Claudia* incident. Although the two guys were mercenaries, we found them to be very genuine and sincere in their dealings with us. We never had any doubts about their honesty in the operation and we had no worries that they would attempt to sell us out.

'The plane flew directly to Libya and loaded up there. We had arranged for the weapons to be landed at a small airport in Farranfore in County Kerry. The airport operated only during the day. We planned to take over the airport for the night and set up our own lighting system to mark out the runway. But on the night the plane was due, it was really wet, a real bad night with a thunderstorm raging. One of our volunteers was aboard the plane, which we could hear circling overhead. But, as with the *Claudia*, we had trouble establishing radio contact.'

With his aircraft running low on fuel and unable to see the runway, the pilot told his republican passenger he would have no alternative but to abort the operation and divert to the international airport at Shannon. The airport authorities readily gave permission for the aircraft to land. 'They regarded us,' the pilot told Cahill later, 'as a couple of crazy but harmless Yanks who were flying around the world.'

The IRA man on board the aeroplane knew there was every chance he would be recognised by Shannon security personnel. He bade farewell to the Canadians and jumped from the aircraft when it touched down, but before it had come to a halt. Although injured in the incident, he managed to run from the glare of the runway lights and make his way to the perimeter fence. Once over the fence, he was in familiar territory and made off into the night.

After completing formalities at the airport, the Canadians left their craft and its illicit cargo at Shannon and booked into a hotel to rest up and await developments. Meanwhile, the injured IRA man contacted Cahill and outlined the situation.

'More gloomy news came when the local OC told us he had been to the airport to study the situation. He had talks with republican contacts there and he was absolutely sure there was no way to get the stuff out,' says Cahill.

Listening to a news bulletin on a radio in a safe house nearby, Cahill heard a report of an explosion in Belfast. A bomb had been detonated in Belfast city centre, inside the newly erected and tightly guarded 'ring of steel' – a network of high steel railings and gates designed to protect the city's main banks, stores and businesses which, in IRA terms, were prestigious 'economic targets'.

The report claimed that schoolboys, members of Na Fianna Éireann, had passed the bomb components through the railings to republicans inside the high security zone, who then re-assembled and detonated the device. According to a person who was present in the safe house, Cahill turned to the local OC and said: 'If the fucking school kids in Belfast can do that, you can get the fucking stuff out of the airport.'

The OC replied that there was one man he wanted to speak to before the operation was abandoned. 'If there is any way to get the arms consignment out of Shannon, this guy will know,' he told Cahill.

Eventually the man, a long-established worker at the airport, was contacted and did indeed come up with a plan. If the plane was taken to a particular hangar at the airport complex, ostensibly for repairs, the situation might well be saved. Asked to cooperate, the pilot assured the republicans that he would 'have no problem developing engine trouble'. The unsuspecting authorities again granted the necessary permission and the plane was moved to the hangar.

As Joe Cahill and his colleagues waited anxiously, a service van driven by a man well known to the customs men at the airport pulled up close to the hangar.

'He somehow connived to get the empty van into the hangar. I don't know to this day how he managed it, but he did. He loaded the stuff into the van and, as he drove out, the customs men knew him so well that they actually saluted him as he passed,' Cahill says.

The elation of IRA personnel at the turnaround in their fortunes was to be dampened shortly afterwards. The arrangement with the pilot was that he was to be paid half his money before setting out for Libya and the rest when the operation was completed and they had returned home. The co-pilot, however, was unhappy about waiting until he returned to Canada to be paid the remainder, and suggested that he and his friend stay in Shannon until the republicans could raise the rest of the cash. According to Cahill, the delay was to prove fatal:

'The storm had eased for a while but, even though it was raging again, the Canadians were anxious to get home after being paid. We suggested that they stay in Ireland for another twenty-four hours to await better weather. The co-pilot in particular wanted to go home as soon as possible and they headed off. They ran into a very severe storm over the Atlantic. We heard shortly afterwards from our contact in Canada that the plane had gone down and the two men were lost.'

CHAPTER TWELVE
Missing the Flight

Cahill found many old friends in Mountjoy prison, including several from Belfast and other areas of the North, and had little trouble settling into the routine. In early June, however, just over two weeks into his sentence, he was to receive bad news from home – his mother had died.

'We were always close as a family and news of Mother's death came as a bad blow. It was my intention to apply for parole and travel to Belfast for the funeral, but it didn't work out like that. In fact, there was a bit of controversy over the application.

'I went before the governor, who told me parole had been granted, I think for forty-eight hours. Normally in these cases, the RUC in the North would recognise parole granted in the South and would not bother someone who came up for a funeral, even if they were wanted there. But the governor said he had been told – and it was the first time in his experience – that my parole would not be recognised by the northern authorities. He said, "I am advising you not to go north." There was nothing I could do.

'After my mother's funeral, my father and most of the family came down to see me in the house of a friend in Dublin. It was very sad. We were a close-knit family and it hurt to miss her funeral.'

Back once more in Mountjoy, Cahill threw himself into the ongoing campaign for improved conditions and the political status which all republican prisoners sought as a matter of course. With the Irish government refusing to meet their demands, the decision was taken to embark on a hunger strike. A request went out for volunteers and Cahill, by now a member of the Camp staff, was one of twelve prisoners selected to begin refusing food in early September. As well as recognition as political prisoners, the republican demands included remission on sentences, free association between 8am and 8.30pm, the provision of recreational facilities, complete segregation from other prisoners and the housing of all republican prisoners under one roof. This last demand referred to the transfer to Mountjoy of sentenced IRA men from the Curragh military camp, part of which was used as a prison.

'We were twenty-one days into the hunger strike,' says Cahill, 'when, unusually, the governor told the staff that he wanted to address the men. We had a staff meeting about it and decided he could address the men, but it would be as a parade. They would be called to attention and stood at ease. It was also agreed that if he offered to answer questions, no one should take up the offer.'

Cahill recalls that the jail OC, Dublin journalist and author Eamonn MacThomáis, assembled the prisoners, called them to attention and then ordered them 'at ease'. He remembers: 'The governor then made a short speech outlining a number of concessions, and said, "You can end the hunger strike, you have got all your demands." He then asked if anyone wanted to say anything. The men stood in silence for a few minutes. MacThomáis called the parade to attention again and dismissed them.

'MacThomáis and myself approached the governor as the men were going away. We told him the staff would meet and then inform him of our decision – whether the hunger strike was over or not. If I remember rightly, we said we would see him within half an hour to give our decision, which we did do. We were brought to his office, and told him the hunger strike was not over. He was dumbfounded. He said, "Sure, you have got everything you wanted." We told him we had not. The most important thing was recognition as political prisoners, and he had made no reference to that particular issue.

'I don't know whether you could believe him or not, but he said he had not realised that this had not been attended to. He would get in touch with the Justice Department and come back to us on it.'

A little over an hour later, Cahill says, the governor sent a message to him and MacThomáis asking for a meeting in his office. The governor held the Justice Department reply to his query in his hand, but did not provide the republicans with a copy. As he began to read, Cahill and MacThomáis realised that the republican prisoners in Mountjoy had made a little bit of history.

'The reply was that since the foundation of the State no group had ever been recognised as political prisoners. Of course that was true, except for internees during the war. But he said the Justice Department recognised the fact that because of the situation in the North, and because so many republican prisoners had been involved in what was happening in the North, they would recognise us as a special category.

'It was a significant victory. The terminology did not matter – they were recognising us, to all intents and purposes, as political prisoners.

'We told him we would have to discuss the special category offer with the rest of the staff. We went back to the wing and held a staff meeting. It was a foregone conclusion that they would accept, but they had to sanction the decision. The staff met and they were quite happy with the terminology. We did not have to go back to the governor; the chief warder was waiting for us and we told him the result and consequently the hunger strike was over.'

Towards the end of the protest, Séamus Twomey, one of Cahill's old colleagues from the Belfast Brigade, arrived in Mountjoy. Twomey, who was known as a straight-talking, no-nonsense northerner, was well respected within republican circles and had replaced Cahill as chief of staff following the *Claudia* affair. Twomey expected unstinting effort from the volunteers under his command, but in return would support them to the hilt. His tenure in the post had lasted only a few months before he was arrested and brought before the Special Court, where he was found guilty of being a member of an illegal organisation.

In Mountjoy, Twomey found that his fellow Belfast man was paying a heavy price for his high-stress lifestyle. Exactly a week after coming off hunger strike, Cahill was paralysed with severe pains in his chest. A doctor summoned to his cell ordered his immediate transfer to Dublin's Mater hospital.

As Cahill was being taken from the wing, the artist in MacThomáis came to the fore. He felt such a solemn occasion could not be allowed to pass without an appropriate gesture.

'I was being carried out from my cell on a stretcher to await an ambulance,' Cahill recalls. 'MacThomáis paraded the men and called them to attention as I was being brought past them. I heard afterwards when I came back from hospital that Twomey had not agreed with MacThomáis's action, and thought it was a bit over the top. He told the OC, "Cahill was only sick, he wasn't fucking dead."'

Cahill had a thorough examination carried out by a heart specialist, who declared that he was out of immediate danger. The same doctor came to see Cahill shortly before he was discharged to say he was unhappy about his patient being returned to a prison cell, but the matter was out of his hands. At the least sign of chest pain, the doctor said, Cahill was to ask to be returned to the hospital.

Donal de Barra, another republican prisoner from Mountjoy, shared a hospital room with Cahill. A native Irish speaker, De Barra was born in the Donegal gaeltacht and, according to Cahill, did not speak English until he went to work in England at the age of sixteen.

'The two of us were put into a private room, probably for security reasons – it helped the Special Branch to keep an eye on us and at the same time kept us away from the main wards.'

Cahill was receiving visits from a Franciscan priest with whom he had become friendly. The cleric often brought a religious relic with which to bless the hospital's patients. On occasion he would bring a glove which had been worn by Padre Pio, the Italian friar who was said to bear the marks of Christ's crucifixion wounds on his body. Each time the stigmata wounds bled, the friar changed his fingerless gloves. The discarded mitts were treasured by Padre Pio's followers. On several occasions, the gloves were said to have been responsible for miracle cures and the friar, who died in 1968, was elevated to sainthood by the Pope in 2002.

'The Franciscan priest came in to our hospital room and was talking to me – he didn't know Donal de Barra at that stage. After he blessed me with the glove, I told him the guy in the other bed was also from Mountjoy, so he went up to have a yarn with him. He also blessed Donal with Padre Pio's glove. That night when Donal's visitors came in, his mother, after talking to him, came down to my bed and thanked me. She said she was very grateful that the priest went to speak to Donal, but even more so for giving him the blessing with Patrick Pearse's glove!

'But,' Cahill continues, 'not everyone in the hospital had been happy to see me there. In fact, I was told the matron was the same lady who was in charge when MacStiofáin was there, and she blamed me for the attempt to rescue him.'

Back in Mountjoy once more, Cahill was still recovering from the hunger strike and his heart trouble when he was informed of a planned escape attempt. IRA escapes were almost always aimed not only at freeing prisoners, but also at winning publicity. As a high-profile prisoner, Cahill was asked if he wished to volunteer to take part in the plan, which involved three other northerners – his old County Armagh gun-smuggling friend Joe B O'Hagan, Séamus Twomey and Tyrone republican Kevin Mallon.

Despite still feeling unwell, Cahill agreed and was told he would receive any help necessary. The date was set for Halloween, 31 October 1973.

Two days before this date, a 'Mr Leonard' entered the offices of Irish Helicopters Ltd at Dublin Airport. Staff said the man, who was in his early twenties and spoke with an American accent, asked if he could hire the services of a pilot and an aircraft. He was a film-maker, he said, and wanted to take aerial photographs of ancient monuments in the Stradbally area of County Laois on the coming Wednesday.

The helicopter he was allocated was a five-seat Alouette II which had seen service with the French air force. President Charles de Gaulle had presented the aircraft to the wife of South Vietnamese leader President Thieu. The South Vietnamese had later sold the machine to Irish Helicopters Ltd.

The mysterious Mr Leonard, obviously immersed in his role, turned up for the lunchtime appointment wearing a white suit and hamming up his mid-Atlantic accent. When they were in the air, he told the pilot he needed to pick up some photographic equipment and asked him to put down in a field beside a farmhouse at Dunmace, near Stradbally. As the pilot stepped from his craft, he was confronted by two men, one armed with a revolver, the other carrying an Armalite rifle. After it was explained that he was part of a prison escape plot, the pilot, accompanied now by the man with the rifle, was ordered to take off and head for Mountjoy prison.

Inside the jail, Cahill says, the republican escape committee had briefed dozens of prisoners, on a need-to-know basis, on the part they were expected to play.

'Gaelic football matches were played every day in the exercise yard, but on that particular day a "needle" match had been arranged. It was October and it was cold. There would not normally be many spectators, so the match had to be of special interest to ensure that all the prisoners would be in the yard to support their team.

'The whole operation was kept very tight as far as inside was concerned. A number of prisoners knew it was coming off and they had a specific job to do on that day. We would have to make our own plans to ensure that the warders on duty in the yard would have no chance to interfere with the escape. They were to be physically held back if necessary.

'The instruction we got from the outside was that the helicopter would land in the exercise yard. It was to arrive before four o'clock – if it did not arrive by that time the operation would be postponed for twenty-four hours. The reason for this was that darkness would descend and the helicopter would have bother landing, but bigger bother in landing at its destination.'

Cahill was still weak and had been advised to sit close to Kevin Mallon as they waited. The pair had known each other since the '56 campaign, when the man from Coalisland, County Tyrone, had been acquitted on murder charges, only to be sentenced to twenty-two years for explosives offences. Mallon was a tough, fit thirty-five-year-old, who would have no trouble carrying Cahill to the helicopter if necessary.

At four o'clock there was no sign of the aircraft, and the escapers were trying hard not to look anxiously at their watches. Fifteen minutes later, with the light fading and the afternoon growing colder, Mallon became concerned about Cahill's health and advised him to go inside.

'Mick O'Connell, from the west coast, was sitting with us,' Cahill recalls. 'I was not aware how much Mick knew about the escape, but he said he would come inside with me and make a cup of tea. We went to his cell and he went out to get the tea ready while I waited. I had just sat down to take the tea when I heard the noise of a helicopter – but it was landing in the wrong yard.

'It was a comment by Mick which made me realise that he knew all about it. He said, "God, what's gone wrong? It's landing in the other yard." He told me later he had been there to help Mallon get me onto the machine.

'We then heard the aircraft lifting up. They had realised, who-ever was in charge of the aircraft, they were landing in the wrong place. It lifted up and landed in the yard where the boys were. Along with Mick, I headed towards the barred gate leading to the yard. When we got to the gate we found the screw already had it locked.'

Cahill shakes his head and smiles ruefully as he once again reflects that he 'was not born to escape'.

'All I could do was look through the bars and watch the helicopter lifting up into the sky.'

The escape was reported in the media as having been carried out with split-second precision. Mallon, Twomey and O'Hagan scrambled aboard the craft as the other prisoners jostled and obstructed prison officers. One of the prisoners – Gerry O'Hare, who was later to become a successful journalist – helped to cram the last man on board before slamming the door.

Scuffles broke out in the prison yard, but the helicopter took off unhindered. O'Hare insists that a warder watching the helicopter rising into the sky frantically called out, 'Close the gates, close the gates,' before realising that the escapers were not using the conventional exits. Delighted prisoners yelled, cheered and applauded as the machine cleared the walls of the old prison and banked towards the Royal Canal before disappearing from view. The pilot was told to take his aircraft to Baldoyle racecourse, just outside Dublin, where he was forced to land on the five-furlong straight, close to the main road. The three escapers and their armed escort ran to waiting cars and were whisked off.

Back in Mountjoy, Cahill says that the prisoners milled around in the exercise yard trying to confuse warders, who were attempting to carry out a headcount to discover the identities of the escapers.

'MacThomáis eventually held a parade in the yard and addressed the men,' says Cahill. 'He was a bit of a comedian and said he had been informed by the prison authorities that a helicopter had landed in the yard and that a number of prisoners had escaped. He said, "I didn't see a helicopter and, this being Halloween, the prisoners who escaped must have went out on witches' broomsticks. I don't see who's missing, but the prison authorities want to do a headcount, which necessitates all men going to their cells."'

A count was carried out as the men filed inside and it was discovered that three prisoners were missing. Their identities were discovered after a cell check.

'Naturally there was jubilation and a lot of talk amongst the men afterwards. Mick O'Connell, the boy who had made the tea for me, his comment was, "Bad heart and all as Joe had, he beat me in the race to the gate. There was not much wrong with him when he was running towards the helicopter."'

The escape of the three northerners, who had all been senior IRA officers at various times, caused severe embarrassment to the Irish government. Normally such an operation would have included prisoners with long terms still to serve, and some republicans expressed surprise that such was not the case on this occasion – Twomey had completed just three weeks of his sentence. However, Cahill and the three others had been chosen because the government had made so much of their arrests, making their escape even more newsworthy.

Mountjoy's location close to Dublin city centre had made the prison seem reasonably secure. Those responsible for security believed that escapers would have to cope with the dense city traffic, which would hamper a speedy getaway. Authorities now feared a repeat performance of the helicopter escapade and moved the entire republican population of Mountjoy and the Curragh military camp fifty miles across country to Portlaoise prison in County Laois. For Cahill, the move was to mark a period of confrontation and conflict with prison authorities, which ended only with his release.

'There was no doubt we were shifted because of the escape. There was no notice – we were just told to pack our stuff, we were being shifted. I actually thought we were going to the Curragh camp, but that was not to be. We were convinced the transfer to Portlaoise was our punishment for the escape. It also meant that prisoners' relatives from the North had a lot further to travel.'

The extra distance was not the only problem. The republicans, already dismayed at the state of the old jail, were to suffer a further blow when they learned that the improved conditions won by the hunger strikers in Mountjoy would not apply in Portlaoise. Worse still, protesting non-political prisoners had smeared excrement on the walls of many cells.

'We arrived sometime in the afternoon. Portlaoise was very dark, a black hole with a very oppressive atmosphere. There had been ordinary prisoners in it and they had been on dirt strike. In fact there was shit everywhere. When they were shifted wherever they were shifted to, I presume it was Mountjoy, the prison had not been cleaned. When we went into it the stench was unbelievable.

'The governor wanted to lock us up as soon as we arrived. This was the same governor from Mountjoy – he too had been transferred to Portlaoise. He said he wanted to get the prison organised and wanted to get food for us, so we would be locked up until the meal was ready.

'We told him we wanted the conditions we had in Mountjoy and there would be no lock-up. We had won those conditions and they had no right to take them away. He agreed that he was not happy with the regulations that they were laying down for us and he wanted to meet the Justice Department to sort the whole thing out. He told us he was going off to meet them right away. In the meantime, we refused to obey instructions from the screws and would not let them lock us up.'

During this period Cahill became caught up in a confused situation brought about by the presence of two camp staffs. The Curragh prisoners were following orders from their own officers, as were the men from Mountjoy. In the mix-up, Cahill was separated from the prisoners who had been moved from Mountjoy. He found himself in the Portlaoise basement, where a number of Official IRA men were being held.

In the meantime the governor arrived back at the jail, accompanied by several Gardaí and the deputy governor who was responsible for security at Portlaoise.

'The governor had a lot of drink taken – he was, in fact, under the weather. He was certainly a changed man in drink. If I remember correctly, he said he was going to enforce the new regulations laid down in spite of the previous agreement.

'At this stage they had started to try to lock people up. The screws in the basement made towards me and said they were bringing me upstairs to lock me up. I said they would have to carry me and I lay down on the floor. Fair play to the Official IRA prisoners who were there – they formed a ring around me and told the screws and Gardaí they would have to deal with them before they got me. It was around this period they decided to leave us in peace and leave the cell doors open until the next day. I always admired those Officials for the way they stood around me.'

Next morning, with the cells doors still open, the republicans took the opportunity to clear up the staff anomaly by electing a new OC. Belfast republican Leo Martin was voted into the post and appointed Cahill as his adjutant. The former OC of the Curragh prisoners was brought on to the camp staff. Shortly afterwards one of the helicopters escapers, Kevin Mallon, was recaptured. He was also incarcerated in Portlaoise.

'We started to get the men organised. We said we would not clean the prison but, once it was cleaned, we would look after it. I think they brought in a squad of other prisoners to do the cleaning.'

Much of the next year, Cahill remembers, was marked by negotiations aimed at improving the lot of the Portlaoise inmates. 'We kept on chipping away at the system, trying to gain rights,' he says, 'but things continued to deteriorate and the conditions gradually got worse, because, I believe, the governor had been told to tighten up. We did try to negotiate and did get bits and pieces, but realistically we were back to square one and had to fight very hard for any improvements.'

Little compromises and token gestures were regarded by both sides as victories, and acted as safety valves in an atmosphere which was rapidly becoming explosive. The government, however, had not forgotten the political fallout from the helicopter escape. They were loath to give the Portlaoise authorities permission to grant concessions which could possibly lead to a repeat of the embarrassment. But republican prisoners were never happier than when the government was embarrassed and, even as the discussions were taking place, a large number of men were working on other unauthorised early-release schemes.

'There were a couple of attempted escapes that year, including one very similar to the tunnel started in the cell in Crumlin Road in 1958. The Portlaoise tunnel was also started in a cell, in May 1974. By June, it was around eighty feet long when the prisoner occupying the cell – he was a bit of a maverick – decided to launch his own protest by setting fire to some newspapers. The screws rushed in and the tunnel was discovered,' says Cahill.

Cahill's old friend from the *Claudia* operation, County Clare man Denis McInerney, was also involved in an attempted escape the same year.

'There was a priest who came to the jail to give a mission [a week-long retreat of prayer and services] and he was the double of Denis. This priest went around the cells meeting prisoners during the day. In one cell his clerical garb and identification documents were taken from him. Denis walked out dressed as the priest. At each of three locked gates he stopped and waited as they were opened for him. He actually got to the main gate when some very alert screw recognised him and raised the alarm.'

Cahill's health was still giving cause for concern and he ruled himself out of the next escape attempt, which was scheduled for August. He was, however, still on the camp staff, and helped sanction the plan as well as give advice and encouragement to the prisoners involved. For the plot to succeed, the escapers needed to acquire the ingredients for two bombs.

'A lot of planning and preparation had been put into it. The important thing was to get the explosives in. That was difficult. They were smuggled in, naturally. Once all that was arranged, a time and date were set. The Laois IRA provided three buses and several cars, which were to be waiting for the escapers when they hit the outside. Once again the plan was on a strictly need-to-know basis. Only the staff, the people who were escaping and one or two others who had jobs to do had any knowledge of what was to happen.

'The bombs had to be manufactured on the day of the escape – we would not have wanted them lying around, risking discovery. They were made up in the cell next to mine, which was fairly convenient to the point where the men would escape from the wing.'

One of the problems facing the escape committee was the lack of secure hiding places for the explosives. The problem was solved by a number of prisoners each scraping away the cement around a brick in the centre of their cell wall. Cahill says that the warders frequently used electronic detectors to scan the walls, but almost always at the top, bottom and sides – seldom in the centre.

Using whatever tools were available – a screwdriver, a chisel or a nail stolen from a workshop – the republicans spent days painstakingly hacking at the wall until the brick was loose enough to be removed. It was then broken up into fragments and taken to the exercise yard, to be thrown over the wall. Gelignite, detonators and fuses were placed in the cavity and hidden behind a false brick made from newspaper and glue. The cells walls were then repainted. According to a contemporary of Cahill's, the warders were only too happy to provide prisoners with copious quantities of paint, which, the authorities believed, kept the men occupied in a relatively harmless and even useful pursuit.

Cahill says security surrounding the escape had been kept very tight, but a small hitch occurred on the day scheduled for the escape. A prisoner from another landing persisted in hanging around the cell where the IRA bomb expert was due to assemble the two devices.

The prisoner, says Cahill, 'did hankies', a reference to the practice of painting Celtic designs or portraits of republican icons onto a handkerchief. These were either presented to relatives or balloted at fund-raising functions organised by the Green Cross, a republican prisoners' aid group. If the work was being sent to a particular area, it was generally signed by any prisoners who lived there.

'The man who was making the bombs had spotted him. He said, "That bloody man is down here again getting hankies signed. Use your authority and send him to the top tier to get him out of the road." I told the man he was always down at our tier and he should get some signatures up above. He was reluctant to go there, because he was always getting kidded and slagged off.

'He went, but grudgingly. He didn't go to the top tier, but returned to his cell where he lay on his bed reading and listening to the radio.'

The plan was put into action after lunchtime, while many warders were watching an All-Ireland semi-final football match between Donegal and Galway on television.

Cahill recalls: 'When everything was ready, the prisoners went to their pre-arranged places. The code word was to be given by Kevin Mallon, who had a hell of a voice. He was to yell as loudly as he could, "Mickey Dubh" [dark or swarthy Mickey]. I don't know where the hell he found it, but that was the signal for the operation to start.'

Amongst those who watched events from the vantage point of a prison landing was a young friend of Cahill's. Martin McGuinness, a sandy-haired Derry youth who was fond of a joke but generally serious beyond his years, was chatting about Gaelic football with another prisoner and a senior warder when Mallon let forth his stentorian roar. McGuinness, who was many years later to become education minister in the Northern Ireland Assembly, had not been invited to take part in the escape, because he had only a short time left to serve.

Prisoners reacted immediately to Mallon's signal, overpowering staff and taking over the first-floor laundry. Here, sturdy rein-forced French windows led to a flat roof. Using a warder's keys, the men opened the windows. They dropped from the roof to a court-yard adjoining the governor's garden, fifty yards away. It was at this point that the first and smaller bomb was placed and detonated, blowing open the garden door.

Irish soldiers who guarded the prison's perimeter began firing at the escapers, but were confused by the fact that some prisoners were dressed in warders' uniforms. They had stripped these from their victims after Mallon's signal. A second, heavier door, leading from the garden to the outside world, was blown open with the main charge, and nineteen republicans raced through the gap. All managed to evade capture, despite a widespread search and the sealing off of the border.

'A few minutes after the escape,' Cahill says, 'a newsflash came on the radio saying there had been an explosion at Portlaoise and that a number of prisoners were missing. The hankie man came flying out of his cell and said, "What's going on? I heard on the radio there was an escape and I knew nothing about it." Little did he realise just how close he had been to the most important part of the operation.'

Government ministers were furious, and their anger was reflected in an even more stringent security clampdown at the jail. The prisoners left in Portlaoise, while delighted for the escapers, knew they were now facing an uphill battle for recognition of the Mountjoy agreement.

'So, whatever conditions we had won or achieved, from arriving in Portlaoise until the escape, went out with the escape. We were back to fighting for an improvement in conditions again,' Cahill says.

There were occasional lighter moments, however, and the prisoners were able to take part in relatively normal pastimes, such as word games.

'We had a very good Scrabble team in Portlaoise and we played when we could. I played with Kevin Mallon, Denis McInerney and Joe Donaghy from Tyrone. It was good craic. Mallon was the man who always caused fierce arguments by making really obscure words. We accused him of making them up, and the argument would go on until a dictionary was produced. Mallon, invariably, was proved correct.'

But it seemed inevitable that the head of steam building up in the jail would lead to serious violence. In late December 1974, the prisoners decided to step up their protests in an attempt to highlight their claims that prison authorities were not honouring agreements reached after the previous year's hunger strike.

'We got so far in the negotiations, but then we hit a stone wall and got no further. Action had to be taken. We decided to put the screws out of the wing, take over the wing ourselves in protest. We planned to take the cell doors off and use them to barricade the entrance to the wing so the screws would not have access,' Cahill says.

'The warders were told to get off; they had no alternative but to go. That part of the operation was the simplest. Although, as it turned out, the removal of the doors – they were wooden doors and steel-plated – that was simple too. I never saw doors coming off as handy in my life. We opened the doors as wide as possible, put books between the door and the frame on the hinge side, then forced the door closed. The result was that the hinges jumped out, screw nails and all. All cells on all tiers had their doors removed and used to block the entrance to the landings. Any doors not needed were thrown out onto the safety grid [strong wire mesh placed between the landings as an anti-suicide measure].

'After we started to put the barricades up, it was realised that there were three or four screws still in the wing. We put them in a cell and told them we were not going to harm them and that they would be okay if they did not attempt to do anything. They were given a radio, a chess set and playing cards to help them while away their time. They were given the same food as the prisoners. The prisoners treated them well, but did not talk to them.'

This incident led to claims that the prisoners had taken the warders hostage to be used for bargaining purposes. Cahill and other republicans, however, remain adamant that the men's presence on the wing was an oversight and they were placed in the cell 'for their own safety'.

Food reserves had been built up from the parcels sent in by relatives at Christmas. Cahill says prisoners did not expect a long siege, but they intended nonetheless to hold out for as long as possible. They settled down to await developments.

'I remember on the night we took over the jail, there were soldiers on the roof and some of the skylights were open. One of the things that sticks in my memory is the sight of a particular officer looking down into the jail and calling my name, making some remark such as, "You are doing great work there, Joe, keep it going."'

Up north, the IRA and the British government had reached terms for what turned out to be another short-lived truce, but, on the landings of Portlaoise prison, open war was about to break out. It took prison authorities around seven hours to muster a force of 200 soldiers and Gardaí to put down the mutiny.

'They did come in during the night and it took them a brave while to get through the barricade. They just battered and battered until they got an opening. There was very little we could do once they had made an opening. There was military, Gardaí and screws. The Army had their rifles trained on us. The Guards and screws were pushed in in front of the military and there was fisti-cuffs, there was a rough house all right. They used high-powered water hoses to force us back. Some hand-to-hand fighting was still taking place, but they had the upper hand in numbers and weapons.'

Cahill says the authorities, after regaining control, carried out what he calls 'an alleged search' of the cells. It was, he insists, more of a punitive mission than a search operation.

'I never saw such an orgy of destruction in my life. Prisoners' clothes were ripped up by screws and Gardaí, and kicked all over the place. Pictures, religious or otherwise, photographs, *et cetera*, were grabbed from the walls, thrown to the ground and walked on.

'Naturally, when the prisoners saw this happening, they tried to stop their property being destroyed, which resulted in many prisoners being batoned and manhandled. Some men were very badly beaten. This lasted all night long and well into the next day.

'Eventually there was some form of negotiation to bring it to an end. Clean-up operations started then. We carried that out ourselves – sorting out clothes, tidying up cells, and arranging for food for the men. Any we had in the cells had been destroyed.

'There was a lot of bitterness between prisoners and screws. We were kept in the wing with a number of Gardaí and screws while all the doors were put on again. This was done through negotiation and we had agreed there would be no interference with the work.

'There were no visits or letters allowed. And no radios, they had all been smashed. There were no newspapers; we did not know what was happening. This concerned us quite a lot, because we were worried about our relatives on the outside.'

From previous experience, the prisoners knew that the rumour machine would be working overtime and relatives would be frantic with worry. Visits and parcels had been stopped and there seemed to be no way of communicating with their families. One republican, however, approached the IRA leadership to say that he was very friendly with one of the Gardaí. There was a good chance, the prisoner said, that the policeman could be persuaded to take out a verbal or written message.

'The camp staff decided to take a chance on this and ask him to take out a written message. When our man approached the Garda he was very reluctant, until he was assured that any message sent out would not contain information about an attack on the jail or any other threatening or violent act. He was told the note was intended solely to stop any wild rumours – to let people on the outside know what was happening; to say that no one had been killed.'

The policeman eventually agreed to take a note out, but told his contact there would be a condition: Joe Cahill was the only man he would deal with. No one else was to know his identity, and Cahill would have to deliver the note to him in person.

'I met him at an appointed time and place in the prison, when he would not be under observation, and brought the message, which gave a full rundown on the situation. It said that while some people had been hurt, no one was seriously injured. I thanked the Garda for taking the trouble to deliver the note. The only remark he passed was that he felt honoured that I was giving him this communication, but that it would be a one-off. It was duly delivered.'

Cahill says 'quite a number' of Gardaí remained on the landings with the warders as negotiations continued between the prisoners' leaders and the authorities. The prisoners' beds were thrown out because, Cahill believes, the legs could have been removed and used as weapons. New mattresses and bedclothes were supplied, but these were placed on the cell floors.

'There were only two people who were given beds – myself and another prisoner who also had a heart condition. This situation lasted a couple of weeks. For that period of time, no one was locked up, not even those who had had their doors replaced. The result of all that was that prisoners slept where they wanted, so you had up to six in a cell, with mattresses thrown on the floor. The craic was good, with storytelling and sing-songs. The prisoners were in high spirits and no one complained about not getting sleep.'

Eventually, Cahill says, the situation returned to 'a sort of normality'. But in general, conditions remained poor and there seemed little chance of a restoration of the agreement made in Mountjoy before the helicopter escape.

'We kept negotiating but made very little progress, with the result that, in early January 1975, it was reluctantly decided that there would have to be a hunger strike. It took a lot of hard thinking before we did decide to go on hunger strike. Volunteers were asked for and the selection made.'

Ten men were selected and began refusing food on 3 January. They were joined by another six a few days later. The government refused to yield to the prisoners' demands and several hunger strikers, after longer than a month without food, were moved to the hospital at the Curragh military camp. One man – Pat Ward, from the fishing village of Burtonport in Donegal – was taken to an intensive care unit in Dublin's Jervis Street hospital, where he was reported to be close to death.

Once more, events in Cahill's life were to take a completely unexpected turn.

'The hunger strike was three weeks on when I was suddenly released, on health grounds. It came as a total surprise to me.'

Cahill had served twenty months of his three-year sentence. Newspaper reports of 24 January 1975 said no official government statement had been issued about his release, but that prison regulations and medical advice left justice minister Patrick Cooney with no option but to free him. Cooney was a member of Fine Gael, a political party traditionally opposed to republicans. He was regarded by republicans as a hard-line justice minister, unlikely to use kid-glove tactics on IRA members.

The clamour for an easing of the regime in Portlaoise jail was growing, with prisoners' relatives and friends, including Annie Cahill, taking part in protests at the prison gates. By now, the hunger strikers had been refusing food for twenty-one days, and there was every indication that they were prepared to fast to death if necessary. No Irish government wanted either the responsibility for a death in such circumstances, or the backlash which was certain to follow. On the day Cahill was released, prison authorities were given the go-ahead to lift the ban on mail and visits that had been in place since the takeover of the jail in December. The final paragraph of a little double-column story in the *Irish Press* gives an interesting clue: 'The release of Mr Cahill and the improvement of prisoners' conditions at Portlaoise were among the suggestions put forward by the Provisional IRA as ways of helping to create a better atmosphere in the context of the recent ceasefire.'

Cahill immediately headed for the home of friends in Dublin who he knew would be in contact with members of the IRA leadership. Soon he was discussing the Portlaoise hunger strike with Daithí Ó Conaill and Séamus Twomey, who was still at large after his aerial escape from Mountjoy.

'They instructed me to take on the job of having the hunger strike settled, brought to a successful conclusion. That was my first task after being released. It appeared to me that others wanted to use me to attempt to bring the hunger strike to an end. I came to this conclusion because I was contacted by a Fine Gael TD, Paddy Harte of Donegal.'

Harte's home county shared a border with three of the six northern counties. He took a close interest in the affairs of Northern Ireland and was a frequent visitor to Belfast. It seemed, therefore, that Harte was a natural person to act as go-between with the government.

Harte asked Cahill to meet him in the Mount Herbert hotel in south Dublin. Cahill knew the hotel well, having used it for meetings with Michael Flannery, the president of Noraid, who stayed there when visiting from the United States.

'There were several meetings with Harte, but they never really came to anything,' says Cahill. 'Any proposals we put to Cooney through Harte were rejected. Harte's message for us was that it was felt we were looking for too much and that the prisoners' demands were unrealistic. After he made that statement I had no further meetings with him.'

A number of high-level intermediaries were working to try and broker an end to the hunger strikes. Twelve men remained on hunger strike, and doctors were soon advising that those in the two hospitals were on the point of death. The IRA leadership decided to make another attempt to contact justice minister Cooney.

'We re-established contact with Cooney through Mickey Mullen, the general secretary of the Irish Transport and General Workers' Union. Mullen was approached by the republican movement to act as intermediary between the government and ourselves. We were in constant contact with Mickey Mullen, it's fair to say he worked very hard and put every effort into it. Through him various proposals were put to Cooney, who adopted a hard-line attitude right up to the Sunday [16 February].

'The final list of demands was given to Mickey Mullen on Saturday, but Cooney could not be found on Saturday night to give an answer. The only reply Mickey got back was to contact Cooney on Sunday morning.'

The following morning, Cahill was in Mullen's house in Cabra awaiting the outcome of the call to Cooney. They were joined by Bob Smith, organiser of Cumann Cabhrach, a republican prisoners' welfare organisation with similar objectives to the Green Cross.

Above: IRA volunteers take aim with a rocket launcher. The man on the left is preparing to reload the weapon, while the man on the right watches the rear. Photograph: Colman Doyle.
Below: The scene of devastation in Magherafelt town centre on 24 May 1993, where a 300lb bomb exploded the night before. This was the fourth bomb attack in four days. Photograph: Pacemaker.

Above: Taking in the washing in Rosemount, Derry, in full view of the watchtower of the nearby joint Army–RUC base. Photograph: An Phoblacht.
Below: An armed soldier does not merit a glance as these children go about their business in Belfast, August 1994. Photograph: An Phoblacht.

Joe Cahill takes a rare break with his wife Annie Cahill and six of their seven children. This photograph was taken shortly after his release from Portlaoise Prison in 1975. Photograph: Colman Doyle.

Above: An IRA patrol on the Ballymurphy estate, west Belfast, in the early 1970s. Photograph: An Phoblacht. **Below**: Violet Street, off Springfield Road, west Belfast. A blast wall built to protect the joint RUC–Army base from IRA rockets and bombs reduced the width of the street to just six feet for much of its length. Residents found it impossible to read a newspaper, even in broad daylight, without switching on the lights. Springfield Road barracks, once RUC headquarters for west Belfast, was closed in September 2002. The street was restored to its former dimensions when the barracks was demolished in early 2003. Photograph: An Phoblacht.

Above: The North's trouble occasionally spilled over into the Republic, as this picture shows. A petrol bomb explodes in Dundalk, County Louth. Photograph: An Phoblacht.
Below: Joe Cahill welcomes Bill Clinton to Stormont in December 2000, during the last few days of Clinton's presidency. Also pictured is leading Kerry republican Martin Ferris, now a member of Dáil Éireann. Photograph: John Harrison.

Above: Children prepare to throw rocks as the RUC and British Army raid homes in Elmfield Street in Ardoyne, Belfast, July 1997. Photograph: An Phoblacht.

Below: In January 2000, Joe Cahill visited Belfast's Crumlin Road prison where he had spent several years, both as an internee and a serving prisoner. The picture shows Cahill in the death cell he shared with his best friend and fellow IRA man Tom Williams. The nineteen-year-old Williams was hanged on Wednesday, 2 September 1942. Photograph: Brendan Murphy.

Above: Joe Cahill makes the traditional keynote speech at the grave of Wolfe Tone in Bodenstown cemetery, County Kildare, in June 1998.
Photograph: An Phoblacht.

Right: The grave reserved for Tom Williams by the National Graves Association, Milltown cemetery, County Antrim.
Photograph: An Phoblacht.

Sinn Féin president Gerry Adams and vice-president Joe Cahill
caught in a reflective mood just before the unveiling of a republican mural
at Ballymurphy, west Belfast, in May 2002. Photograph: An Phoblacht.

'The message that Cooney gave back to Mullen on Sunday over the telephone was that the governor would be instructed to meet with the IRA staff in the prison. Cooney was told that Bob Smith and I needed access to Portlaoise, the Curragh prison hospital and Jervis Street hospital – we needed to talk to the prisoners' staff and to the hunger strikers. He had no hesitation in acceding to that request.'

Cahill had a number of meetings with the prisoners' staff officers, who would have the final say in whether or not to end the hunger strike. Leo Martin, Dan Hogan from County Mayo, Cahill and Smith were present at the final meeting with deputy governor William O'Reilly.

'We went through the points on demand and O'Reilly's reply to each of the demands was, "That's reasonable." The use of the word "reasonable" occurred so often that Leo Martin, when he was speaking to O'Reilly, would refer to him as Mr Reasonable. In this way we went through all the points. The OC said he would have to report back to a full meeting of the camp staff. We already knew the outcome, it was a foregone conclusion at this stage. The prisoner's demands had been met, but Martin still had to consult the rest of his staff.

'There was an adjournment in the talks while Leo and Dan went to talk to the others and we enjoyed the hospitality of the prison, with tea and the best sandwiches I have ever tasted. After a short period, Leo and Dan came back and said the staff were satisfied with the progress made and they would ask the men to end the hunger strike. Leo's parting words to us were, "As quick as you can, get on your way."

'At this stage, every minute was important and could mean the difference between life and death. We went immediately to the Curragh first and the military police were actually waiting on us arriving. They escorted us without any nonsense to the military hospital and brought us straight to the ward where the men were.

In the shortest vocabulary, we told them they had won, we had been with the staff in Portlaoise and they had instructed the men to finish the hunger strike.

'We certainly felt that some were very near death. Gerard McCarthy from Cork, when we went to speak to him, he was not too sure who I was. When he did recognise me he passed the remark, "Joe, you are my friend, I was floating on clouds, to where I don't know." He was not even able to raise his hand to shake hands, I had to take his hand in mine.

'We then went to Colm Dalton, who was so near death that he did not know what I was talking about. Joe Buckley was in the same condition. It was hard to get through to them that they had won their demands and that the hunger strike was finished. Nicky Keogh – I have always retained a very vivid recollection of Nicky. He was very young; he looked like a child lying in a cot. The hospital medical staff, who had been on standby, proceeded to administer whatever medical attention was necessary for men coming off hunger strike.'

Outside the Curragh, republican supporters had set up a caravan to use as a base for their semi-permanent protests. Four people were there, collecting signatures for a petition to be sent to the government. Cahill and Smith paused briefly in their race to Jervis Street to tell them the good news. They left the scene with the cheers of the protestors ringing in their ears.

'We headed then to the hospital to let Pat Ward know he had been successful. This, incidentally, was Pat Ward's second hunger strike within a year, and it had a serious effect on him. Physically he was badly affected, particularly his speech. But mentally he was very clear. He never recovered full use of his speech. Pat died at an early age and I have absolutely no doubt that the hunger strikes were a contributory factor in his death.'

Cahill's first task for the IRA after his release had been successful. There is no evidence, however, to suggest that he rested on his laurels. In June, on Bodenstown Sunday, journalists noticed that he did not make the obligatory appearance at the Wolfe Tone commemoration ceremony. A headline and subhead in the *Irish Press* the next morning read: 'Joe Cahill on Libyan visit. Purpose still unknown.' Some people, rightly or wrongly, believed the old warhorse was back in harness.

CHAPTER THIRTEEN
From Pistols to Politics

The political situation facing Cahill on his release from Portlaoise in early 1975 was very different from when he was arrested on the *Claudia* almost two years previously. It was, however, only after the ending of the Portlaoise hunger strike that he found time to draw breath and take stock.

As a result of a meeting with northern Protestant clergymen in the County Clare village of Feakle in late 1974, the IRA had agreed with British officials to take part in a short negotiated truce. Many initially believed the cessation was aimed at giving IRA volunteers a break over the Christmas holidays, but it had in fact been called to facilitate secret talks between republicans and British government representatives. The ceasefire was extended until 17 January, abandoned for a period when the talks ran into difficulties and then reinstated in February. Finally it was declared open-ended when republicans were convinced the officials were advising their government to announce a withdrawal from the North.

Despite the ceasefire in the North, Cahill found that Garda Special Branch, now nick-named the Heavy Gang by republicans, were taking a much tougher line with political activists in the South.

'It was the time of the reign of the Heavy Gang,' says Cahill. 'They got their name from their tactics. Their role was to terrorise people by consistently raiding homes and stopping people in the street and questioning them. They had added this wee subtlety: if they spotted a republican talking to someone or in the company of someone who was not politically involved, that person's name and address was noted and their home raided.

'It was not so much that they had found new suspects, but more of an attempt to isolate republicans, to make people feel uneasy or even fearful of being associated with them. In some cases, they actually succeeded in isolating support for the republican movement.

'A series of protests was launched. These were attended not only by republicans but many others who were involved in human rights and civil rights. One man in particular who was very active in this field, well, because of the treatment he received and the harassment, he actually left the country – he felt terrorised and was practically forced to leave.'

Cahill now found that no matter where he travelled, undercover Special Branch officers were certain to be in the vehicle behind.

'It became a battle of wits to throw them off your tail before you arrived at your destination. Quite often we drove for miles just to give them the runaround.'

On one occasion, Cahill and Ruairí Ó Brádaigh had been meeting two United States congressmen who were in Ireland on a fact-finding mission. The politicians were running late for a meeting with the taoiseach at Leinster House and their taxi had not arrived. Cahill offered to run them there himself. Cahill says that his car was stopped on the way by members of the Heavy Squad, who were particularly nasty to the Americans but did not pay much attention to him.

'They grabbed one man, Chris Dodd, flung him over the bonnet of the car and searched him very roughly. One of the Branch men asked me who they were. I told him that whoever had sent them on this particular mission had put them on a bum steer. I told him they were American congressmen and I was taking them to Leinster House to meet the taoiseach. Their attitude changed immediately – while they did not apologise, they gave us an escort to Leinster House, driving ahead and clearing the road with their flashing lights.'

Dodd, a United States Democratic congressman from 1974–80, later became a senator and played an influential role in the Irish peace process during the presidency of Bill Clinton.

'Some years later I was on a visit to America, and I happened to be visiting Hartford, Connecticut. Chris Dodd was seeking re-election and was holding a fund-raising breakfast. One of his election agents asked me to attend it. I said it was entirely up to Dodd, whether he wanted me to appear or not, because I didn't want to cause him any embarrassment. The election worker got back to me and said Chris would be delighted to have me present. When he arrived at the breakfast, he said he wanted to welcome a very special guest and told the story of his first meeting with me in Dublin and his encounter with the Special Branch.'

✠ ✠ ✠

Meanwhile up north, the ceasefire, which had started on a such promising note, was being breached so often that it was turning into a disaster. Seven incident centres set up across the North were manned by republicans, working in liaison with British government representatives to monitor the ceasefire. British officials had met some of the IRA's demands, but, according to Cahill, were holding back on others.

'It's true that the British had released some internees and scaled down troop activity in nationalist areas, but it is now acknowledged that they had no intention of carrying out the promise the truce was based on – a declaration of their intent to withdraw.'

By autumn, both sides had accepted that the 'phoney truce', as it came to be known, was about to collapse. In Derry, where opposition to the ceasefire was strong, republicans permanently closed their incident centre in November, by blowing up the building it was housed in. Two days later, secretary of state Merlyn Rees closed the other six. Although there was no formal announcement, the ceasefire was effectively over.

It had been a bad year for the IRA, whose northern units were involved in the resurrected feud with the Officials. At the same time, republicans had been engaged in retaliatory attacks on loyalists, who had stepped up their campaign of assassinating Catholics. The ceasefire had ended without political advantage and a British withdrawal seemed as far away as ever. Recruitment had dropped off, morale was not high and questions were being asked about the strategies being embraced by the leadership.

The phasing out of detention without trial was followed by a more considered British strategy – one of criminalising republicans and rescinding any official acknowledgement of their claim to be political prisoners.

'It was a strange time,' recalls Cahill. 'Even while the Brits were talking to our people, they were planning more draconian actions and they were building the H-Blocks in Long Kesh. I believe it was at this time they were working on their strategies of Ulsterisation, criminalisation and normalisation. They did announce the ending of internment that year, but only because it was an international embarrassment to them and anyway, they had found that the no-jury Diplock courts were more efficient.

'When the last internees were released in December, it coincided near enough with the new policy of criminalising republicans, removing all traces of political status for republican prisoners. Rees announced that after a certain date, March 1976, the special status won by the prisoners would end. Everyone convicted under the special legislation after that date was to be treated as a criminal.

'There were few people found not guilty in the Diplock courts – in fact, I don't know of any that were. The difference between Diplock and the special criminal courts in the South was that you had three judges in the South, but the results were much the same. Although I have to say that it was a special criminal court which ordered my release in 1972.'

In 1972 prisoners in Crumlin Road jail, under the leadership of

Cahill's old colleague Billy McKee, had won special category status – the same terms and status later wrung from the Irish government by the Mountjoy hunger strikers. After Rees's cut-off date, plucked quite arbitrarily from the calendar, those convicted under the emergency legislation were expected to serve their sentences without special or 'political' status. This meant an end to the cherished republican desire of segregation from non-political prisoners. Republicans would now have a much-reduced say in the running of the prison, be expected to carry out prison work, revert to the older, less favourable visiting hours, have shorter periods of free association and, most objectionable of all, be forced to wear prison uniform. This last was total anathema to those who regarded themselves as prisoners of war.

Special category prisoners had been moved to Long Kesh in 1973, and were housed along with the internees in what they termed 'the cages'. These consisted of old-fashioned Second World War Nissen huts, surrounded by secure wire mesh fencing topped with barbed wire. However, the new 'non-political prisoners' would be placed in the neighbouring specially-built H-Blocks, so-called because the prison wings and connecting corridor, seen from the air, formed that letter. Whatever the intentions of the government, the new terms meant just one thing to republicans – the battle lines were once again being drawn in the age-old struggle between IRA prisoners and the authorities.

Cahill recalls: 'People on the outside began protesting publicly about the loss of political status in early 1976, but the practical effects were not felt in the North until later that year. Over in England, Irish prisoners were already paying the price of the fight for political status. Michael Gaughan, who was from Ballina in County Mayo, had died two years earlier after being force-fed while on hunger strike in Parkhurst jail, on the Isle of Wight. His body was brought home and he was buried in the republican plot in the Leighue cemetery in Ballina, with full honours.

'Frank Stagg, who was also from Ballina and who was a good friend of Michael's, died after sixty-two days on hunger strike in Wakehurst Prison in England, in February 1976. He had asked, in the event of his death, to be buried next to his friend.

'I was still in Portlaoise when Michael died from complications caused by the force-feeding, but I was outside when Frank died. We wanted, naturally, to give him a republican funeral, but two or three members of his family objected. We spent three or four hours in a room at the Ormonde hotel in Dublin, trying to convince them that Frank should have a volunteer's funeral with the full honours, and that they should agree to it. Most of the family had agreed, but no amount of talking could convince the others.'

Cahill joined Stagg's mother – 'a lovely lady' – and other family members at Dublin airport, where the body was due to arrive. There was a delay of several hours and the party spent the night in a room provided by airport authorities.

'We had not been given a definite time for the arrival of the flight, but we wanted to be there when the remains came. It was actually an airport worker, whom I knew well and who was also a member of the movement, who came to the room and called me out. His message was that the flight had been diverted to Shannon and Frank's remains had been hijacked by Gardaí.'

The Irish government had indeed ordered the re-routing of the flight and, from that point on, no republican was able to get near Stagg's coffin. The body was taken to Leighue Cemetery, but not to the republican plot as Stagg had wanted. Several family members refused to attend the funeral because of the security presence. The family was further aggrieved when concrete, to a depth of eighteen inches, was poured over the grave. The cemetery, says Cahill, was 'an armed camp' and, with over 1,000 Gardaí and Irish soldiers on guard duty, it was impossible to even approach the grave.

The huge security presence was still in place next morning,

when members of the Stagg family arrived at the cemetery to attend a commemoration ceremony. Cahill presided over the ceremony and delivered an oration, before 'a powerful turnout' of republicans and supporters. Despite being surrounded by Irish security forces, volunteers fired a volley of shots over Frank Stagg's grave.

Cahill had been heartened by a message he had received earlier, and he gave a hint of its contents in his final brief statement at the graveside. Newspapers of the day reported him as saying: 'I pledge that we will assemble here again in the near future when we have taken your body from where it lies. Let there be no mistake about it – we will take it, Frank, and we will leave it resting side-by-side with your great comrade, Michael Gaughan.'

There must have been some present who thought of the solid foot-and-a-half of concrete covering the grave and the apparently permanent police guard around it, and wondered if Cahill was indulging in a piece of rhetoric. He wasn't.

'A local Sinn Féin activist pointed out that there was a vacant grave beside the spot where Frank was buried. Sinn Féin should buy that grave, he said, because it would be important when the time came to reinter the body. We took his advice.'

The republicans of County Mayo watched and waited for many months before they were able to put their plan into operation. After several weeks, the round-the-clock guard on the grave mounted by Irish security forces was proving expensive. There was also the feeling in government circles that the Stagg issue was becoming less contentious. After six months, the Garda complement in the graveyard was stood down. In November 1977, under cover of darkness, local republicans began digging in the Sinn Féin-owned plot beside Stagg's grave. Once below the depth of the concrete covering, they starting working at an angle towards the IRA man's coffin.

Stagg's remains were located and gently eased from the grave.

The coffin was lifted onto the shoulders of IRA volunteers and ceremonially carried the 250 yards to the republican plot, where his dying wish was fulfilled as he was buried beside his friend, Michael Gaughan. A Catholic priest was in attendance as the six-hour operation came to an end with the firing of a single shot over Stagg's new resting place.

'I was not in the country – I may have been in the United States – when the remains were reinterred,' recalls Cahill, 'but I found a postcard waiting for me in 44 Parnell Square [Sinn Féin's Dublin office] when I returned. It said, "We regret we were unable to contact you before we lifted Frank's remains, but we know you were there in spirit." It was signed, "the Grave-diggers". Frank's mother was very pleased.'

Cahill remembers that criminalisation was well under way in the North when the British government initiated Ulsterisation, the second strand of its new policy. This plan called for the British army to be reduced to a back-up role in the conflict, with the bulk of house searches, arrests, roadblocks, checkpoints and covert operations carried out by the RUC and the Ulster Defence Regiment (UDR).

In late March 1976, Merlyn Rees revealed his hand during a debate in the House of Commons. The RUC, he said, would now have 'primacy' in all security operations in Northern Ireland. In effect, police officers were now to be regarded as senior to army officers of equivalent rank, with the RUC chief constable in over-all command of the security situation. Shortly afterwards, Rees withdrew 1,000 troops from the North. It was, says Cahill, the beginning of Ulsterisation:

'It was very much like Vietnamisation, and I think they actually based the plan on that. Ulsterisation was meant to take the British aspect out of the war. It was to give the impression that it was not a war between the IRA and Britain, but a purely sectarian war. It was also about trying to reduce the number of body bags returning to

Britain, because ultimately the people there didn't care too much about the RUC or UDR. They weren't regarded as British – they were Irish. It was in keeping with the old British colonial custom – when fighting wars in other people's countries, use locally-recruited forces.'

The next stage, he says, was 'normalisation', which was meant to convince people that 'everything was okay'. The Northern Ireland Office, proving that they could come up with catchy slogans to match the IRA's series of 'year of victory' battle cries, launched an extensive advertising campaign around the catchphrase 'Seven years is enough'.

'It wasn't long before some wit came up with an answer to that one,' recalls Cahill. 'I remember seeing the NIO slogan on a wall in Belfast, but now it read, "Seven years is enough, but 700 years is too much." So here were the Brits attempting to win over the people with silly advertising campaigns and building leisure centres in nationalist areas, as though somehow leisure centres were proof that their lives had changed for the better and the political situation had improved.

'Of course it was all part of a propaganda exercise. But all the time they were doing this, they were carrying out their strategy of jailing political opponents as easily and as quickly as possible, while portraying the struggle as crime. All this was also meant to hit at international support, to reduce support for the republican struggle, particularly in America where the Brits had been embarrassed politically.'

✠ ✠ ✠

In September 1976, Kieran Nugent, a fiery young red-haired IRA man from west Belfast, became the first person to be sentenced under Rees's criminalisation policy. Five days earlier Rees had been replaced as secretary of state by Roy Mason, a tough and uncompromising little former coal miner, who was determined to defeat the IRA.

Nugent was taken to the reception area of the new H-Blocks at Long Kesh. He was stripped, but refused to accept the regulation clothes from prison warders.

'If you want me to wear a prison uniform, you'll have to nail it to my back,' he is reported as having said. Nugent was handed a blanket to cover his nakedness, and locked in a cell. Refusal to wear uniform meant that Nugent was a non-conforming prisoner and, as such, he was continually punished by three-day periods of solitary confinement 'on the boards', when the bed, table and chair were removed from his cell. In addition, he forfeited all privileges, visits and remission of sentence. In the following months, as the H-Blocks began to fill, other republicans sentenced under 'scheduled offences' followed his example. The blanket protest was under way.

Meanwhile, Cahill was now being given the chance to put into practice his long-held theory that the movement could not expect to advance without a sound political base. Increasingly, his energies and efforts were being channelled into the rebuilding and reorganisation of Sinn Féin. Almost before he knew it, he found himself a member of the *Ard Comhairle*, the party executive. Later – he is unsure about the exact date – Sinn Féin's long-term treasurer, Tony Ruane, retired and Cahill was voted into the post. He was to remain in charge of Sinn Féin's finances until the late 1990s, when the party honoured him by making him vice-president for life.

'A lot of the *Ard Comhairle* work involved holding public meetings, organising functions, meeting people individually, in general endeavouring to rebuild support. By this time there was a realisation that Sinn Féin was not an effective political party – it was more of a protest party. It was actually a republican support organisation, supporting the IRA and taking up causes, like the internees' cause or the prisoners' cause. There may have been a vague anti-imperialist position, but it was not in any real sense viewed as a functioning political party. So we had to get our heads around that situation, to begin to mould the party into a political force.'

Cahill was based mainly in Dublin during this period, only occasionally seeing Annie and the children, who were still living in Belfast. An indication of the austerity of his lifestyle can be gauged from his answer when asked what part of Dublin he had been based in at that time. 'Anywhere I could get a fucking bed,' is the rather curt reply.

His views on restructuring Sinn Féin were endorsed by younger republicans like Martin McGuinness, who had looked on the older man as something of a father figure and a fount of wisdom since they were in Portlaoise together. Jimmy Steele's protégé, Gerry Adams, had been released from prison in 1977. He now carried considerable clout within the republican movement and was instrumental in pushing for the development of a solid political base.

'The building up of Sinn Féin,' Cahill says, 'came about through debate on policy, on tactics. I found that in this phase of the struggle – the past thirty years – there was more talk among the activists than there had ever been before. You did not have the strong political organisation in my young day; you did not have any effective republican political party at all. It was all purely military, and in a military organisation you get an order, you obey it, you do not question it. During this phase of the struggle, when Sinn Féin was becoming stronger, it meant that people had an outlet to voice their thoughts, to put ideas forward. I think it created a really good, strong bond among republicans when everybody had a say in what was happening.'

Cahill is one of only a handful of senior republicans who felt, from the outset, totally comfortable with the ideas of the younger generation, who were advocating the development of republican politics. A partial explanation for his thinking is reflected in his occasional references to the strategies conceived, but not fully developed, by the Three Macs – Paddy McLogáin in particular.

'I remember in my young day, Paddy McLogáin, when he was president of Sinn Féin, always said the IRA could not win a war on its own – it needed a political back-up. He maintained that you could not win by physical force alone; you needed a political wing. Physical force would not succeed without the support of the people, and you should always strive to have the backing of the people.

'This seemed to develop in the 1960s, but, in my opinion, the movement went astray by going completely political to the detriment of the physical force tradition. But now – and this is one of the great strengths of the republican movement over the past thirty years – we have had the support of the people, the people backed the IRA, the people backed the republican movement and the strategy.'

Nonetheless, the Diplock courts and the new set of British strategies were taking their toll on republicans. The IRA leadership realised that they too needed to change if the organisation was not to be wiped out.

'The second half of the 1970s were not good years for republicans. The armed struggle was continuing all right, but there were many volunteers being killed or lifted. In many ways, the Brits' strategy was working and the movement had been caught flat-footed. Sinn Féin was beginning to reorganise but so too, by all accounts, was the IRA,' Cahill says.

The IRA had begun a complete restructuring operation, aimed at rendering the organisation more effective, countering British initiatives, making infiltration more difficult and protecting its operatives. Attitudes were changing regarding a quick victory and early British withdrawal. The first public references to the change in strategy came at Bodenstown in 1977. Belfast republican Jimmy Drumm warned in his keynote speech that year that the organisation was in for a long haul. The lesson of the disastrous ceasefire had been bitter, he said. Far from being on the brink of announcing a withdrawal, as some republicans had thought, the British were digging in, pouring in vast sums of money in a bid to stabilise the political situation. Republicans, Drumm said, must now prepare for a long war, a war of attrition.

'That was the first inkling for most people that it was going to be a long, hard struggle,' says Cahill. 'There were no more annual slogans of this year or that year of freedom. The thinking had developed that you certainly could not drive the Brits into the sea. That was when the leadership realised the importance of political backing, particularly in the South, to defeat the laws used against republicans. The "long war" theory proved to be right – it was a long war.'

Evidence of the IRA's intention to change tactics became public knowledge later that year with the arrest of Séamus Twomey, who was chief of staff once again. Twomey had a number of documents in his possession when he was captured, but one in particular caught the imagination of the media.

The document painted a gloomy picture of the state of the IRA, suggesting that a number of factors were responsible: the tough new laws, confessions obtained using controversial interrogation techniques in police holding centres, the plethora of informers – all had contributed to a haemorrhaging of the membership. The present command structure of brigade–battalion–company–section was proving to be unwieldy and, worse, easily infiltrated, because it was too structured and formal.

A root-and-branch restructuring of the IRA was recommended. Sleepers (volunteers not known to security forces) should be put in place with a view to long-term operations; small cells should be set up to reduce the risk of infiltration by informers or agents.

Each cell would consist of a small group of people, numbering from five to seven, who would specialise in particular tasks – intelligence work, planting bombs, sniping, etc. Only one member in each cell would be in contact with a senior officer, so that even if a volunteer broke under interrogation, there was a limit to the amount of information he or she could divulge. The organisation's structure should revert to the old system of Northern Command and Southern Command, which had died along with the 1940s campaign. This meant that decisions on day-to-day IRA operations would be taken, not by a somewhat remote Dublin-based GHQ staff, but by those closest to the action.

The contents of the document, made public when Twomey appeared in court, were seized upon by the newspapers and made headlines. Cahill maintains the document was, in fact, one of a number of discussion papers in Twomey's possession when he was arrested.

'This one document was hyped up in the media and described as a staff report,' says Cahill. 'It's my understanding that it was just one of several documents found on him. They were not actual strategy papers from the IRA. They were suggestions for the IRA to consider, to talk about and, if seen to be good, then adopted. At that particular time, the different areas were asked for ideas on the structure of the IRA and how it could be restructured. This happens from time to time.

'Over the years, structures evolved – they were not imposed or thought out. At that particular stage of the struggle, from what I gather, it was believed necessary to restructure the Army, make it more effective and it would survive. Areas were asked, as were prisons, to produce documents on how they thought the Army would be most effective. A lot of ideas came out of the republican universities, the think tanks – the jails.

'It's common knowledge that there were other papers caught that day, but they seemed to hype up that particular plan without reference to the other documents found on him. He was chief of staff at the time; he had the documents; he was studying them; they were in his possession when he was arrested. That's why it was believed they were so important, that it was the new structure. The army did not say it was the new structure; Twomey did not say it was the new structure; no one has said since it was the new structure. It was other people surmising that it was the new structure.'

Cahill admits, though, that the republican movement appeared to take on board many of the suggestions outlined in the discussion paper. Although he was deeply involved in helping to strengthen Sinn Féin at the time, he was, he says, conscious of the fact that the new strategy had resulted in a turnaround of the IRA's fortunes:

'Yes, it certainly marked a turning point. It led to a lot of good, sensible thinking and the present strategy. I thoroughly agreed with the cell system. It had been used with the sanction of GHQ in Belfast years before. But following the truce of 1975–6, the IRA had been an organisation which was too open. It would have been difficult, with its structure then, to build security within the organisation. Because it was so open, the IRA risked infiltration by British intelligence, but some of the ideas suggested in the Twomey paper, such as the cell structure, were adopted and helped to protect against touts and informers. After the introduction of the cell structure, the internal security of the IRA became quite effective and became a big problem for the Brits.'

✠ ✠ ✠

If Jimmy Drumm's 'long war' speech and Séamus Twomey's captured document together marked an important milestone for the IRA, it was in the H-Blocks of Long Kesh that a battle was about to take place that would send Irish republicanism hurtling off in a direction that few could have predicted.

Kieran Nugent and the other prisoners on blanket protest in the jail found their protests making little impact on northern secretary Roy Mason, whose avowed aim was to defeat the IRA on all levels. 'The prisoners were criminals,' Mason said in his memoirs, 'and I was determined to treat them as criminals.'

In 1978, with the protest in its third year, the prisoners felt they were making no headway. Reports reaching the outside claimed the men were being regularly beaten and kept hungry. Cell furniture was broken in clashes with wardens and was eventually removed altogether. The protestors at this stage were allowed out of their cells only to go to Mass, to wash, or to empty their chamber pots. When a dispute broke out over the circumstances in which they went to the washrooms, the men decided not to leave their cells. The blanket protest had now escalated into a no-wash protest. There were frequent clashes between prisoners and warders, who objected to having to empty chamber pots. Soon cells and mattresses were saturated with urine. Prisoners responded by throwing their waste out of the windows, until these were blocked. Urine was then poured away through the cracks; excreta was smeared on the walls. Prisoners claimed they were periodically taken from their cells, hosed and scrubbed down with coarse brushes. Outside, the IRA responded by shooting warders. Nineteen were killed between 1976 and 1980.

Cahill recalls that the protest was receiving little publicity in the South. Supporters had an uphill battle trying to explain the motivations of over 300 'non-conforming prisoners', as they were termed by government spokesmen.

'I was one of the people who were going around the country trying to mobilise support for the protests. It was very difficult, very hard work. People knew very little about conditions inside the H-Blocks, or what the prisoners were protesting about. A lot of that was due to the censorship laws in the South – Section 31.'

Section 31, in force since 1972, was the piece of legislation which banned IRA and Sinn Féin members from being interviewed on the Republic's radio and television stations. Cahill admits that the ban made life difficult for republicans. It was 1988 before similar broadcasting restrictions were placed on republicans in the North.

An explosive new element was about to be added to the deteriorating situation in the H-Blocks. The general election of May 1979 saw Conservative leader Margaret Thatcher become the first British woman prime minister. If republicans believed that Roy Mason had been intransigent, they would soon be forced to reassess the meaning of the word. The Iron Lady, as she was dubbed by the press, came to power with her own ideas on how to settle the Irish question. Only weeks previously she had lost her close friend Airey Neave, when his booby-trapped car exploded as he left the House of Commons car park. The Irish National Liberation Army (INLA), a militant group which had split off from the Officials, claimed responsibility. Twelve weeks into her premiership, Lord Mountbatten, seventy-nine-year-old cousin to Queen Elizabeth, was killed along with three others when an IRA bomb exploded on his boat at Mullaghmore, County Sligo. Within hours, eighteen soldiers died in an IRA ambush at Narrow Water Castle near Warrenpoint, County Down. Thatcher was in no mood to grant concessions to Irish republicans.

In a bid to increase pressure for a return to political status, the protesting prisoners decided in late 1980 to embark on a hunger strike. The IRA leadership attempted to talk the men out of such a drastic step, but the protesters were determined. The seven volunteers who began the protest ended their fast shortly before Christmas, when they were given to understand that they had won significant concessions from the British government.

Claiming they had been deceived into ending their protest, the prisoners announced that a second hunger strike would commence in March 1981. Once again the leadership objected strongly, pointing out that the loss of several lives was extremely likely under the current British administration. After a hectic exchange of contraband communications, GHQ staff conceded that they had lost the argument and gave their full support to the men.

The second protest was to be phased, with IRA and INLA prisoners joining the hunger strike at regular intervals. The dirty protest was now called off, but the men still wore only blankets. Bobby Sands, IRA OC Long Kesh, began refusing food on 1 March 1981. The scene was set for one of the great prison struggles of the twentieth century, one that was to impact hugely on the future of Irish republicanism.

'Most of us,' Cahill says, 'were worried that Thatcher, who had little regard for the lives of Irish republicans, would let all the hunger strikers die, in spite of the fact that the five demands were legitimate and were only what was due to political prisoners. But once the prisoners had convinced the leadership they would go ahead with the hunger strike regardless of outside opinion, everybody threw their weight behind the campaign.

'There was a feeling amongst the leadership that Bobby believed his death was inevitable, and that Thatcher would be compelled to compromise before anyone else died. But, as it turned out, she was such a cold and ruthless person that her lust for Irish blood was not satisfied with the death of just one person.'

Around this time, Cahill was despatched once more, illegally, to the United States. He went on a tour of the main cities, raising funds and garnering support for the prison protest.

Bobby Sands was five days into his protest when Frank Maguire, independent nationalist MP for Fermanagh–South Tyrone, died suddenly. After consultation with the Maguire family and the various H-Block support groups, the republican movement came up with a masterstroke that would put the plight of the hunger strikers centre stage, and highlight what was viewed as British intransigence on the prisons issue – they would nominate Bobby Sands for Frank Maguire's vacant Westminster seat.

Nationalist representatives pulled out of the election, leaving Sands as the sole non-unionist candidate. The various strands of unionism had also left the field clear for their strongest contender, former Stormont minister Harry West. West polled 29,046 votes, to Sands's 30,492. It was a public relations disaster for Margaret Thatcher, who had declared that she would never concede political status to hunger strikers 'or any others convicted of criminal offences'.

In the H-Blocks, the prisoners were ecstatic. One prisoner in each block had possession of a smuggled crystal set – a tiny and extremely basic radio receiver. In H-5, the first man to hear the election result, a prisoner from the Short Strand enclave in east Belfast, quickly passed the news to the next cell through a tiny gap where the heating pipes entered the wall. The word spread along the wing within seconds, and throughout the entire block in a minute or two. The prisoners had been warned by camp staff to observe strict silence and not to react to news stories in case warders became aware that they had a source of information.

'But the wing just erupted,' the prisoner recalled. 'The lads were banging on the pipes and yelling and screaming. I heard two screws talking outside my cell door and one said, "Those fucking orderlies must have told them the election result."'

Momentous though it was, Sands's victory failed to move Thatcher. She steadfastly refused to intervene in the hunger strike, and Bobby Sands died in the early hours of 5 May. More than 100,000 people attended his funeral. The role of the second man – Francis Hughes, from Bellaghy in south Derry – now became pivotal. Starkly aware now that Thatcher was prepared to let them die rather than compromise, Hughes knew that he too was facing certain death unless he gave in. If he came off, the whole hunger strike would be in danger of collapsing. He stayed on the protest.

'I was in the Noraid office in New York,' says Cahill, 'when Martin Galvin [a prominent Irish-American republican supporter] came in and said he had received a message from Ireland that Bobby Sands had been nominated to fight the election. It was news to me. I was surprised, but I thought it was a very good idea. So I was in the States when he was nominated, when he was elected and when he died, and I was there when the next three died. I think I spent around four months in the States that time, and was able to put a big effort into publicising the protest and explaining the issues.'

Sands's election agent, Owen Carron, stood in the by-election caused by the hunger striker's death and won. Encouraged by these successes, republicans put prisoner candidates forward for the general election in the Republic. Two H-Block prisoners, Ciaran Doherty and Paddy Agnew, won Dáil seats. Mairead Farrell, who was serving a sentence in the women's jail in Armagh, also polled strongly. Joe McDonnell missed being elected by 315 votes. The election results were being noted by Sinn Féin strategists. Doherty and McDonnell were to die on hunger strike in the following days. Farrell and two male IRA colleagues were later shot dead in controversial circumstances by undercover soldiers of the Special Air Services (SAS).

'I remember I was in Philadelphia,' says Cahill, 'when Raymond McCreesh became the fourth hunger striker to die. I was present at an open-air meeting attended by 7,000 people. The families of the first four men came to the States and I met them in a house in New York. I remember Seán Sands [brother of Bobby Sands] saying that Haughey had extracted a promise from the British government that no more would die. I don't know any more about it than that, but obviously more were allowed to die.

'I was back home a few days later when the fifth man, Kevin

Lynch, died, and I was asked to speak at the GPO. We were using the back of a lorry as a platform. I remember being disappointed at the crowd that turned out – it was quite small, around 1,000. I saw a face I half-recognised, a woman on the edge of the crowd. It was a woman from Philadelphia. She said that a few days previously in the States we had 7,000, and asked why the crowd was so small in Ireland. She said the attendance was so poor that it was frightening. I couldn't explain, because I had been shocked myself.'

Cahill discussed the fall in attendance numbers with others, and came away with the impression that people from the various H-Block support committees who had wanted to attend a dignified protest had been upset when some rallies had ended in violence.

'In Dublin, shop windows were broken in O'Connell Street. People did not want this. The leadership had called on people not to do these things; some people felt offended and stayed away. It was a culture shock to come home to that. There had been riots in O'Connell Street while I was in America, and people there did not believe it was doing any good. They asked if the movement was behind it. I said no. I was 3,000 miles away, and could only hazard a guess that it was the spontaneous reaction of people against the twenty-six-county government, because they were doing nothing. It was also likely that some were reacting to provocation from the Gardaí.'

Despite the pounding she was taking from the world's media, Margaret Thatcher refused to bend. Ten men in all – seven IRA and three INLA volunteers – were to die before the hunger strike was called off. Shortly afterwards, the prisoners were granted all their demands. Cahill recalls being in the Mountjoy Square headquarters of the hunger strike supporters when he heard the news that the protest was over.

'Bernadette McAliskey [prominent civil rights activist and republican socialist] and Jim Gibney [senior Sinn Féin member] were there when the word came through that the hunger strike was ended. We were kind of surprised that it ended so quickly. We knew that negotiations were going on within the jail and outside, but we did not expect it to finish as quickly as it did.

'The families were taking the strikers off. They were being force-fed while unconscious. The momentum was being lost. The decision was taken within the jail to end it. I remember Bernadette, who was inclined to be annoyed that it was over, said they could have won if they had held out.'

Years later Cahill, on yet another illegal trip to the United States, was taken to see a hunger strike memorial in Hartford, Connecticut.

'In the main street in Hartford, there is a beautiful monument erected by the local council to the memory of the hunger strikers. There is a horseshoe of shrubs around it. There are three flower beds – green, white and orange – and that is something to see when they are in bloom. The guy responsible for it was showing me around. I told him he had made a mistake in the number of shrubs – there were only thirty-two counties in Ireland, and he had thirty-four shrubs there. He said, "I'll be damned, it took someone to come out from Ireland to see that." That evening, two were taken out.'

Cahill believes the hunger strikes were responsible for awakening republicans to the tremendous potential in entering the political arena.

'Thatcher claimed victory over the prisoners, but the international support shown for the hunger strikers showed who were the real winners, who the real people of principle were. The hunger strikes of '81 gave republicans a sense of how elections could be used to the advantage of the struggle. The results achieved gave great encouragement to the party and showed what was possible. It was those results which led Sinn Féin to review its electoral strategy.

'That was our entry into the political field in a strong way. Up to then it had been purely military thinking. That was the public image of things, but there was hard work going on in the background to develop politics.'

Sinn Féin, Cahill says, decided to test that strategy at the next opportunity. The chance came the following year, when Thatcher's northern secretary, Jim Prior, called elections for a power-sharing assembly. Prior's initiative was the latest in a series of abortive attempts to return some form of devolved government to the North. Republicans had not participated in elections to any of the previous bodies. Their participation in this poll would be on an abstentionist basis.

'In the main, Sinn Féin was ridiculed by the media and regarded as outsiders, no-hopers,' says Cahill. 'All of the opinion polls had us coming in last in any electoral contest. To the surprise of the electoral experts and, I may say, to the embarrassment of the media, we pulled out ten percent of the vote, and won five seats. We were unlucky not to win a number of others.

'Gerry Adams, Martin McGuinness, Danny Morrison, Owen Carron and Jim McAllister were all elected to the Assembly. The election results proved that the vote during the hunger strikes was more than just an emotional reaction by the people. It proved that Sinn Féin had a significant core support. In my opinion, this was the point when many republicans come to realise the potential of politics, to understand that we could advance our objectives politically.'

While the five Sinn Féin Assembly members did not take their seats, they opened offices from which to conduct constituency business. Soon there were twenty-eight such offices across the North, most with an enthusiastic team of young party workers prepared to deal with the problems of the community.

'There was another grand boost for Sinn Féin the following year – 1983 – when Gerry Adams took the Westminster seat. Danny

Morrison just missed the mid-Ulster seat by seventy-eight votes. Later that same year, Adams became party president.'

June 1983 also marked the election of west Belfast republican Alex Maskey to Belfast City Council, the first Sinn Féin member to take a seat there since 1922.

'Alex's election was a big breakthrough politically, because, at the next local government elections, several other councillors won seats. Our support increased from that time on; the party is currently the largest on the council.

'He had a tough time as the first Sinn Féin councillor. Every time he rose to speak at a council meeting, he was met with a barrage of noise from the unionist benches – they sounded off hooters, whistles and things like that. But Alex weathered all that and eventually, in June 2002, he wrote his own wee bit of history, by becoming the first republican mayor of Belfast.

'Sinn Féin had fought local government elections before, but in the North we were prevented from taking seats because councillors had to take an oath of allegiance to the British Crown. That had been in place since the 1920s and remained on the books until it was lifted in 1973 by the Whitelaw administration. It was the same oath which Catholic nurses, teachers and civil servants had to take if they wanted to work.'

Things were moving fast. In 1984 the republican leadership thought it was time to ensure that the American support base was kept abreast of developments. Cahill, by now regarded as Sinn Féin's unofficial, and still illegal, ambassador to the United States, was accompanied by two other veterans on his trip to take the message to the faithful.

'Joe B O'Hagan, Jimmy Drumm and myself went out. The normal practice was that, if arrested on these missions, you would accept voluntary deportation. In this particular case, Joe B was stopped going into the country and arrested. He was deported within two days. Jimmy Drumm and myself got through. We had gone separately, of course. When in America we didn't go about as a group.'

Cahill was heavily disguised when he arrived at Kennedy Airport. He had grown a moustache for the trip and was wearing spectacles, not normal practice for him at that time. His thinning hair was hidden by a luxuriant wig, which he had bought in a store in Dublin a few days before his flight. Cahill was travelling abroad so often now that he had a range of wigs which he used to help create different characters.

'I was travelling on a passport in the name of Jimmy Dowling. At the airport's reception area I was stopped by customs people and questioned. They then sent for a superintendent, who asked me about the purpose of my visit. I explained that I had a daughter in the United States and would be staying with her. It was just a cover story of course. He asked for her address. I told him I was to ring her, but had come away without her telephone number. I would ring my wife and get the number from here. He asked me if I knew what I was doing, and said that it would be like looking for a needle in a haystack. He said I didn't realise the vastness of the country.'

As Cahill was being questioned, other customs men had upended his suitcase and were going through his belongings.

'The superintendent was a nice guy. He told them to put everything back exactly as it was. He said I appeared to be an honest-to-Jesus man, wished me luck in finding my daughter and directed me out of the airport. I was relieved to go.'

Cahill took a bus to another New York airport – La Guardia – where he telephoned his contact, who lived fifteen minutes away in the Bronx.

'This man, Chris Dixon, was typical of the people we met in the States. I couldn't thank them enough. Their doors were always open to us, and nothing was too much trouble. For instance, when the families of some of the hunger strikers came to New York they were being billeted in different places. They were not too happy about that, because they hadn't been in the States before. A New York couple didn't hesitate – they took all eight people to stay with them. Chris Dixon worked for the state and, if the authorities had known what he was doing, he would have lost a good job. I stayed at his house quite a lot and he drove me around. Nothing could repay those people for their generosity.

'There was another good guy, who worked as an undertaker. Once he decided to take me to Long Island for a break. On the way he remembered he had a job to do. I said, forget about the trip, go ahead and do your work. He told me there was no rush and said, "It's okay, he's in the glove compartment."'

Cahill was around three weeks into his proposed four-week tour when, quite by accident, he met up with Jimmy Drumm. Drumm was booked on to a flight to another city the next day. Finding themselves in the same house, they agreed to go together that night to a meeting where Cahill was due to speak. Around thirty supporters had gathered in the private house where the function was to take place.

'We were driven to the function and when we arrived the area was deserted, except for a telephone company truck and some people with it who were working at the bottom of the street. Our driver pulled in close to the steps leading to the house. Just as we got out of the car, the customs men seemed to grow out of the ground. I heard a voice saying, "Hold it there, Joe, don't move."

'They got Jimmy and the driver as well and held us for a couple of minutes, until a number of police cars came to take us away. I discovered later that the men posing as the telephone people gave the signal that we were arriving.'

Jimmy Drumm, says Cahill, was travelling on his own passport. Although he had been interned, he had no convictions apart from a three-month sentence imposed in the 1930s. Drumm accepted voluntary deportation and was sent home within forty-eight hours.

'I would have accepted voluntary deportation, and did offer to accept it, but they brought a charge against me of violating a previous exclusion order. I was brought before the court, because I had been deported before and told not to enter the country again. I was also charged with possessing the false passport.'

Cahill was granted bail of $1 million. This seemed to pose little problem, as there were a number of supporters in the courtroom willing to put their homes up as surety. He was released into the custody of a probation officer, but not before the judge voiced his opinion of Irish republicans.

'He lacerated me,' says Cahill. 'He said he had no time for people like me because he believed I would have no compunction in blowing up his court, which is what he said we did back in Ireland. Yet despite this, the judge said, the court was full of people willing to go bail for me.'

Cahill was ordered to report to a probation officer each Monday until his next court appearance. The probation office, he said, was just a block away from the home of an Irish immigrant with whom he was staying.

'I turned up on the first Monday and the probation officer said he had discovered I had a heart condition. He told me I needn't travel to his office, but just to telephone. It was a rare stroke of luck. For the next twelve weeks I rang him every week. I made the phone calls from wherever I happened to be on Monday – Chicago, Philadelphia or San Francisco. I called him and was still able to travel freely and do the work that I went out to America to do – to organise support, keep supporters informed and collect money.'

The tangible fruits of his tour were witnessed in the following weeks, with the flood of Irish-Americans travelling to Ireland on holiday.

'The fund-raising part had been very successful. The money was brought over by people coming home on holidays. They concealed it on their persons. In those days, more money came over hidden in brassieres than any other way.'

Cahill describes the following year, 1985, as 'a measure of Sinn Féin's evolution into a political party'. The party did indeed have more electoral success when, for the first time in the North, it fought local government elections, putting forward eighty candidates and taking fifty-nine seats on local councils.

The British and Irish governments, alarmed at the growing support for Sinn Féin, hammered out the Anglo-Irish Agreement. This agreement, in Cahill's view, was aimed at undermining his party while winning support for the moderate nationalist Social Democratic and Labour Party (SDLP). Signed by Margaret Thatcher and taoiseach Garret FitzGerald, the agreement provided for an intergovernmental conference and the setting up of a full-time secretariat staffed by Irish and British officials. It also gave the Irish government a consultative role in British policy on the North. Unionists were infuriated by what they viewed as southern interference in their affairs, but the agreement was warmly welcomed by the SDLP leadership, regarded by both governments as the acceptable face of nationalism.

'The Anglo-Irish Agreement was supposed to be constitutional nationalist Ireland coming to an agreement with the British government. This would give more power, more influence to the nationalist side. The message was that you would be better off supporting the SDLP than Sinn Féin,' says Cahill.

'But it didn't quite work out like that, for a lot of reasons – not least because the British government did not honour any of the promises that were made. Also the promises were exaggerated and hyped, the most famous being Garret Fitzgerald's remark that the "nationalist nightmare" was now over. The problem was that if you were a nationalist living in Tyrone or Fermanagh, the UDR were still giving you hassle, still messing you about, still abusing and harassing people, still raiding. Discrimination was still going on. All the problems that existed before the Anglo-Irish Agreement still existed afterwards, and in some cases got worse.'

It was after the signing of the Anglo-Irish Agreement, Cahill insists, that the British government introduced what he calls 'political vetting'. He points to Conway Mill as an example: Cahill's younger brother, Frank, had the idea of buying and renovating the old semi-derelict mill on the Falls Road for the promotion of community projects. Gerry Adams, MP for the area, and pioneering west Belfast priest Des Wilson were also involved in developing the idea. Conway Mill was soon housing several small businesses and further education classes.

'People who previously could only dream of running their own business or achieving a qualification were flocking to the Mill. But the British were always suspicious where republicans were involved, on the basis that if known republicans were involved in anything, it must be bad. Projects like the Mill were denied funding and had to struggle for financial support. It is only now, many years later, that some projects have started to receive funds. It brought out their opposition to republicans being involved in a political process.

'The British tried to close down projects they thought were too republican-orientated, but they were missing the point. People saw the projects as community projects, not republican projects. It was seen as an attack on the community by a government which was supposed to be an ally of the SDLP and was supposed to be giving more power to the SDLP. The SDLP couldn't stop them. It didn't help the SDLP much and it also made nationalists wary of the Irish government, which for so long had ignored what was happening in the North, but then got involved, produced an agreement and found they could not deliver on it.'

Cahill's job as party treasurer was by now taking him all over the twenty-six counties. He was travelling more miles than any other member of the republican leadership. He was already well known to many republicans in Belfast, Dublin and Dundalk, but his work now was to ensure that his face also became familiar to Sinn Féin branches the length and breadth of the island.

His personal popularity and an almost legendary capacity for hard work were to stand the party in good stead during its next big step forward. Since the early 1980s, an internal debate had been taking place within Sinn Féin over its abstentionist policy in the Republic. In the North, the party had one Westminster MP, five Assembly members and fifty-nine local councillors. In the South, where Sinn Féin had been contesting council elections and taking seats for many years, they had thirty-nine councillors. They had no seats in the Dáil, however, and no real prospect of gaining any, since southern voters tended to regard support for an abstentionist party as wasted votes.

According to the new young leadership, personified by Gerry Adams and Martin McGuinness, the party needed to build support in the South and widen its power base. The way to do that, they argued, was to remove the barrier to Sinn Féin deputies taking seats in the Dáil.

Cahill had no problem with the dropping of the abstentionism clause from Sinn Féin's constitution as far as Leinster House was concerned. It was, after all, one of the ideas he had favoured since the late 1940s:

'My view was that we should contest elections in the South with the view to taking seats in Leinster House if elected. I had certain reservations about Stormont. In the early days, taking seats there was out of the question because that required an oath of allegiance to the British Crown to be taken. Also, because of the legislation and the political situation in the North, it would have been futile to take seats in Stormont. I would be entirely opposed to taking seats in Westminster.'

By 1986, those senior members who favoured dropping the abstentionism policy regarding the Dáil were ready to put their case to the *Ard Fheis*, held that year in November at the Mansion

House, Dublin. To be successful the proposal, Motion 162, needed a change in the Sinn Féin constitution, and that required a two-thirds majority. Opposition to the proposal was expected from traditionalists such as Ruairí Ó Brádaigh and Daithí Ó Conaill. No one was quite sure how much support Ó Brádaigh and Ó Conaill could muster, but there was a very real danger of a split in the movement.

'Many people,' says Cahill, 'were wondering what the IRA's attitude would be to the proposal. The army's constitution banned volunteers from even talking about taking parliamentary seats. A second clause banned volunteers from supporting anyone who did. So no one was going to go against the army.'

A split in Sinn Féin was one thing; a split in an armed organisation was altogether more dangerous. The Official–Provisional schism in the early 1970s had resulted in a number of deaths and left a legacy of bitterness which lasted for many years.

The IRA's answer came in an army council statement published three weeks before the *Ard Fheis*. The statement contained a report of the first General Army Convention to be held since the gathering in 1970, when Cahill had attempted to change the name of the IRA. A new twelve-member executive had been elected and had in turn elected an army council, which had appointed a new chief of staff. Several sections of the IRA's constitution, the statement said, had been amended and approved by more than the two-thirds majority necessary. Elements of the constitution had been rewritten in non-sexist language. But of particular interest to those concerned with the abstentionism debate was the news that two clauses had been amended to allow for the taking of Dáil seats. Delegates to the *Ard Fheis* were left in no doubt about the IRA's views on the issue.

'Everyone knew the depth of feeling about the abstentionist argument and it was expected that those opposed to dropping the clause would walk out of the *Ard Fheis* after the vote. Gerry and

Martin had a meeting with Ruairí and his people at lunchtime to try to prevent a walk-out. Adams asked them to stay with the movement. He told them that maybe, in time, they would either win the argument or see the sense of our argument. He said they shouldn't turn a tactical position into a principle position. Adams said afterwards that they were not prepared to listen,' Cahill says.

There were others at the *Ard Fheis* that day who had misgivings regarding the change of strategy, but who were prepared to listen to the arguments. Many of the younger people looked to the older generation for guidance and noted the stance of veteran republicans whom they admired and respected – people like Cahill, Seamus Twomey, John Joe McGirl and Joe B O'Hagan.

Powerful and persuasive speeches were made for and against Motion 162 during the debate, but it was Cahill's heartfelt plea for republican unity which made a huge emotional impact on his audience. Dropping abstentionism, he insisted, would not make anyone less of a republican.

'I haven't changed,' he told delegates. 'The dedication and commitment which brought me to the foot of the scaffold in 1942 is the same in my heart today as it was then, and it will be until the day I draw my last breath. The only thing that has changed, as far as I am concerned, is that age is against me and I can't be in the field with the freedom fighters today because of that.'

Cahill recalls that he then appealed to the old traditionalists 'not to walk away from the struggle'.

'In particular, I made a personal appeal to Ruairí Ó Brádaigh, who was suspected of being about to walk out. I said if they believed the policy of Sinn Féin was wrong, as was being put forward at the time, not to walk out. I pointed out that I had made one mistake in my life – in the 1960s, when I resigned from the republican movement, thinking that it would rally support and highlight what was going wrong with the republican movement, I was completely isolated. I used that as an example in '86 and appealed to them not to walk out. I asked them to stay in, fight their corner and work for change.'

The atmosphere in the Mansion House was tense as party chairman Sean MacManus called delegates to order before reporting: 'The result of the vote is as follows. In favour of Motion 162: 429. Opposed: 161. I thereby declare that Motion 162 is carried by the necessary two-thirds-majority-plus-one.'

The announcement was the signal for Ruairí Ó Brádaigh and Daithí Ó Conaill to lead between twenty and thirty supporters from the hall.

'Some may have heeded what I said,' says Cahill, 'but the rump led by Ó Brádaigh walked out. There was a commotion in the hall. It was realised that people were walking out in protest and this led to a great sense of sadness. Some of these people had, for a long time, been part of the movement which had brought us so far. They had made a big input and it was sad to lose them. But they had their minds made up that they were going to walk out. No amount of coaxing or reasoning was going to persuade them to change their minds. They had already arranged a venue to hold a meeting following the walk-out.'

That venue was the West County hotel in Chapelizod, where Ó Brádaigh and Ó Conaill immediately announced the establishment of Republican Sinn Féin. The schism, while engendering a certain amount of bitterness, never came close to descending into violence.

'Fewer than thirty people walked out of the *Ard Fheis* that day,' says Cahill. 'It was a split of sorts, but it was not as bad as it could have been. It would have been better if it hadn't happened. There were people in the media who exaggerated the importance of Ó Brádaigh and Ó Conaill's walkout. We actually needed more than a two-thirds majority. If there had been two-thirds voting for and one-third voting against it, that would have been a big split. It could have been very bad for the party and hampered its development.

'The people who walked out as a result of that decision represented between five and six percent. More than ninety percent supported the proposition, or, if some did not support it, they stayed. The number who left was much smaller than it might otherwise have been, so the damage that they thought they were probably going to be able to inflict did not materialise.'

The dropping of the abstentionism clause, says Cahill, marked the beginning of a transitional period for the republican movement, from war to politics. A few days later the IRA leadership issued another statement, saying they fully supported the outcome of the *Ard Fheis*. The seeds had been planted within the republican movement for what was to become a peace strategy.

'That period was the beginning of an effort by Sinn Féin to get our heads around this word "peace". For years it had been hijacked by others, who kept beating us over the head with it. Republicans, they said, were only interested in violence; everybody else was only interested in peace. It was the first public sense of Sinn Féin trying to develop a peace strategy.'

But, even as Sinn Féin was preparing to embark on a trip into the unknown territory of peace-making, the IRA was all too obviously still involved in armed struggle.

Cahill may have claimed in his *Ard Fheis* speech that he was too old for active service, but there is little doubt that the infrastructure put in place by him in the early 1970s was still being put to good use by the IRA of the late 1980s. Libya, it appeared, was still providing arms, and the IRA was still accepting them. But, as Cahill well knew, not all shipments reached their destination.

In October 1987, French customs officials boarded a Panamanian-registered ship off the coast of France. This was the conclusion of a surveillance operation which had involved British and French intelligence services, a Royal Navy hunter-killer submarine and a French security forces spotter aeroplane.

As the boarding party began to search the old vessel, the *Eksund*, they realised she was tilting well forward and was, in fact, sinking. The crew of five Irishmen, who were wearing rubber wetsuits, had broken out two inflatable dinghies and were preparing to abandon ship. Below decks, the forward ballast tanks had been flooded. This was no accident – an attempt was being made to scuttle the ship. A lesson had evidently been learned from the capture of the *Claudia* fourteen years earlier.

In the *Eksund*'s holds, the French team discovered a cargo of 150 tons of modern weaponry, including twenty surface-to-air missiles (SAMs), 120 RPG7 rocket launchers, 1,000 AK47 assault rifles, 1,000 mortar bombs, a million rounds of ammunition, 600 grenades, fuses, detonators, ten DShK heavy machine guns and two tons of Semtex, the most modern and deadly plastic explosive then available.

In the days following the arrest of the Irishmen, it emerged that the gunrunning trip had not been an isolated incident. Four previous shipments had already been landed in Ireland, and distributed in dumps all over the country. The capture of the *Eksund*, which was carrying the largest tonnage of all five trips, was a blow to the IRA, but still left it more heavily armed than it had ever been in its history.

'We heard about the *Eksund* at the 1987 *Ard Fheis*,' remembers Cahill. 'A reporter told me that news was coming over the wire that a shipment of arms had been intercepted by the French, in French waters. There was a lot of speculation about the ownership of the cargo, but no one could enlighten us at the time.'

It was abundantly clear that, while the seeds of a peace formula had found fertile ground within Sinn Féin, the IRA was now better equipped than at any time in its history. It was able and willing to carry on its 'war of attrition' indefinitely.

Cahill by now had experienced three heart attacks of varying intensity and had not enjoyed full health for several years. Despite this, he continued with a punishing schedule which, colleagues say, would have exhausted men half his age. But he was soon to be struck by an ailment that he could not work through or shrug off.

In 1988 three IRA volunteers on an operation in Gibraltar were killed by undercover troops of the British Army's SAS regiment. Several senior republicans had gathered at Dublin airport to receive the bodies of Mairead Farrell, Dan McCann and Seán Savage. Part of the ceremony entailed Cahill stepping forward to place the national flag on McCann's coffin.

Sinn Féin vice-president Pat Doherty was standing beside Cahill and noticed that he was swaying slightly from side to side. Cahill, determined to tough it out, attempted to walk towards the coffin, folded tricolour in hand, when he appeared to stumble. Doherty held him firmly by the elbow and guided him forward. Cahill completed his part of the ceremony, but colleagues afterwards insisted that he go to hospital for a check-up. After several tests, he was found to have cancer of the colon.

Dessie Mackin, who worked with Cahill in Sinn Féin's accounts department and later became the party's director of finance, said Cahill had to be practically ordered to rest after coming out of hospital.

'Accommodation was found for him in Dundalk, County Louth, and Annie came down from Belfast to help nurse him back to health. With the children occasionally visiting from Belfast, it was the nearest they had come to a bit of family life since 1969,' Mackin recounts.

As soon as he was able, Cahill, self-admittedly a bad patient, was back on the road, commuting daily between Dundalk, Dublin and anywhere else that he was needed. Then aged sixty-eight, he found himself, as a member of Sinn Féin's executive, receiving briefings suggesting faint but exciting possibilities of peace. After a shaky start in 1988, a relationship was built up between Gerry Adams and John Hume, leader of the SDLP. From 11 January until 5 September that year, a series of meetings took place, initially between Hume and Adams only and then along with party delegations. The parties also exchanged detailed papers outlining their respective views of the conflict. Some areas of agreement were reached and, while the talks ended in September, these formed the basis for further private discussions between the party leaders and were later to re-emerge in the Hume–Adams statements and agreement.

Cahill recalls: 'Republicans kept everything under wraps for a long time, for fear of raising hopes of peace falsely or too quickly, but there was an awful lot going on behind doors. Gerry Adams was consulting the *Ard Comhairle* on his talks with John but, to the best of my knowledge, John was not briefing his party. In 1990 we also began to get briefings about renewed contact between republicans and the British. An old channel, actually referred to as the "back channel", had been used by the two sides over the years. It had been reopened and messages were passing back and forth between them.

'The communications between republicans and the British hit a few bad patches, but managed to continue for the next few years. They eventually broke down in November 1993. As for the Adams–Hume talks – they resulted in an agreement between the two which opened up the real potential for a peace process. London and Dublin rejected Hume–Adams, but eventually, in December 1993, produced the Downing Street Declaration. It fell short of what republicans wanted, and many more months of negotiation and discussions followed.'

Significantly, however, the Letterkenny conference conceded that the declaration 'marked a further stage in the peace process'.

'The Hume–Adams document,' says Cahill, 'was read out at the Letterkenny conference, but no copies were handed out because it was a private, confidential document. It was the first time the rank and file of the republican movement had heard its contents, apart from speculation about it which had appeared in the papers, but, as I said, the *Ard Comhairle* had been kept fully briefed and had ratified the talks.

'There was a great fuss made by the media after the conference, because of the expectation that an announcement would be made concerning an IRA ceasefire. The fact is that the leadership believed that all the conditions would be right, all the pieces of the jigsaw would be in place, by the time the conference came around, and the cessation could be announced. But not everything was in place at that time, and so the announcement couldn't be made.'

By August 1994, all but one of the pieces of the jigsaw were in place. Cahill was given the crucial task of completing the picture.

CHAPTER FOURTEEN
Peace?

The IRA leadership and the Sinn Féin *Ard Comhairle* knew that conditions were now almost right for calling the long-awaited ceasefire. However, outside of that relatively small group, the public feeling was a mixture of expectation, confusion and doubt.

In the republican heartlands in Belfast, Derry and across the North, there was an air of suppressed excitement, coupled with not a little anxiety. People wondered what form the ceasefire would take, if it came at all. Was there compromise involved? Had too much been given away? Would all the deaths and the years of sacrifice be in vain? Would an agreement bring a just and lasting peace? Would it lead to a thirty-two-county Irish republic? There were those too, who feared that a cessation called on the wrong terms could lead to what republicans dreaded above all else – a split.

The pieces of the jigsaw referred to by Cahill were a series of public statements made by parties interested in the success of the Irish peace process.

'These statements were meant to set the scene, to create the context for the ceasefire and to reassure not only republican activists, but the whole community, that the IRA was embarking on a huge endeavour, a genuine effort at peace-making. They were also aimed at letting people know just how wide support was for the political alternative to armed struggle that Adams and others had been working on for years.

'It all came together, more or less, towards the end of August. The first statement came on Friday, 26 August, from the Connolly House group, as they were known. These were influential Irish-Americans who had been involved, successfully, in lobbying president Clinton for the visa that Gerry Adams needed to get entry into the States earlier in the year.'

This group was comprised of former congressman Bruce Morrison, billionaire businessmen Chuck Feeney and Bill Flynn, Niall O'Dowd, publisher of the New York-based *Irish Voice* newspaper, and trade union executives Joe Jamison and Bill Lenihan. Some members had been involved with the peace process almost since its inception. The group took its name from Connolly House, Sinn Féin's Belfast headquarters, where they met party leaders when in the city.

'They had been back and forward a few times and had met the loyalists, the unionists and us. They landed in Dublin on the twenty-fifth and came to Belfast the following day, when speculation about the IRA cessation was at its height. They came to meet us and they did so with the full knowledge of Clinton. They made a very positive statement afterwards about the potential for the peace process.'

Bruce Morrison said after the meeting he was 'hopeful of a dramatic breakthrough'. That optimistic message by the Connolly House group was followed by two others to be released that same week.

On the following Sunday, Gerry Adams and John Hume put out a joint communiqué on their aspirations for the peace process. It concluded: 'We are indeed optimistic that the situation can be moved tangibly forward.'

Hours later, taoiseach Albert Reynolds reaffirmed his commitment to the reunification of the country by peaceful means.

Cahill recalls: 'Sinn Féin was now able to put a very strong case to the IRA to announce a cessation. The input of the Americans showed the success of the leadership's attempt to create international support for Sinn Féin's peace efforts. We were not alone. This was in spite of the British government, which had always referred to the situation here as an internal matter that had nothing to do with any other country. It was not until 1985 that they allowed the Irish government to have even a limited input into the situation up here.

'Albert Reynolds as taoiseach was also behind the process, and that strengthened the North–South connection. His statement meant that the Irish government was supporting the peace efforts. The joint statement by Gerry and John showed that the leaders of nationalism and republicanism in the North were agreed on the way forward.'

It was a rare set of circumstances indeed which had brought the Irish peace process to this juncture: a republican leadership determined to follow a particular political course; a president of the United States strongly interested in bringing peace to Ireland; influential Irish-Americans willing to act as honest brokers; a taoiseach with a close understanding of republicanism, and a willingness to take risks; and a remarkable priest, whose insight into the process was probably as deep as that of any of the principals.

This priest, Father Alex Reid, was a member of the Redemptorist Order based in Clonard Monastery, just off the Falls Road in west Belfast. The full part played by Father Reid in the peace process will probably never be made public, but all players acknowledge the importance of his role as mediator, counsellor, courier, facilitator and one-man pressure group. The fact that the Irish Republican Army was on the verge of calling a ceasefire was due in no small measure to the efforts of this quiet, unassuming clergyman.

That, then, was the situation leading into the last week of August.

Gerry Adams met the IRA leadership and gave them his assessment of the situation. The IRA, however, needed just one more assurance before the final piece of the jigsaw would drop into place. There remained one element of the wider republican support base, a very important element, which needed to be reassured that there had been no sell-out, no abandonment of principle – that element was Irish-America.

The importance of the role played by republican supporters in the United States has often been underestimated, but the leadership in Ireland knew the value of their power base there. Many Americans were even more hard-line in their republicanism than people in Ireland. If the announcement of a cessation was not handled properly, there was as much chance of a schism in the movement occurring there as in Ireland. It was imperative, therefore, that an emissary be sent to the USA to brief the support base when news of the cessation broke.

As far as the republicans were concerned, there was only one man who had the necessary authority and respect, and whose word was most likely to be accepted by Irish-Americans – that man was the unofficial ambassador, Joe Cahill.

'We knew that if the IRA decided to go for a ceasefire it would come as a surprise, even to a lot of active republicans. There was an air, an impression, that something was happening, but, because of the type of talks that were taking place, the information was kept within a very tight circle. It would be important to keep everybody on board, both at home and in America.

'There was a lot of concern about the American support base, that it would come as a shock to them because they had absolutely no knowledge of what was happening. It was felt that there needed to be somebody in place in America if a ceasefire was announced, someone who would be fully briefed and would be acceptable to the American support base. I had a fair innings with people in America, so it fell to my lot to go out, to be in place. I would then immediately begin to travel the country to brief different Irish groupings in different cities and different states, basically to calm nerves and assure them there was no sell-out.'

Cahill had been advised by the Sinn Féin leadership to apply for the visa and did so. He knew there was political involvement at a high level in pushing his case, but it was only later he became fully aware of just how close the application came to being thrown out.

It was soon to become obvious to him that his record had come under recent scrutiny from the American authorities – he was as notorious within the United States government as he was popular with that country's Irish republicans. He had, after all, been convicted on a murder charge and sentenced to hang, as well as being a convicted gunrunner.

But the IRA had staked much on Cahill being in the States at the right time. A refusal to grant him entrance would have had serious implications for the possibility of a ceasefire and the peace process in general. Brought to basics, the message was stark – no visa for Cahill, no ceasefire.

Once more, Father Reid proved to be hugely influential as he worked in the background, constantly providing Albert Reynolds with analysis and updates while urging him to contact president Clinton. The priest wanted Reynolds to impress upon Clinton the importance of granting a waiver of the ban on Cahill entering the United States. Reynolds was, of course, very supportive of the ceasefire attempts but, at the height of the holiday season, he was having great difficulty in contacting his usual channels to Clinton.

'Jean Kennedy Smith,' Cahill recalls, 'was the American ambassador to Ireland during that period, and she was always willing to help. She was very interested in the peace process. But she was on holiday in France. After being contacted several times by Reynolds, she broke her holiday and returned to Dublin to see what she could do. I remember later going to her and apologising for upsetting her holiday plans.'

The ambassador's first move was to contact Nancy Soderberg, staff director of the National Security Council and one of Clinton's leading foreign policy advisers. Kennedy Smith rang Soderberg several times, but found she was reluctant to get involved. Soderberg had used her good offices earlier in the year to provide a visa for Gerry Adams, on the understanding that it would help achieve an IRA ceasefire. Adams had had a hugely successful visit to the

United States, but now Soderberg wanted the ceasefire signed, sealed and delivered before she considered any more concessions.

Only the insiders knew that if everything was favourable, the IRA would announce a cessation of military operations on Wednesday, 31 August. Reynolds, at Kennedy Smith's instigation, was regularly on the telephone to Nancy Soderberg. On Monday evening, 29 August, he made his final pitch, shamelessly attempting to capitalise on the fact that the American was one-quarter Irish. Soderberg eventually agreed to contact Clinton who was holidaying at Martha's Vineyard, an island resort just off the coast of Massachusetts. The result was that Clinton telephoned Reynolds.

'[Reynolds] said to Clinton in a telephone call during the night that it was imperative that I be in America,' says Cahill. 'I assumed that Clinton knew by now just what was happening, because he had asked to see the file on me. He got back on to Reynolds and he asked him if he had seen my CV – did Albert realise what kind of man he was seeking a visa for? Reynolds is said to have passed some remark like, "What did you expect, a parish priest?"

'Reynolds told him that if things didn't work out, he could send me back home on the next plane. I think at this stage that Clinton was on the verge of taking the decision to grant a waiver, but Albert still had a wee bit of work to do.'

Clinton then turned to the subject of Pat Treanor, a Monaghan Sinn Féin councillor and ex-prisoner, whom the republican leadership wanted to accompany Cahill on his tour of the United States. Clinton told Reynolds that Treanor had been stopped at Kennedy airport just a few days previously, and sent back to Ireland. Reynolds replied that Cahill's health had been poor recently and Treanor was needed to help look after him.

The president was still not totally convinced. He was clearly unhappy that he was now being asked to grant waivers for two republicans who had served prison sentences for IRA activities.

'Bill Clinton asked Reynolds about the proposed wording of the ceasefire statement,' says Cahill, 'but Albert said he would have to get back to him on that. Albert contacted Father Reid and was then able to ring Nancy Soderberg and tell her a bit about the form the statement would take. From what I heard, Nancy was excited and contacted another senior foreign policy advisor, Tony Lake. They then immediately informed Clinton of the wording.'

The few lines from the IRA statement had helped Clinton to make up his mind. He told Reynolds to 'have the two gentlemen' at the American embassy in Dublin at 9am the following morning. Meanwhile Cahill, who had been joined at this stage by his wife Annie, was waiting on tenterhooks for Clinton's decision:

'The evening before I was due to fly out, there were several phone calls. It was a case of, maybe it's on, maybe it's not. There was nothing clear. The last phone call that I got – fortunately I had a phone beside the bed – was early on the morning of the day I was to go to America. We were booked onto a flight at midday. Annie was going with me, because my health was not good. I think she was getting a bit browned off with the phone calls – she said to me to tell them to go to hell.

'That last call told me I had to be at Hume House, across the road from the embassy at Ballsbridge, at nine o'clock. I was to be there in the anticipation that I was going to America, but at this stage, at 6.30 in the morning, there was nothing definite. I arrived at Hume House at nine. There were officials waiting and they ushered us into an office. We were offered tea and biscuits. I still didn't actually know what was happening at this stage, because no one had said you are getting your visa or not getting it. They came over to ask the odd question or some clerk would come in to have some form filled. Around ten o'clock in the morning, I was told I was being granted a visa. The flight was just two hours later. We were standing at the airport, with our suitcases and ready to travel, and we still did not have the visas. They were eventually delivered to us by courier.'

Just before he left for the airport, Cahill privately received confirmation that the cessation statement would be released the following day.

Few journalists linked Cahill's trip to the USA with speculation about an IRA ceasefire. It was, however, a different story on the other side of the Atlantic.

'There was no great sign of media interest in Ireland about me going to America, no media at Dublin airport. But when I arrived in America, I was surprised to be informed by people who met me that there was a big lot of media waiting outside. Rather than go through the crowd, it was arranged that we would use a back entrance at the airport.'

The party managed to avoid the press, except for a couple of enterprising photographers who had staked out the rear entrance and managed to get some shots of the group as they headed for their waiting car.

'The day we arrived in America I attended a function in Hartford, Connecticut. This was accepted as an ordinary Northern Aid function with nothing special to it. But I have a very vivid memory of talking to people that night and knowing that the next morning, at around six o'clock American time, the ceasefire was to be announced. It was sort of a wee bit strange. I was talking to them about support and continuing their work for prisoners, and the political work that they were doing, and all the time knowing that within a few hours this whole thing would be changed. I had to be very careful.'

The next morning in Dublin, a journalist working for the national broadcasting service, RTÉ, played an audio-taped IRA statement to his excited bosses. It had been handed to him earlier by a republican source. The contents were revealed to the Irish public in a newsflash at 11.25am. Contrary to everyone's expectations, the IRA army council had not put a time limit on their ceasefire. It was to be open-ended.

'Recognising the potential of the current situation,' the IRA statement went, 'and in order to enhance the democratic peace process and underline our definitive commitment to its success, the leadership of Óglaigh na hÉireann have decided that as of midnight, Wednesday 31 August, there will be a complete cessation of military operations. All our units have been instructed accordingly.'

In west Belfast, Gerry Adams needed the services of several stewards and Sinn Féin councillors to guide him through a phalanx of cheering supporters on his way to a hastily-erected platform outside Connolly House. It took the beaming Adams several minutes to negotiate the few yards from his car to the platform. At one stage he looked to be in real danger of being overwhelmed. Everyone, it seemed, wanted to slap him on the back or shake his hand. Dozens of women, including one foreign journalist who momentarily abandoned all pretence of objectivity, hugged and kissed the Sinn Féin president. A stream of cars, adorned with Irish tricolours and with passengers hanging out of every window, blared their horns as they passed Connolly House, to be greeted with cheers from the crowd.

Over in Connecticut, Cahill had stayed up all night. He found he was somewhat surprised at his own emotions as he watched media coverage of reaction to the cessation. He had worked towards this day for years, had indeed been one of the leading advocates of the Irish peace process. Now that it had arrived, he felt more melancholy than elated.

'I still clearly remember watching the announcement of the ceasefire on television next morning and seeing the celebrations in Belfast, Derry and elsewhere – the car cavalcades, the joy in the faces and expressions of the people. I felt isolated and away from it all, and I felt sad that I was in America and not in Ireland. I was also afraid that people might have gone a bit overboard. As I watched the television pictures, I said to myself that if the talks didn't work out it would be a terrible disappointment to people, and we could lose support if the IRA had to go back to war.

'That night I was doing a function in Philadelphia. Before I went on to the stage, I was still unsure what the reactions of the people would be. But there was absolutely no problem among the supporters in Philadelphia. They were fully supportive of what was happening and the reaction I got fully endorsed what was happening back home. It did me good and it compensated for what I felt I had lost by being in America.'

Cahill says that he and Treanor then set out on what turned out to be a punishing round of briefings, aimed at explaining the cessation to Irish-American communities in as many states, cities and towns as possible.

'Pat Treanor was invaluable when we reached the States. Generally we did joint meetings, but sometimes it was necessary to split up because it would have been impossible for me to cover the entire country on my own. Pat would go to one state while I went to another.'

Cahill's regard for Treanor did not, however, prevent him from an occasional piece of mischief-making at his friend's expense, especially in front of their American audiences.

'A while back Pat was taking some overseas visitors from Monaghan into the North, where he wanted to show them around. They were stopped by the RUC and Pat was arrested and put into their vehicle. On the way to the barracks the IRA opened fire on the RUC vehicle. The only person injured was Pat, who was hit in the hand and sustained the loss of a finger.

'Shortly after the incident, Pat walked into the special meeting at Letterkenny with his hand heavily bandaged. Some people asked what was wrong with his hand and he said the IRA had shot him. No one believed him, of course. And when he was in America with me and there were times I was introducing him to the audience, I would explain what had happened. I would say they may have noticed that Pat is minus a finger – his only regret about that is he's not able to pick his nose.'

Despite the warmth of their welcome, many American supporters made plain to Cahill and Treanor that they did not intend to blindly accept a ceasefire at any price and demanded explanations:

'When I say we were very well received, that's not to say that people did not ask questions. People were worried. They were asking why a ceasefire was called at this stage, what was the reasoning behind it. Naturally they had awkward questions to ask. Some of our supporters were ex-IRA who had set themselves up with a new life out there, and people of that ilk can be very critical.

'At the same time, while there were people who asked awkward questions, there was nothing asked that I couldn't answer. I was able to satisfy everybody there was no sell-out or anything like that. I assured them that no deal had been done, that the ceasefire was called to allow negotiations between republicans and the British. As far as the ceasefire was concerned, I said, it was a unilateral cessation, which left the IRA in the position that if negotiations failed, they could go back to war. The reception everywhere was beyond our expectations. Supporters were optimistic, and even in a jubilant mood.

'We started off with that first meeting in Hartford, Connecticut, and kept up a hectic pace for three weeks. After Hartford, we went to Philadelphia, then the Midwest, Chicago, Cleveland, then headed west to San Francisco, Los Angeles and Santiago. Then it was back to the east coast, where I did several meetings in and around New York, including Long Island and New Jersey. After that it was up to Boston. We did three or four meetings in that area and then, very tired, headed back to New York and home.'

Back once more in Dublin, Cahill said he was relieved to find that people were not regarding the ceasefire as a victory – which was what the leadership feared – but were just happy that the IRA had called a cessation to pursue a changed strategy.

The IRA's use of the term 'complete cessation' took practically everyone by surprise. Even the RUC chief constable of the day, Sir Hugh Annesley, with his extensive intelligence network, expressed surprise that the IRA did not put a time limit on their ceasefire.

Cahill says that, like Annesley, most people had assumed that if a cessation was coming it would be finite, lasting perhaps a few days, a week or a month.

'It was for many republicans a deep psychological shock, even though the process had been underway for some years. The strategy had been outlined in terms of building alliances with other political forces in Ireland and outside Ireland, of trying to build a peace process which would deal with the core issues, including the British presence. This initiative, an open-ended cessation, was huge in republican terms, enormous.'

Sinn Féin leaders, who had persuaded the IRA to call the cessation, now wanted to move the peace process on, with an early meeting with British ministers. They knew, however, that it would be an uphill task to make progress, and had frequently warned their membership that negotiations would be difficult and protracted. As Cahill himself has frequently pointed out: 'It's easy to make war, it's hard to make peace.'

But even the most pessimistic of republicans must have been surprised at the response to the news by British prime minister John Major, who had succeeded Margaret Thatcher when she was dropped by her party in 1990.

'The first thing Major said,' says Cahill, 'was that there would have to be a "decontamination" period before anybody could talk to Sinn Féin. It was quite insulting, but we bit our tongues and didn't allow his comments to put us off our strategy. We kept focussed on that.

'I believe that Major and the British government were unhappy with the peace process, unsure about engaging with it. They were afraid it was going to take them to positions they did not want to go, so they tried to keep us at arm's length. The cessation was at the end of August, and the first discussions we had with British government officials were in early December, over three months later. Even then, the discussions were inconclusive. They staggered on for months, getting nowhere. The British would not engage properly in negotiations.'

Cahill suspects that Major had been advised by his intelligence agencies to use the cessation in the same manner as Harold Wilson's Labour government used the 1975 ceasefire.

'I think Major's government saw the peace process as a means of defeating republicans, who were investing time and energy in it and who had persuaded the IRA to take huge risks by calling a cessation. All previous cessations, mainly in the 1970s, had been disasters. The 1974–5 cessation in particular had been an unmitigated disaster for republicans. It dragged on for a long period, they got nothing out of it and all the time the Brits were moving ahead on criminalisation and Ulsterisation and building the H-blocks. It was all a con. It was all about keeping the IRA quiet while they were building the blocks. Many of our people said they would never go down that road again. That ceasefire caused all sorts of ructions within the republican movement; some of the leadership lost credibility over the way it was handled.'

To the casual observer, the political scene in the following months seemed to be a series of stand-offs and stalemates – Sinn Féin was busily seeking negotiations with government ministers, while John Major was doing his best to deny them access to anyone other than senior civil servants. Cahill says there were few who realised that British procrastination was causing intense frustration, not only within Sinn Féin but also, according to soundings, at the highest levels of the IRA:

'Major appeared to be interested only in creating obstacles to progress and setting preconditions. First it was the decontamination period. Then he would not allow his people to talk to Sinn Féin unless the IRA said the ceasefire was permanent. No talks had yet taken place on the issue of the release of prisoners. Then Major and the unionists raised the issue of arms decommissioning. Meaningful talks, substantive talks, the Brits said, could not begin until the IRA handed over its weapons.

'The British seemed to think they could prevent change while keeping republicans locked into a process that had no momentum and was going nowhere. They believed that if they kept that up long enough, republicanism would implode, time would pass without violence and republicans could not go back to war. And actually, there were some republicans who also believed that the IRA could not go back to war once the momentum was lost.'

The situation, from a republican perspective, was not helped when Albert Reynolds, one of the stalwarts of the Irish peace process, resigned in November 1994 after a political crisis and his Fianna Fáil government collapsed. The party lost the general election the following month and Fine Gael leader John Bruton became taoiseach. Bruton was viewed with suspicion by the Sinn Féin leadership, and their dismay was compounded when the new taoiseach appeared to adopt an approach close to the British line.

'Somebody once said John Bruton was like a cushion, because he always bore the impression of the last person to sit on him,' says Cahill, 'and I can't help thinking that was true. He had a meeting with Major just days after winning the election, and immediately afterwards said there could be no progress until the IRA moved on decommissioning.'

In November 1995, the British and Irish governments brought in respected former US senator George Mitchell to head up an international team to compile a report on the issue of decommissioning of republican and loyalist arms. President Clinton attempted to inject movement into the stymied peace process with his first visit to Ireland the same month. He was given a rapturous reception in Belfast and Derry, but failed to persuade Major to engage fully with republicans.

The stalled peace process brought vigorous protests from Sinn Féin, but there were also dark murmurings emanating from the IRA.

'I was always afraid, and I said it many times, that if the Brits did not deliver on this peace process and if they failed to honour their commitments, the IRA was quite capable and able and, arguably, could go back to war,' Cahill says. 'It was the day before Clinton was due that it dawned on John Bruton and John Major that they would have to make a move. They met at midnight and hammered out a paper on a twin-track approach, which referred to the arms issue being dealt with as the parties talked.

'President Clinton arrived and got this huge welcome – he was seen by people at the time as the Seventh Cavalry coming over the hill to the rescue. The process was in crisis; it was about to go down. Everybody knew the twin-track approach agreed by the two governments was only there because he was coming. The governments did this to accommodate him.'

George Mitchell's report, produced after Christmas, was fairly well received by Sinn Féin. Mitchell reported that prior decommissioning – the handing over of weapons before entering talks – would never be accepted by the IRA. The team recommended parallel decommissioning, as described in the twin-track paper. But, once again, republicans felt they were getting sand kicked in their faces when Major, as Cahill describes it, 'binned the report in the House of Commons'.

'Major said he was going to hold elections to a new forum in May, which was what the unionists had been demanding. The unionists were depending on their inbuilt majority to veto progress. The SDLP said they didn't want an election. We said we didn't want it. The Irish government said it didn't want it. Major gave the unionists what they wanted.'

The election meant that the long-delayed high-level negotiations between Sinn Féin and government ministers were again put on the long finger. For republicans, it was the final insult.

At 5.40pm on Friday, 9 February 1996, London police began to receive calls from a number of news organisations reporting that the IRA had issued a statement ending their ceasefire. Police confirmed the authenticity of the statement at 7pm. One minute later a 1,000 pound bomb, concealed in a lorry in an underground car park, exploded beneath an office building at Canary Wharf, one of London's most important commercial districts. Two men were killed and 100 people injured. More than £850 million of damage was caused.

The Canary Wharf bomb marked the start of a limited campaign by the IRA, confined mainly to Britain and Europe. Other bombs followed. The heart was torn out of Manchester city centre by another massive explosion and a British army base at Osnabrück in Germany was mortar-bombed.

'The interesting thing,' says Cahill, 'was that the IRA went back to war in February and there was an election to the forum in May. The forum was basically a debating facility. We and the SDLP contested the elections on the basis that we were not participating. Sinn Féin got around fifteen people elected. Our vote was up. It scared the hell out of the Brits and our opponents, who probably thought we were going to get hammered as a reaction to the IRA going back to war. In fact the reality was that most people didn't want the IRA going back to war, but understood that the British had been messing.'

But if Sinn Féin supporters understood, the British government took a different view and broke off contact with the party. Sinn Féin, however, was still kept in the political picture through the Dublin-based Forum for Peace and Reconciliation, established during the premiership of Albert Reynolds. Party president Gerry Adams was also travelling regularly to the United States, where, to the disgust of John Major, he had been welcomed by President Clinton.

It was not until October that the IRA switched their attention back to the North. Their target for one of the most audacious attacks in twenty-five years was the British Army's Northern Ireland headquarters at Thiepval Barracks in Lisburn, Country Antrim, probably the most closely-guarded complex on the island. A warrant officer was killed when two car bombs exploded inside the barracks grounds within a few minutes of each other.

'There was more or less political stalemate for the fifteen months or so of the IRA's return to war,' says Cahill. 'At the forum elections in May 1996, Sinn Féin's vote had risen to 15.5 percent. In the British general election of May 1997, the party did even better, taking almost seventeen percent. Sinn Féin won two Westminster seats. Gerry Adams regained his seat, which he had lost in the previous election, and Martin McGuinness was elected in mid-Ulster. Major was kicked out of office at that election and Tony Blair's Labour party had a big majority.'

In the Republic, John Bruton was toppled in the same year, with new Fianna Fáil leader Bertie Ahern becoming taoiseach in a coalition government. Suddenly, the auspices for the Irish peace process seemed brighter. The approach to the process taken by the new Irish and British leaders was in stark contrast to their predecessors. In June the previous year, Sinn Féin had turned up at all-party talks from which they had been excluded. The British and Irish governments said the party could only take part in the discussions after the IRA had reinstated its cessation of violence. Cahill says that Sinn Féin rejected this and pointed to its substantial electoral mandate, which had increased in the Forum elections two months earlier. 'We had a democratic mandate and the governments had to respect it. We went to Stormont that day to make a stand,' Cahill recalls.

Photographs of the party leadership snapped through the bars of the gate at Stormont may have had much propaganda value, showing up Major's perceived intransigence, but did little to progress the process. Now Ahern and Blair were determined to get proceedings back on track. Blair appointed the popular Mo Mowlam as secretary of state for Northern Ireland and promptly announced his government's intention to take part in exploratory talks with Sinn Féin. The IRA responded by calling a second cessation on 21 July. Compared to the 1994 cessation, reaction was low-key, with the news being greeted more with relief than celebration.

'We got the British to accept that the IRA would call a cessation on the same terms as the first one,' says Cahill. 'The difference was that Blair was interested in peace. Major's government had basically wanted an IRA surrender – they were not keen on a peace process. They had looked at the South African model and realised that peace processes are dangerous. Parties and governments get involved in peace processes and nobody knows exactly where they are going to go.

'This was borne out when Sinn Féin met the National Party. They told our people that they had engaged with Mandela and the African National Congress on the basis that the ANC were such a disparate, disorganised bunch of people that they would fragment; that the National Party and the white government would talk rings around them and it would be twenty years or longer before there would be black majority rule.

'But once they got locked into the peace process, despite their security forces carrying out mass killings of black people and Inkatha getting involved in a war with the ANC – despite all that – the peace process created a dynamic, and within three or four years Mandela was president.

'People say that David Trimble is not a de Klerk, but the reality is that de Klerk was not a de Klerk. He only became a de Klerk after four years of the peace process. At the end of that time, I think the guy was still scratching his head and wondering how in hell he ever got there.'

Blair announced that Sinn Féin would be invited to take part in all-party talks six weeks after the announcement of the cessation, and in September the first session took place at Castle Buildings at Stormont. The Reverend Ian Paisley's hard-line Democratic Unionist Party, which had participated in the talks from the previous June, now refused to take part, but the Ulster Unionists, under new leader David Trimble, decided to attend. The British prime minister arrived in Belfast in October to give a boost to the negotiations. When he shook hands with Gerry Adams, it was the first such gesture between republican and British leaders since 1921.

'The venue for the talks was moved between Belfast, Dublin and London. A loyalist was killed in Belfast in February '98, around the time that a session was due to be held at Dublin Castle. The IRA was blamed and Sinn Féin was expelled for a while,' says Cahill. 'A couple of people were arrested and charged with the killing but the charges were subsequently dropped. It just proved there had been no basis for Sinn Féin's exclusion at all.

'It's part of the problem we still face now – if the chief constable of the RUC, or somebody else who is a securocrat, makes an accusation against republicans, it creates a crisis. You can't allow that to continue as a means of excluding people from a political process, because it would be done every day. The process would fall apart, because these people have their own agenda. Sinn Féin has a democratic mandate; our electorate has rights and entitlements. The British have to learn to respect these.'

Senator George Mitchell had now moved from chairing the decommissioning body to chairing the talks. There were many ups and downs, rows and recriminations, but, against all the odds, heading into Easter 1998 an agreement had begun to take shape. In a bid to pressurise the participants into producing a result, Senator Mitchell announced a deadline of midnight on Thursday, 9 April.

'Ten days of intensive negotiations at Castle Buildings came after that, sometimes all day long and all night,' recalls Cahill. 'I attended the talks on a number of occasions. Sinn Féin had a big team there, at least twenty people. There was the main team of negotiators, including Martin McGuinness and Gerry Adams, then a team drafting and formulating arguments, plus publicity people to handle the media. There was also our secretariat, working on eight computers and laptops. We also had the services of lawyers and senior counsel to help out with the legal stuff.'

The rounds of talks were conducted at a hectic pace and, as the deadline approached, fatigue was clearly visible on the faces of the participants when they emerged from Castle Buildings to stretch their legs in the car park. Journalists too were feeling the strain, with print and broadcast personnel barely able to catch a few minutes sleep on a plastic seat in one of the mobile offices provided for press use.

'Our people worked around the clock,' says Cahill. 'The Sinn Féin leadership was in constant contact with taoiseach Bertie Ahern and senior members of the SDLP. Gerry Adams also spoke regularly on the phone to Bill Clinton. All sides were exchanging position papers, then hammering out amendments and suggestions – putting in bits, taking out bits. Bertie Ahern was a regular visitor during the most intensive period of negotiations. He actually left his mother's wake in Dublin when he was needed in Belfast, and then had to rush back home for her funeral. Tony Blair came over for the last couple of days.

'The two last issues, the sticking points, were prisoners and policing. We wanted a new police service, not a reformed RUC. The prisons issue was particularly important – we needed our prisoners out as soon as possible.'

The Good Friday Agreement, a wordy masterpiece of compromise, language manipulation, vagueness and deliberate ambiguity, was finalised after a particularly fraught all-night session involving

George Mitchell, Bertie Ahern, Tony Blair and the negotiating teams. A deal was finally struck in the afternoon of 10 April – Good Friday.

Among its many clauses, it provided for a devolved government assembly. While republicans did not want this, they accepted it after safeguards were built in to prevent the abuse of power by a unionist majority. A far-reaching review of policing was to be carried out; equality and human rights agendas were to be implemented; a ministerial council of Ireland was to be established, and another council set up to explore cooperation between Ireland and Britain.

Cahill says Sinn Féin could not sign up immediately to the Agreement – it would have to be taken back to the *Ard Comhairle*, and then put before the whole membership at the *Ard Fheis*. There was, he points out, a historical precedent, when a document had been signed by a negotiating team and the result had been disastrous for the Irish nation:

'On Good Friday, when agreement was reached, a round-table conference was held with Blair and Ahern present. Trimble said he was accepting the Agreement and the other people accepted it. Gerry Adams said that Sinn Féin did not have the authority. We were not going to do a "Treaty". The people who signed the Treaty in 1921 got into all sorts of trouble. The Sinn Féin delegation which took part in the negotiations leading to the Good Friday Agreement were there as negotiators on behalf of the party. The delegation could not be given *carte blanche* authority to sign up to the agreement. Only the party had the authority to ratify what was agreed.

'What Gerry had to do that day was say all the positive things like, we think it's a good agreement, *et cetera*, and it is now a matter for Sinn Féin to take the decision on that. He said the party would hold a special conference, where the delegation would argue that Sinn Féin should endorse and support the Agreement.'

A special *Ard Fheis* with a one-item agenda was held on 18 April at the RDS, a large entertainment and conference complex in Dublin. Cahill spoke in favour of the Good Friday Agreement. The *Ard Fheis* had agreed to discuss and debate the implications of the document and then adjourn until a later date when it would be voted on.

'The Good Friday Agreement is not a settlement,' Cahill says. 'It's not perfect, it has faults, but it's a basis for progress. It could and should be a stepping stone to a thirty-two-county republic. I see it as a new line of strategy.'

✠ ✠ ✠

Alongside his political work, Cahill, with his colleagues in the National Graves Association (NGA) had been heavily involved in the campaign to have the remains of Tom Williams exhumed and reinterred in the County Antrim memorial plot in Belfast's Milltown cemetery.

A grave had been reserved for Williams for many years, but at times Cahill almost despaired of ever seeing the day when his friend's remains would be, as he puts it, 'brought home':

'We seemed to have spent years trying to contact Tom's surviving family, because it would be necessary to have their permission to have him buried in the grave reserved for him. We found some cousins, but in the event of Tom's remains being released, they wanted him buried in one of two family plots. Their preference was a cemetery in Bryansford, County Down. The republican movement always respected the wishes of dead IRA volunteers. Whilst our preferred option would be to have Tom buried in the grave reserved for him for so many years, we were happy to agree to the compromise reached – to have Tom buried along with his mother Mary. At least he would be staying in his home town.'

Part of the sentence of an executed prisoner was that the body would be buried in unconsecrated ground, in an unmarked grave within the prison walls. The NGA had been making little progress with polite requests to the Northern Ireland Office, and decided to take legal action. After a judicial review, the courts ruled that the Northern Ireland secretary of state had the power to commute the part of the sentence confining the body to the prison grounds. In August 1995, Queen Elizabeth signed a warrant removing the relevant clause.

Meanwhile Cahill and his colleagues had contacted other members of the Williams family – two half-brothers and a half-sister, all of whom lived abroad. The next problem was to locate the grave. Many people who had been inmates of Crumlin Road in 1942 were interviewed and gave their opinions on where they believed the remains lay. The jail closed in 1995, but the prison service had been ordered to keep it in a habitable state as a precautionary measure. Cahill was one of a small group who travelled to the jail in December 1998, to view the plot where it was believed Williams was buried.

'The directions we had been given were very good,' he recalls. 'I stood in the spot where we had been told Tom was buried. I looked slightly to the side at the wall and there, in faint letters, the prison authorities had scraped "TJW" on a brick. We had been told the letters were put there after Tom's burial. It was the last bit of confirmation we needed.'

An emotional little ceremony followed, with Cahill laying a wreath on the newly-located grave.

The battle for custody of the remains dragged on, however. It was not until 1999 that an official decision was taken to permit exhumation. In August of that year, the remains were finally removed from the prison grave.

On the evening of Tuesday, 18 January 2000, a group of elderly republicans stood rigidly to attention and formed a guard of honour as Tom Williams's coffin was taken from a hearse and carried into St Paul's church on the Falls Road to await requiem Mass next morning. One of the pall-bearers was Joe Cahill. Now approaching eighty, Cahill hardly felt the chill air of the winter evening as he left St Paul's that night, scarcely daring to believe that one of his dearest wishes was about to come true.

'Tom's closest family members preferred him to be buried with his mother, Mary, so at least he would be in Milltown where we could visit his grave and say a prayer,' Cahill says.

Following requiem Mass in a packed St Paul's next morning, Williams's coffin was carried from the church and placed on trestles. Cahill stepped forward, a folded tricolour in his hands. As he and fellow NGA member Liam Shannon spread the flag over the coffin, thousands of mourners pressed forward, anxious to witness the remarkable scene. The cortège then moved off on the journey to Milltown. Black flags and Irish tricolours fluttered from almost every lamp post on the two-mile route.

'It was a very moving sight. Tens of thousands of people attended the funeral. It was a remarkable display of respect, even affection, for a man who died fifty-seven years ago. I think people felt they were taking part in a wee bit of history. I hadn't seen such crowds since the funeral of Bobby Sands. I heard later that right across the country, in every community where there were republicans, black flags were flown in honour of Tom.'

Apart from Cahill, three other members of Williams's original active service unit remained alive and attended the funeral – John Oliver, who had been reprieved along with Cahill; Madge Burns, now Mrs Madge McConville; and Margaret Nolan. These last two were to have disposed of the active service unit's weapons back in 1942. All four veterans declined the offer of a lift, opting to walk behind the coffin.

Thousands of mourners joined the cortège, while many thousands of others lined the route. At Milltown cemetery, the procession was held up for several minutes while stewards walked ahead attempting to clear the way.

'Tom's relatives were completely overwhelmed at the numbers who attended the funeral, at the respect shown and the solemnity of the whole thing. They were fine people and I think they were glad then that they had agreed to have him buried in Milltown,' Cahill says.

On the following Sunday, the republican movement paid its own tribute to Tom Williams. Again, the survivors of that ill-fated IRA operation in 1942 – Cahill, Madge McConville, Margaret Nolan and John Oliver – took part. Madge McConville placed a wreath at the site of Williams's old home at Bombay Street in the Clonard area. The procession then began the journey to Milltown.

Cahill says the crowds on Sunday were even larger than those attending the funeral the previous Wednesday.

'People had a bit more time and were able to come from all over Ireland for the commemoration. Marie Moore – the child who was in the house all those years ago – acted as master of ceremonies and spoke a few words. She was, at that time, deputy lord mayor of Belfast. After that, Gerry Adams made a speech. The crowds were so huge that Adams, from his vantage point on the platform, mentioned that people were still arriving at the gates of Milltown twenty minutes after the ceremony had started.'

Then it was Cahill's turn to address the crowd. A hush fell over the packed cemetery as he began to speak. Those still filing along Milltown's narrow pathways halted in their tracks, people stopped shuffling and edging towards better positions, and children fell silent, as though sensing the uniqueness of the occasion.

His strong deep tones occasionally cracking with emotion, Cahill spoke of his friendship with Williams, the execution, the long struggle which had resulted in the release of his remains and the ideals they had both embraced.

A tumultuous roar rose from the crowd as he ended his tribute with Williams's own words, when the condemned man had urged his friends 'to carry on the struggle until that certain day', a reference to Irish unity.

The tricolour, the Citizen Army's starry plough ensign and the flags of Ireland's four provinces were lowered by standard-bearers as a trumpeter played 'The Last Post'.

The cemetery was once again hushed as Annie Cahill sang 'The Ballad of Tom Williams'. Her voice undiminished by the years, she received a massive ovation with her ad-libbing of the last line of the song, changing the words from 'a lad who lies within a prison grave', to 'no longer lies within a prison grave'.

Cahill recalls with a little smile: 'The IRA's longest-serving prisoner had come home at last.'

Epilogue

Some weeks before Tom Williams's funeral, a journalist had applied to the Northern Ireland Prison Service for authorisation to take a small group, including Cahill, on a tour of Crumlin Road jail's C wing. By coincidence the date for the visit, selected at random, was Friday, 21 January 2000 – two days after Williams's funeral and two days before the commemoration parade.

Cahill was asked if he wanted to postpone the visit in case it proved to be emotionally exhausting for him. With typical stubbornness, he insisted on keeping the appointment.

So it was that, at the end of the third week of the new millennium, Joe Cahill travelled back to Crumlin Road prison, where he had spent so many years of his life. The changing political climate in the North, the republican and loyalist ceasefires, and the resulting relaxation in the strict Northern Ireland Office rules governing its Prison Service, had led to the thaw which made the visit possible.

For once Cahill, four months short of his eightieth birthday, was able to wander the deserted landings and empty cells without escort. No jangle of keys followed his every move; no door slammed metallically behind him; there was no rasp of steel on steel as bolts were rammed home. The authorities had thrown open the forbidding steel gates of C Wing, where Cahill and his friends had been incarcerated after being sentenced to death for the killing of constable Murphy. Almost sixty years later – despite efforts to keep the old Victorian prison in 'warm storage', in case the jail was needed in an emergency – the yellow-painted walls and cell doors failed to disguise the oppressive atmosphere.

The ground-floor cells were known to prisoners and warders as 'the Ones'. The first and second landings housed the 'Twos' and 'Threes'. On this occasion Cahill entered C wing through a heavy steel door at the end of the corridor, which would seldom have been opened while he was an inmate. Prisoners normally came onto the wing through the Circle, where the entrances to all four wings met, like spokes at the hub of a cartwheel. In prison parlance, prisoners always came 'on to the wing', never 'into' the wing.

Cahill's small group was guided to C wing by a single warder, a civil and knowledgeable man with a keen sense of the old prison's history. The officer's job was now more akin to that of a museum curator than a gaoler.

After taking a few seconds to re-acclimatise himself and allow his eyes to adjust to the gloom, Cahill walked directly to the condemned cell near the end of the corridor and pushed open the unlocked door. It was an emotional moment. This was the double cell occupied by Cahill and his friend Tom Williams while they awaited the attentions of the British hangman. It was empty now, except for the large, empty wooden cabinet that covered most of the wall furthest from the door, concealing the entrance to the gallows chamber next to the death cell.

Those around Cahill could not help but be moved when, speaking softly in his distinctive, rumbling bass tones, the old republican pointed first to one wall and then to another, saying: 'Tom's bed was just there, and mine was there.'

On the wall beside the dresser, the marks of a bricked-up doorway were still visible. This door originally led to a small room equipped with a toilet for the use of the condemned men. This little luxury was not only for the convenience of the doomed prisoners, but mainly to avoid contact with other inmates.

Perhaps appropriately, the end room was even more gloomy than the others. The L-shaped gallows chamber had seen considerable renovation in recent years, but still bore telltale signs of the trapdoor in its floor.

Cahill, showing eminent good sense as it transpired, declined an invitation to go below to the basement. It was into this under-ground cellar that the body of the executed man dropped.

A second, smaller trapdoor at the back of the gallows chamber concealed a staircase leading to the basement. These stairs were used immediately after an execution by the assistant executioner, the doctor who pronounced the prisoner dead and a priest or other clergyman who would administer the last rites. Almost forty years after the last execution in Crumlin Road prison, the heavy pall of death still lingered.

Once away from the chamber, Cahill was in his element, remi-niscing on this incident or that, pointing out the cells of colleagues and conducting tours of the little prison chapel and C wing exer-cise yard.

Cahill and the warder had given a fascinating insight into prison life in the first half of the twentieth century, but when the visitors left Crumlin Road jail on that crisp January day, the sunshine seemed just that little bit brighter on the other side of the wall.

✠　✠　✠

Looking back on the years and months since the Good Friday Agreement negotiations, Cahill says that political progress, while not impossible, had been difficult.

'A lot of the trouble comes from the fact that unionists find it very difficult to cope with change. They are afraid of change but, when you look at it, all they are being threatened with is equality. They used the decommissioning issue to stall and stymie progress and, each time the situation looked like settling down, they threatened to collapse the institutions. They have already carried out their threat on a number of occasions.

'Bertie Ahern and Tony Blair put together a plan in July 1999 which provided for the establishment of a devolved government within days. Ulster Unionists didn't turn up at the Assembly building to nominate their quota of members on the Executive, and the whole effort collapsed.'

The Assembly Executive was eventually formed in November, with Sinn Féin being allocated two ministries. They chose education and health, the two portfolios generally regarded as the poisoned chalices of Northern Ireland politics. But in February 2000 the new northern secretary, Peter Mandelson, suspended devolution after Trimble threatened to resign if the IRA did not hand over its weapons. The power-sharing government was restored in late May.

'That set the pattern – the Assembly is working; the Assembly is not working. Sinn Féin has played its part, the IRA has made seismic shifts, and still it is not enough. For example, in June 2000 the IRA permitted the inspection of two arms dumps by international arms inspectors. As Gerry Adams said at the time, there has not been an initiative like that in 200 years,' says Cahill.

The dumps, believed to be in the Republic, were rendered useless, with the arms inspectors placing electronic seals at their entrances. The inspectors were later to report that the IRA had built on the June initiative by 'putting the weapons beyond use'.

✠ ✠ ✠

Shortly after the Agreement negotiations, Cahill felt it was time to hand Sinn Féin's financial dealings completely over to his joint treasurer, Dessie Mackin. The tiny operation nurtured by Cahill had grown into a busy department, with five staff. In 1998 Cahill resigned as treasurer and, to thunderous applause and a standing ovation at the *Ard Fheis*, was made honorary vice-president of Sinn Féin for life.

In 2000, Cahill finally came face-to-face with Bill Clinton, the man whose belief in the Irish peace process led him to risk censure by granting a visa to an IRA ex-prisoner.

'We eventually met at Stormont in December 2000, in the last few weeks of Clinton's presidency. Gerry Adams was about to perform the introductions, but the president recognised me right away. He said, "This man needs no introduction," and I replied, "I'm still not a parish priest."

'We chatted for a while and my parting remark was that even though he would soon be leaving the White House, he could still do a lot for us here in Ireland afterwards.'

Far from enjoying the quiet life, Cahill continues to throw himself into new enterprises. His diary is as full as it ever was, and it is still difficult to catch him at home. He was one of the main organisers of the huge *Tír Ghrá* (love of country, patriotism) commemoration function in Dublin in 2002, when the families of deceased republicans were honoured.

Despite health problems and protests from friends, Cahill insisted in May 2002 on travelling to the Republic to help with Sinn Féin's election campaign. He canvassed in several constituencies. In the week that he celebrated his eighty-second birthday, and sixty years after escaping Thomas Pierrepoint's noose, he returned from electioneering to his new home in Belfast, his first permanent residence since 1970. A little tired, but looking fitter than he had done in years, he relaxed on a couch under the gaze of Tom Williams, whose portrait hangs on the opposite wall. The election results, he says, had been gratifying. He had enjoyed seeing five colleagues elected to Dáil Éireann, or, as he insists on calling it, 'Leinster House'.

'It is generally believed, and I believe this myself, that the changes that have taken place make it possible to work effectively politically now to achieve a united Ireland. You hear people shouting that republicans are only interested in a united Ireland, and they are dead correct. That is republican policy. Our goal is a united Ireland, and the strategy we are using today is directed to taking us to a united Ireland by peaceful means.'

Dessie Mackin on Joe Cahill

Dessie Mackin is Sinn Féin's Director of Finance. He has known and worked with Joe Cahill for many years. Here he speaks frankly of his friendship with a man he admires and respects, and their sometimes stormy relationship:

'We were reforming and reorganising the Fianna in Belfast after the [1969] split. One of the people I first dealt with, and who provided assistance and guidance, was Joe. I remember going to his house when I was fourteen or fifteen years old. I thought he was an old man, because he was baldy and I was young.'

Mackin went to the United States in 1976 to drum up support for the blanket protest in Long Kesh. His colleague Fra McCann, a Sinn Féin colleague who was later to become a Belfast city councillor, was deported, but Mackin spent two years in jail fighting extradition.

'Joe was republicanism's main ambassador to the States from '71 into the 1980s. There is no other way to describe it, he was the face of the republican struggle in the United States at that time, without question. He used to go under the name of Joe Brown, or Father Brown – it was almost as well known as Joe Cahill.

'During that time if Joe was out in the States, he had the cheek to ring me in jail. When I rang a house and he was in it, I talked to him on the phone. He was good to my wife and child. He was there illegally, so he could not visit me, but we certainly had a few telephone conversations. I came back home on New Year's Eve 1981. As you can imagine, everyone, even republicans, were long gone at that time of year, but old Joe was at the airport waiting for me along with my family.'

The two men found themselves working closely together when

Mackin was made general manager of *An Phoblacht*. He was based at 44 Parnell Square in Dublin, from where Cahill also carried out his work as Sinn Féin national treasurer.

'I had not seen him in a while. Walking into the 44 [Parnell Square] I saw him just basically working in the hallway. His only office was a desk and a big wooden cabinet in the hall. He was sitting there, wrapping up stuff and folding calendars for the post, and you said to yourself, "This guy is the national treasurer of the party." I know it is a cliché, but no job was too big or too small for him. There he was, sitting in this draughty hallway, folding calendars. Joe never had the "general syndrome", no illusions of grandeur. That probably gave him a lot of clout, because he did it all himself.'

However, Mackin says that Cahill viewed innovations such as computers with suspicion.

'He denies it, but he is very much a Luddite. He and I would have sparked on this sort of stuff. It would not have been a highly technical argument on the pros and cons of computerisation, it was more like him asking, "Why the fuck do you need that crap?"'

'There was not even a safe in the building. All the money coming in, from collections around the country and all the sales, was stuck in different cupboards. Joe worked off an old ledger. His handwriting is very difficult to decipher, and he had his own system. He created his own accountancy system. He was sometimes obsessive about trying to trace three pence, when anybody else would have written it off in a column at the end: "leakage 3p." But he just had to track it down. He would have put you mental running around the place looking for it.

'He was living with families at the time and at Christmas he went to a caravan and brought Annie and the girls down. I say caravan, but it had no electricity and no running water – very, very basic. I remember going over at Christmas Eve, and he would be sitting there going mental, doing the books. Our books had to be completed by 31 December, and had to be ready for the *Ard Fheis* early in the new year. The Sinn Féin constitution requires the books to be inspected by the *Ard Comhairle* and then included in the financial report at the *Ard Fheis*. Joe used to get up during the private session and say, "We got something like £70,000 last year, spent £68,000, we have £2,000," and then sit down.

'We first noticed he began to lose his balance, and sometimes would stagger like a drunk, in 1988, the year of the Gibraltar shootings. I thought it might have been a brain tumour, but it turned out it was colon cancer.'

Mackin said he visited Cahill in hospital, just before he was about to undergo an operation, to discuss a brief note Cahill had left for him about Sinn Féin finances.

'I went up to visit him in hospital every day and on this occasion I asked him, "Joe, where are the books?" He asked why I wanted the books. This was in Joe's nature, because he was always very, very careful. I said, "Joe, I'm looking after things and I have to get the books. Where are they?"

'He said, "They are here." I said, "What do you mean, here?" They were under the mattress in the hospital. These were Sinn Féin's books, going back since the start, under the bed. I said, "Joe, I'm not going to run away with them." He said, "They are safe enough here. You just take a note."

'He was quite ill for a while. We got him settled in Dundalk and Annie came down. We just told him. It was put to him as a *fait accompli*. He was not consulted.

'Joe had never lived with his family. His attitude was that if he had his family down here in Dublin, he would not have been able to give the commitment and do the work that he did. It was a great sacrifice of his family and a sacrifice of his home life. The way he looked at it, he could have been going into jail tomorrow. Annie could have moved down, but if she gave up her home in Belfast and he was arrested, she would have no home and no one. He made a calculation.

'So he settled in Dundalk and we started daily commuting together then. We travelled together five days a week, sometimes six, until 1995. His energy for a man of his age was tremendous. I was a lot younger than him and it was taking a lot out of me, so what was it doing to him?

'The worst thing was getting into the car for the hour-and-a-half drive home. It was not only white-knuckle driving, but also everything that had cropped up that day, aggravating stuff, all the frustrations of the day, were coming out. So you were living this every day, fighting like mad on the way home. It was all right in the office – if we fell out in the morning we could avoid each other all day – but then you had to get into the same car together. It was a great source of hilarity for everyone.

'The silence would be broken by him nearly killing us, so then he had to start talking. He is still driving. He was recently done for speeding. He has been done twice in the last eighteen months. I was stopped in the car with him once. The cop looked at him, with the cap and big overcoat and all, and says, "Sir, do you know you were doing over seventy?" Joe said, "I know, but why did you only stop me?" and the cop said, "Because, sir, we can only stop one at a time." Diplomatically, I started driving more and more over the years.

'I used to be partial to an oul' drink at the weekend and occasionally felt like taking Monday morning off, but there was just no way of getting away with it. Everyone else in this movement could bullshit and say they had to meet a *cumann* in Connemara. But old Joe knew all my movements. It was like being in school, there was just no break from it. Even mentioning going on holidays gave you a guilt complex – he was not a great believer in holidays. He would just go to that wee caravan.

'The caravan was in a field, it was winter and he is the worst driver in the world. Joe wheels in, the wee caravan is sitting there – you could have blown it over, it was a wreck. Joe hits the brakes, he is on grass, it's raining. The car does not stop, it keeps going, smack, right into the caravan. Damaged the caravan and knocked the door off it. I told the then editor of *An Phoblacht* and he put it in the paper. Joe was not too well pleased. He said we had endangered his security, even though we did not mention what county the caravan was in.

'We worked on together, and built up the new finance structures. The Sinn Féin national draw was Joe's idea and we have developed it – it now raises over £100,000 a year. It is the mainstay of our Irish fundraising.

'The only way to work with Joe Cahill is to be as tough as him, he is more comfortable with that. That's his nature. Joe has always lived on the edge and has always been driven – what has to be done today has to be done.

'The role of vice-president was created for him. He sometimes acts as a troubleshooter. If you had a problem or fall-out over policy, Joe would go in as a sort of elder statesman and help sort it out, give guidance. People respect him and listen to him.

'Joe has a reputation for being a hard man of republicanism – down the line, a traditionalist and whatever else. He is all those things. But when it came to key decisions, he could be quite pragmatic – for example, on the dropping of the abstentionist rule by Sinn Féin in the South. I knew it was personally difficult for him, but once he decided that was the way to go, just as in the peace process, he threw himself into it and argued and fought. He was one of the most key people, particularly at that time.

'Quite a few of the southern leadership were totally opposed to dropping abstention – Daithí Ó Conaill left, Ruairí Ó Brádaigh left. It could not have been sold unless Joe Cahill was pushing for it. Such was Joe Cahill's influence in 1986. He was critical in that one.

'In the peace process, too, we all had to make big decisions on going into Stormont. Once he worked it out and went with it, he was the biggest pusher and brought people with him.'

Martin McGuinness on Joe Cahill

Derry republican Martin McGuinness is a senior Sinn Féin member, and Assembly Education Minister. He was a young man when he firdt met Cahill. The men became firm friends in Portlaoise prison in 1974:

I really got to know Joe Cahill in Portlaoise, although I may have met him once or twice prior to that. He had a tremendous presence. Young people of my generation – at that time I was in my early twenties – all of us looked up to Joe Cahill and had a great deal of respect for him and the quality of leadership he provided for people in Belfast, in what were some of the city's darkest days.

'All of us were very conscious of the history of this man and of the decades and decades of struggle that he had been involved in. This was people like myself, who had only been republicans for a year or two, knowing and understanding that we were talking to a man who had given his whole life to the republican struggle and who had done so when it was not popular to be an Irish republican, who had stood up consistently for his principals, who had faced the hangman's knot and who had refused to lie down and be subdued or conquered by anyone.

'We held him in tremendous regard. I have to say that when I saw him then I thought he was ancient, so what is he now, thirty years later? What are twenty-year-olds thinking about me now?

'I always sought to learn from conversations with him. The role that someone like Joe played for people like me would have been as a leadership figure rather than a father figure, someone who was at the spearhead of the struggle. He was from Belfast, and was seen as the epitome of the courage of the nationalist republican people of Belfast at a very difficult time in the history of those people within the northern state.

'We looked up to people like Daithí Ó Conaill, Joe B O'Hagan, Ruairí Ó Brádaigh and Seán MacStiofáin, but it is important to say that because Joe came from the city of Belfast, a city that had suffered greatly down the decades, there was a particular admiration for him. He had been a republican in the place where it was most difficult to be a republican. To be a republican in Roscommon isn't as difficult as being a republican in Belfast.

'Joe nearly died on us one night about twenty-eight years ago. We were somewhere in the middle of the west of Ireland when he took ill, and we rushed him to hospital. When he left us, we thought it was the last we would see of him. It was heart trouble. But he has come back to haunt us ever since. Now, I don't think he is ever going to die. Some of us believe he has been around since the days of Wolfe Tone.

'Joe Cahill is the embodiment of the spirit of Irish republicanism. I don't think people of my generation see him, at fifty or sixty years of age, running about the streets with an AK47 over his shoulder. He is about more than that – he represents the continuation of an unbroken line of Irish republicanism back to 1916. His value to the movement is in his spirit and in his wisdom, and principally in his ability to take on board new ideas from upstarts like myself and Gerry Adams, to listen to our views and at times be critical of them and help us to re-evaluate how we should approach a situation ... and bring to a successful conclusion the strategy of the reunification of Ireland and the establishment of a thirty-two-county republic.

'He is a very honest man. If he thought we were going down the wrong road, he would not be behind the door in articulating his view. He was a very steadying influence over the course of maybe the last fifteen or twenty years, going back to the decision to fight the Assembly elections in 1982, and of course the big decision which was made in 1986 to end abstentionism in the South.

'Joe Cahill's status was so immense in the aftermath of 1986 that if he had decided to walk away, it would have seriously undermined the strategy we were attempting to put in place. His support was critical.

'Joe, whatever way the British tabloid media and others try to portray him, is a very political person. I was given the responsibility of building a bridge to the British government, building contacts, which I worked away at from the late 1980s right through to the present day. We were involved in talks with the Irish government, we were in talks with the SDLP leadership, and Joe Cahill was kept informed of it and was fully supportive and encouraging every step of the way.

'At the beginning of the 1990s, Joe Cahill was seventy years of age. Even though he would be regarded as the father figure, which he clearly is, of republicanism, he is a man who was prepared to take on board new concepts, new ideas. In many ways I suppose that shows the youthfulness of Joe Cahill. He has a sharp mind, a sharp intellect and a willingness to absorb and be part of new ideas and new approaches.

'He is the butt of many comments, because of his role within the finance department. At the same time, even though people would have commented on his miserliness, his Scroogeness, people always understood that he was ultra-protective of the finances of Sinn Féin. You could not have had a more honest man dealing with the finances of the party. He was so honest, he wasn't prepared to give anything away to anybody, not even the republicans who needed it. I have to say the comments made about all of that are exaggerated, that Joe was scrupulous – and ruthless.

'Did anybody tell you about his sandwiches at *Ard Comhairle* meetings? Well, you were lucky to get one. People would come from all over Ireland to Parnell Square in Dublin – from Kerry, Galway, Dundalk, Derry, Belfast, everywhere. For years and years and years, you were lucky if you got an egg and onion sandwich and a cup of tea during the interval. Thankfully, we have now graduated to pizzas.

'This man has had an extraordinarily hard life. His wife Annie, and his family in general, have suffered unbelievably as a result of the conflict that has existed on the island of Ireland and because of Joe's participation in the republican struggle. This man has spent periods in prison and, even when he was not in prison, he has lived in the most Spartan conditions that you can imagine and has managed to remain cheerful and active and whole-hearted about his involvement in the republican struggle. We were overjoyed to see that he was able to go back to a house in Belfast again.

'It is okay for people to go through maybe a phase of a struggle for two, three years, and put up with those types of conditions. Sometimes it is extraordinary that people will put up with them for five years, and, of course, many people went to prison for ten or fifteen years. It is almost as if Joe Cahill has been doing this all his life. When you consider that from fifteen years of age – for sixty-five years – this man has been going through the most awful deprivation – that's something to be admired, big time. That shows an incredible commitment to Irish republicanism, and dedication as an Irish republican.

'What politician in the world would go through that? He is comparable, maybe, to Nelson Mandela in terms of willingness to make sacrifice.

'Many people would be content to sit in retirement when they come to sixty-five or sixty-seven or seventy. This man has never stopped. This man has always been part of the republican struggle and has always been putting himself forward to do whatever he can. If anybody is the epitome of what Bobby Sands said – "Everybody has a part to play" – he is. You would think that when it came to his later years, he would be thinking of winding down and doing nothing, but Joe Cahill would go on forever. As long as the man is healthy and able to walk and move and think, he would be willing to drive tonight from Belfast to Cork and back again, and it would not cost him a thought.

'He is a republican from the end of the hairs on his head, what's left of them, to the tip of his toes.

'When strategy changed and we were accused by some people of selling out, Joe had the foresight and insight to see where the struggle was going, that it was a consistent struggle. He is probably the longest-serving political activist in Ireland of any political party.'

BIBLIOGRAPHY

Bew, Paul and Gillespie, Gordon, *Northern Ireland: A Chronology of the Troubles 1968–1993*, Dublin, Gill and Macmillan, 1993.

Collins, Stephen, *The Power Game: Fianna Fáil since Lemass*, Dublin, O'Brien Press, 2000.

Coogan, Tim Pat, *The IRA*, London–Glasgow, Fontana Books, 1972.

Connolly O'Brien, Nora, *We Shall Rise Again*, London, Mosquito Press, 1981.

Elliott, Sydney and Flackes, WD, *Northern Ireland: A Political Directory*, Belfast, Blackstaff Press, 1999.

Farrell, Michael, *Northern Ireland: The Orange State*, London, Pluto Press, 1976.

Feeney, Brian, *Sinn Féin: A Hundred Turbulent Years*, Dublin, O'Brien Press, 2002.

Kenna, GB, *Facts and Figures: The Belfast Pogroms 1920–22*, Dublin, O'Connell Publishing Company, 1922.

King, Cecil, *The Cecil King Diary 1970–74*, London, Jonathan Cape, 1975.

Moore, Steven, *Behind the Garden Wall*, Antrim, Greystone Books, 1995.

MacEoin, Uinseann, *The IRA in the Twilight Years 1923–1948*, Dublin, Argenta Publications, 1997.

McKittrick, David, Seamus Kelters, Brian Feeney, Chris Thornton, *Lost Lives*, Edinburgh–London, Mainstream Publishing, 1999.

McKittrick, David and McVea, David, *Making Sense of the Troubles*, Belfast, Blackstaff Press, 2000.

MacStiofáin, Seán, *Memoirs of a Revolutionary*, Gordon & Cremonesi, 1975.

McVeigh, Jim, *Executed: Tom Williams and the IRA*, Belfast, Beyond the Pale Publications, 1999.

O'Clery, Conor, *The Greening of the White House*, Dublin, Gill & Macmillan, 1997.

Ó Muilleoir, Máirtín, *Belfast's Dome of Delight: City Hall Politics 1981–2000*, Belfast, Beyond the Pale Publications, 1999.

Phoenix, Eamon, *Northern Nationalism*, Belfast, Ulster Historical Foundation, 1994.

Rees, Merlyn, *Northern Ireland: A Personal Perspective*, London, Methuen London, 1985.

Taylor, Peter, *Provos: The IRA and Sinn Féin*, London, Bloomsbury, 1997.

List of Sources

Interviews with Joe Cahill, 2000–02.

Interview with John Kelly, Sinn Féin Member of the Northern Ireland Assembly, 2001.

Interview with Dessie Mackin, Sinn Féin Director of Finances, 2002.

Interview with Father Malachy Murphy, Parish Priest, St Paul's, Falls Road, Belfast, 2001.

Interviews with Richard McAuley, aide to Sinn Féin president Gerry Adams, 2000–02.

Interview with PJ McClean, member of the Northern Ireland Civic Forum, 2001.

Interview with Martin McGuinness, Northern Ireland Assembly Minister for Education, 2002.

Interview with Aidan McAteer, Sinn Féin advisor to Martin McGuinness, 2002.

Interview with Dr Eamon Phoenix, historian, lecturer and journalist, 2001.

Interviews with senior officers of the Royal Ulster Constabulary, 2001.

Interviews with republican ex-prisoners.

Belfast Central Library, Royal Avenue, Belfast.
The Linenhall Library, Donegall Place, Belfast.

Newspapers and Magazines:
Belfast Telegraph, Daily Express, Daily Mail, Irish Independent, Irish News, Irish Press (defunct), *Irish Times, An Phoblacht, The Listener, Irish Weekly* (defunct), *Sunday Times* (London), *Times* (London).

INDEX